DIANA PRESTON is a writer and historian who read Modern History at Oxford. Her book, *Before the Fall-Out – From Marie Curie to Hiroshima*, won the *Los Angeles Times* 2006 Prize for Science and Technology.

READ FEB 2016

A FIRST RATE RATE TRAGEDY

DIANA PRESTON

CONSTABLE • LONDON

Constable & Robinson Ltd
55–56 Russell Square
WC1B 4HP
www.constablerobinson.com

First published in the UK by Robinson,
an imprint of Constable & Robinson, 1997

This edition published by Constable, an imprint of Constable & Robinson, 2011

A copy of the British Library Cataloguing in Publication
Data is available from the British Library

UK ISBN: 978-1-84901-724-4

Printed and bound in the UK

MIX
Paper from
responsible sources
FSC
www.fsc.org   FSC® C018072

To my husband
Michael

Contents

Illustrations

Acknowledgements

At South Hampstead High School for Girls, a quotation written in large Gothic script and framed in oak used to catch my eye as I hurried between the classes: 'Had we lived I should have had a tale to tell of the hardihood, endurance and courage of my companions which would have stirred the heart of every Englishman – R.F. Scott.' Many years later I decided to tell that tale both for its innate power and enduring poignancy and for what it says about the British character and our perception of what constitutes a hero. While researching, I learned that South Hampstead was one of the many schools to be stirred by Scott's 1910 expedition and to respond to his appeal for dogs and ponies. The reason why his words were still displayed so prominently fifty years after his death became clear at last.

I am indebted once again to my husband Michael for help and advice throughout and for the considerable amount of research and editing he undertook. I am also grateful to Lord Kennet for his kindness in allowing me access to the Kennet Family Papers, lodged in the Cambridge University Library; to Elspeth Huxley for her insight into the personalities of some of the chief players; to Bob Headland, Shirley Sawtell and Philippa Hogg of the Scott Polar Research Institute for their help with consulting the original sources held by the Institute; to the London Library for their efficiency and patience in supplying me with many of the most important published sources; to Clive Bunyan, Assistant Curator Aeronautics Collection, the Science Museum, for advice about developments in aviation in the early years of the century; to Deirdre Sheppard of Antarctica New Zealand, Paul Chaplin of the Antarctic Heritage Trust and Baden Norris, Antarctic Curator, the Canterbury Museum, Christchurch, New Zealand for insight into Scott's visits to New Zealand and into the condition and preservation of Scott's huts at McMurdo Sound; to my agent Michael Thomas for his encouragement; to Vera Faith for her research among the newspapers of the time; to Kim Lewison for constructive criticism and advice at a crucial stage; to the Cunard Line for enabling me to visit Cape Town, as Scott did, by sea to carry out research; to Air New Zealand and Mount Cook Airlines for helping with flights to New Zealand's South Island to enable us to join up with an Antarctic expedition, and finally to Southern Heritage Expeditions Ltd, Christchurch, New Zealand, for making possible an attempt by my husband and myself to visit Scott's and Shackleton's huts on McMurdo Sound.

In revising this book in 2009, I am grateful in particular to Susan Solomon for discussing her work on weather conditions, to David Crane for invaluable insights into the character of Scott, to Lady Kennet for renewed access to the correspondence between Captain Scott and his wife Kathleen, to David Wilson for information about his great-uncle Edward Wilson, to Wendy Driver of the Friends of the Scott Polar Research Institute for help and information and to the staff at the Institute for access to the manuscript collection. I am once again grateful to my husband Michael who took a major part in the revision. I am also indebted to Hapag Lloyd and to Quark Expeditions for finally making it possible for

ACKNOWLEDGEMENTS

me to visit the Ross Sea and Scott's huts. Last but not least I would like to thank my editor at Constable, Leo Hollis, as well as of course Bill Hamilton and Charlie Brotherstone at A.M. Heath

Explanatory Note

Unless otherwise stated all distances are given in geographical, i.e. nautical, miles. One geographical mile is equivalent to $1^1/_7$ statute miles.

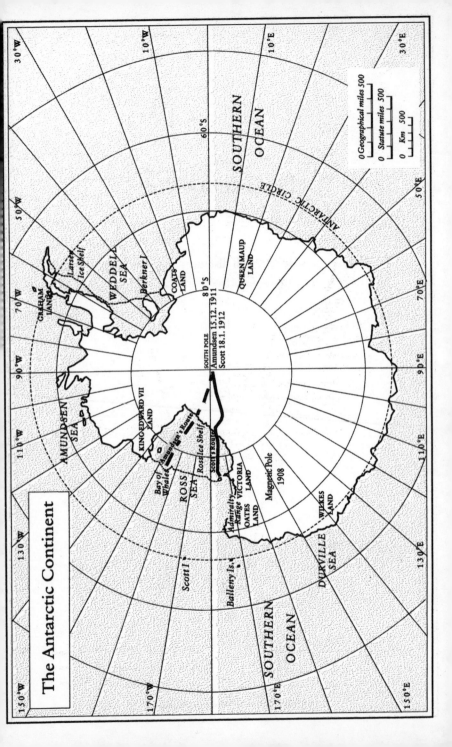

The Antarctic Continent

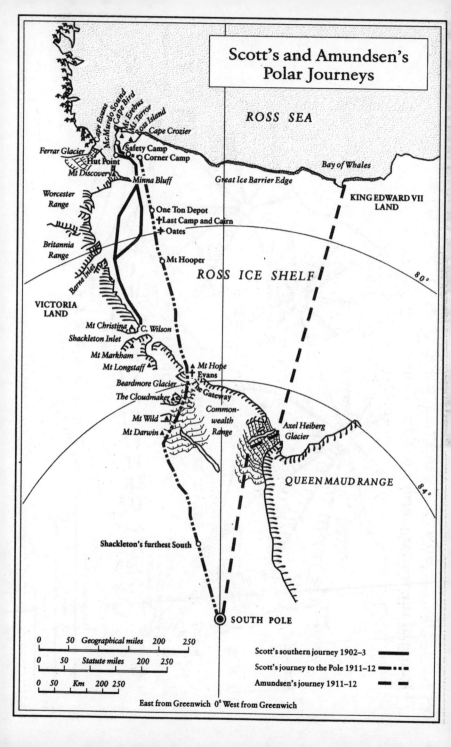

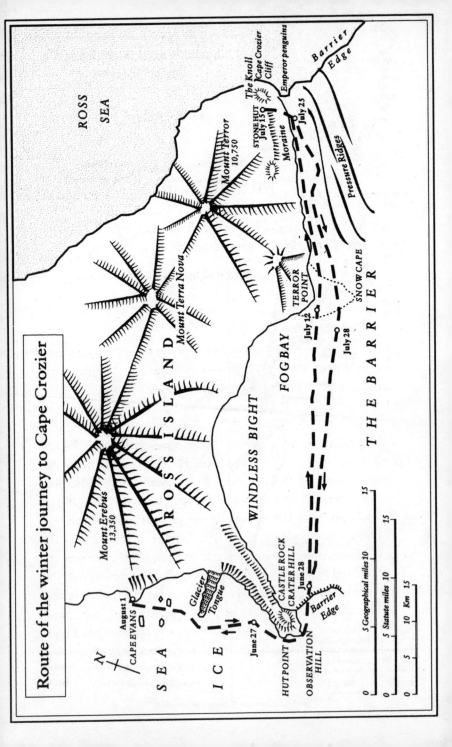

Route of the winter journey to Cape Crozier

Introduction

And so this hero of heroes said, 'I am going to find the South Pole. It will be a big adventure.'

From 'Like English Gentlemen' – Anon.

'It has happened! We have found what we sought! Good God, what a twist of fate.' So the young Norwegian Tryggve Gran recorded a grim discovery on 12 November 1912 by a search party trekking across the blinding whiteness of Antarctica's great Ice Barrier. They had found the snow-covered tent containing the bodies of Captain Scott and his two companions Edward Wilson and 'Birdie' Bowers. They had died just eleven miles from the depot of food and fuel that might have saved them. Of the two other members of the Polar party, Captain Oates and Petty Officer Edgar Evans, there was no sign. However, Scott's diaries and letters, by his body, recounted their terrible fate. It was a story that would resonate throughout the world and make heroes of them all.

Scott and his four comrades had set out over a year before from Cape Evans on McMurdo Sound to plant the British flag at the South Pole and should have returned no later than early April 1912. Yet for some weeks afterwards the party back at Cape Evans had continued to hope. In Antarctica the strange light effects play

1

tricks on the eyes. Sometimes the watchers thought they could see distant specks on the horizon, men with sledges moving purposefully forward, only to find that it was a mirage or a party of seals lolloping over the ice. Sometimes the sledge dogs would begin to howl as if in greeting and the men would rush outside, shouting out to the cook to get moving, that the Polar party was back, that someone should put a record of the national anthem on the gramophone. On 24 April the sunless Antarctic winter with its 'nightmares of the darkness'[1] descended, extinguishing any lingering hope.

The question now was how had Scott and his comrades perished? Had they ever reached the Pole? Had they fallen into a crevasse taking their secrets with them? When the sun returned the other members of the expedition felt it was their duty to discover the truth. The search party found their answer just 148 miles from their base. A dark patch revealed itself to be the top of a tent. It was several hours before they could bring themselves to enter and the task fell to the senior officer, Dr Atkinson. What met his eyes was a truly Arthurian scene: the dead hero, Captain Scott, lying frozen in his reindeer-fur sleeping bag, his arm flung out towards Wilson as if seeking comfort. Bowers and Wilson lay on either side of him like faithful acolytes.

However, in November 1912 the wider world guessed nothing of the disaster. The expedition's only means of contact with the outside world, their ship the *Terra Nova*, had departed for New Zealand in March before there was any reason to fear that Captain Scott had come to grief. What the world did, however, know was that the Norwegian explorer Roald Amundsen had reached the South Pole and had beaten Scott. The news that Scott and his four companions had also reached the Pole but died during their return did not break until early February 1913.

When it did, the story was rendered even more poignant because Scott's widow, Kathleen, was then sailing to New Zealand to be reunited, or so she thought, with her husband, unaware, as the newspapers were quick to point out, that she had been a widow for nearly a year. Neither was she aware of the great memorial service held in St Paul's Cathedral on 14 February, just two days after the news had been announced. Crowds jostled to join a congregation headed by the King himself.

The tragedy had a profound effect. Scott immediately became and remained a far greater hero than if he had survived. But why? What was it in the achievements of a man who all his life had felt himself caught in the machine 'that grinds small',[2] a man who never felt quite master of his own destiny, who believed himself to be inherently unlucky, and who ultimately failed, that so caught at the British soul?

Partly, of course, heroes who die at the apex of their achievement such as Nelson or Wolfe cannot by their later actions fall from grace. Partly, the British have always loved plucky losers and heroic failures, even in Scott's day. Though Britain dominated the 1908 Olympic Games, held at London's White City, outclassing the Americans, the public took their triumph for granted and reserved their admiration for an Italian marathon runner who collapsed near the finishing line, while leading, and was disqualified for receiving help across the line. Queen Alexandra presented him with a gold cup and he was inundated with offers to appear in the music halls.

However, one of the key reasons was the context of the times. The Britain of 1913 was increasingly unsure of her place in the world. H.G. Wells, looking back from 1914, described the ripples of uncertainty and self-doubt that were troubling the nation: 'The first decade of the twentieth century was for the English a decade of badly strained optimism. Our Empire was nearly beaten by a handful of farmers [the Boers of South Africa] amidst the jeering contempt of the whole world – and we felt it acutely for several years . . .'[3] The dismay and self-doubt at the loss of the 'unsinkable' *Titanic* in April 1912 exemplified the nation's waning self-confidence. At the same time, the heroism of the men who calmly loaded their wives and children into the insufficient lifeboats knowing that they themselves would go down with the ship seemed the very apotheosis of noble self-sacrifice.

This was a period when old and new ideas were colliding with some force. In parliament the Liberal Party was locked in a struggle with the Lords over Lloyd George's 'People's Budget'. The army and the navy were each engaged in soul-searching arguments about how to modernize their methods and equipment. This was the era of the Dreadnought and the machine gun. The capability of the submarine and the aeroplane were hotly debated. Other difficult issues clouded the scene – Home Rule for Ireland, confrontation between unions and employers, the increasingly stormy suffragette battle. Moral values and the established social order were under increasing challenge as the certainties of Victoria's golden age faded away. Marie Stopes was advocating birth control. D.H. Lawrence was working on his first book, *The White Peacock*. As Balfour put it, Victoria's death 'affects us not merely because we have lost a great personality, but because we feel that the end of a great epoch has come upon us'.[4]

The novelist Elinor Glyn, she of 'Would you like to sin with Elinor Glyn on a tiger skin', wrote that in observing Victoria's funeral cortège she was witnessing 'the funeral procession of England's greatness and glory'.[5] Comparisons were increasingly made between the decadence and decline of the Roman Empire and Britain's position. People like Baden-Powell worried over signs of physical degeneracy in the British, warning that one cause of the downfall of the Roman Empire was the fact that the soldiers 'fell away from the standard of their forefathers in bodily strength'.[6] Scott's last letter to his wife, addressed unsentimentally to 'my widow', reflected that distaste of growing 'soft': 'How much better has it been than lounging in too great comfort at home.'

Britain's sense of security, of her ability to fill her rightful pre-eminent place in the world was faltering before new threats and challenges. The greatest threat of all was war with Germany. Before he set out in 1910, Scott asked the editor of the *Daily Mail* when he thought that war might break out. With surprising accuracy he advised Scott to complete his expedition by August 1914! A Scottish traveller, Campbell MacKellar, recorded with concern that 'an impudent native' had approached him in Java and said: 'All German man now. Englishman no good now.' The traveller mused over how this idea had spread so quickly but concluded that it was partly 'because it was true!'[7]

Against this background there was much about Scott's Antarctic odyssey that struck a reassuring note. It was brave and daring to venture into the unknown continent where British men would prove that the old values of courage in adversity, cheerfulness, persistence, loyalty and self-sacrifice had not died. Scott's letters and diaries were greeted with deep emotion because they showed that he and his colleagues had held true to these ideals until the end. 'My companions are unendingly cheerful,' he wrote, 'but we are all on the verge of serious frostbites, and though we constantly talk of fetching through I don't think any one of us believes it in his heart.'

The very language in which they were couched – and Scott had considerable literary talent – could not fail to appeal to the heart of a nation that was losing confidence. 'Had we lived I should have had a tale to tell which would have stirred the heart of every Englishman' was his message from the grave. The account of Captain Oates, tortured by frostbite, staggering out to his death in the blizzard to save his friends, with merely the terse comment that he might be 'gone for some time', could have come from the pages of *Boy's Own*. Here was the very epitome of the English officer and gentleman doing his duty without fuss.

Apart from the heroism there was the human interest. Through Scott's diaries the public, then as now, could relive the details of moving events as they unfolded. They could share the awful disappointment and psychological effect of reaching the Pole only to find that Amundsen had stolen the prize; the frustration at the weather conditions which held up the party's dash to safety; the shock and surprise at the weakening of the first and supposedly strongest member of the party, Petty Officer Edgar Evans; the dismay at finding that some of the vital supplies of fuel, carefully depoted, had evaporated; the pain of living with gnawing starvation and frostbitten limbs; the pathetic deterioration of Captain Oates; the tantalizing knowledge that at their final camp they were only eleven miles from a large depot of food and fuel but prevented from reaching it by violent blizzards; the wistful hope that a search party would find them in time; the picture of men lying helpless in their tent hoping above the shrieking of the blizzard to catch the eerie barking of the sledge dogs that would mean salvation; their strong desire to survive, coupled with the knowledge that they would not. If Scott and his party had vanished without trace, if there had been no diaries and letters and messages, he might perhaps have faded from memory.

Another important factor was Amundsen. Here, in the eyes of many at the time, was the villain and foil to Scott, the British hero. Foreigner, interloper and rival he was the man who had sneaked out of Norway in the *Fram*, 'the Viking ship of the Twentieth Century' as another Norwegian Antarctic explorer Borchgrevink called her, concealing his intention to go south rather than north, until Scott was already on his way down to Antarctica. He was the man who turned reaching the South Pole into a race, the 'professional' who, by superior technique with skis and dogs and better luck and preparation, pipped Scott, the 'gifted amateur', at the post and stole the prize. Indeed, Amundsen himself called his journey 'a sporting stunt'.

Amundsen was not perceived to have played the game and his achievement, which had not relied on hauling sledges himself, seemed less virile and manly than Scott's. Scott had written ten years earlier that: 'No journey ever made with dogs can approach the height of that fine conception which is realised when a party of men go forth to face hardships, dangers, and difficulties with their own unaided efforts, and by days and weeks of hard physical labour succeed in solving some problems of the great unknown.'[8] This ethos still underpins British Antarctic ventures, such as the unsupported trek across the continent by Ranulph Fiennes and Michael Stroud, Roger Mear's attempt to walk alone to the Pole and Ranulph Fiennes's abandoned lone trek across the continent.

The sheer mystique of Antarctica, the last frontier, also contributed. As exploration in the southern regions had gathered pace at the turn of the century the popular imagination had become gripped by descriptions of a place of surpassing beauty, mystery and danger. The accounts from both of Scott's expeditions and from other explorers were lyrical and exhilarating. Tryggve Gran described how 'It was as though we lived in a gigantic, wonderful fairy tale; as though we sailed over an ocean where thousands of white lilies lay rippling in the night air. And when the sun rose the white lilies took on a violet hue and the whole of fairyland lay in rosy light'.[9]

And there was the wildlife. Scott's men left wonderful accounts of such curiosities as the little Adélie penguins. Apsley Cherry-Garrard wrote that:

> The life of an Adélie penguin is one of the most unchristian and successful in the world . . . Some fifty or sixty agitated birds are gathered upon the ice-foot, peering over the edge, telling one another how nice it will be, and what a good dinner they are going to have. But this is all swank: they are really worried by a horrid suspicion that a sea-leopard is waiting to eat the first to dive . . . What they really do is to try and persuade a companion of weaker mind to plunge: failing this they hastily pass a conscription act and push him over. And then – bang, helter-skelter, in go all the rest.[10]

Such anthropomorphism was typical of a sentimental age which produced *The Jungle book*, *The Wind in the Willows* and *Peter Rabbit*. However, there was perhaps a deeper reason why such descriptions appealed. By pretending that an ordered animal world replicated the human one, the Edwardians rejected the possibility that baser 'animal instincts' could motivate human actions. Even if there was increasing acceptance of Darwin's theory that man was descended from animals, Freud's emerging theories of the human psyche and its motivation surely could not apply. Scott and his companions seemed to epitomize the nobler side of man, demonstrating self-sacrifice for the benefit of others, loyalty in death and the paramountcy of man's quest for knowledge. Half-frozen and starving, they had continued to 'geologize' on their return from the Pole and had dragged their heavy specimens with them till the end.

If Britain had needed heroes in 1913, she had an even greater thirst for them as the First World War progressed and a generation of young men obeyed the call to unquestioning sacrifice. However, after the war came the doubts. What had it all been for? Was the terrible cost justified? Scott's heroism achieved an even greater prominence. His sacrifice in the pure clean wastes of Antarctica remained comfortingly unsullied amid doubts about what the mud, pain and squalor of Flanders had achieved.

The mystique and enduring power of Scott's last Antarctic expedition lie in all these things. Of course, the modern age is less comfortable with heroes, cynically eager to show its sophistication and scepticism and dig for the feet of clay. There has been much debate in recent years about the scale of Scott's achievement and he has been compared unfavourably with Amundsen. It is of course possible to pare the story down to clinical discussions of logistics, to a debate about methods of transport, the merits of dogs versus ponies, the quality of rations, the effectiveness of the planning, the routes which were followed, the risks which were run. Yet, while these things have their place, there is the danger of losing sight of the essential humanity of what happened out there in that forlorn and silent world.

It is important to strip away the improving tales that accrete to heroes and to reveal the true characters underneath. However, to believe that Scott and his companions achieved something heroic is not to imply that they were perfect. Heroes are not required to be. Scott undoubtedly made mistakes. He could be difficult, impatient and short-tempered. He suffered crises of confidence and periods of abstraction and depression but that does not detract from his stature. In the same way, the story of the South

Pole expedition of 1910 continues to fascinate and inspire but is not without light and shade. It is a tale of perseverance and unquenchable spirit in the face of terrible odds but it is also a story of stubbornness, sentimentality and of men who were deeper and more complex than we sometimes acknowledge. Heroes, but humans too.

1

The Early Heats of the Great Race

The history of Antarctic exploration is a curious story of bursts of activity succeeded by long periods of apathy and neglect. Man was slow to penetrate the mysteries of Antarctica. Vikings roamed the frozen seas of the Arctic but when Wellington fought at Waterloo there was still an undiscovered continent in the south. It was not until 1820 that a human being first glimpsed the Antarctic mainland. When Scott set out on his first expedition with the *Discovery* in 1901 less was known about it than about the moon before the lunar landing in 1969.

Antarctica is still the least-known of all the continents, the least hospitable and the most dangerous – colder, higher and more isolated than anywhere else on earth. A landmass of some five and a half million square miles, all but two per cent of it is covered by a huge ice sheet with an average thickness of 6,000 feet. Seen from space the ice cap shines like a great white lamp. Over 90 per cent of the world's snow and ice lies on or around Antarctica. At the Pole itself the sun does not rise above the horizon for six months of the Antarctic winter. On the Polar plateau temperatures as low as -124°F have been recorded. Around the Pole the annual mean temperature is some -65°F. Hurricane-force winds whip across its surface, driving the snow into thick clotting blizzards. Yet, once tasted, Antarctica has a potent effect. Diary after diary of those who have explored describe a world of spell-binding beauty but also a place of such awesome solitude and melancholy that it can drive people insane.

For centuries Antarctica's very existence was doubted and debated, although the idea of a southern continent was an ancient one. Aristotle believed that the earth was a sphere and that there must be a counterbalance to the Arctic zones. The Romans tended to agree with the Greeks, but the medieval ecclesiastical mind retreated from ideas it found too disturbing – St Augustine condemned the idea that men could 'plant their footsteps opposite to our feet'.[1]

The crossing of the equator by Lopo Gonçalves in the fifteenth century awakened interest in the idea of a lush, rich kingdom to the south. For a while – until Bartholomew Diaz nosed his way around the Cape and east into the Indian Ocean in 1487 to be followed ten years later by Vasco da Gama's more extended voyages – some believed that the coasts of south-west Africa might be the northern tip of the great southern continent. When attention switched to South America many believed that Antarctica adjoined it, others that Tierra del Fuego was the northern tip of a southern landmass.

Francis Drake disposed of these ideas. His circumnavigation of 1577–80 proved that no southern continent adjoined South America and that 'the Atlanticke Ocean and the South sea meete in a most large and free scope'.[2] However, the belief in a temperate southern continent spreading northwards persisted for two more centuries, despite strong evidence to the contrary from the buccaneering activities of men like Bartholomew Sharpe and

William Dampier who cheerfully sailed their ships over what, according to the maps, should have been dry land.

The growing enthusiasm for colonial expansion in the eighteenth century meant that governments found exploration strategically too important to leave to merchant adventurers and other freelances. Instead, it became the preserve of national navies. Britain, France and Russia all sent expeditions south. For Britain Captain James Cook led the way. Cook chose ships of shallow draught, similar to the colliers of his native Whitby, capable of plying close inshore and was thus able to conduct the first hydrographic surveys in Antarctica. Science as well as imperialism was becoming a powerful motive in exploration.

Cook's achievements were extraordinary. On 17 January 1773 his little 460-tonne ship the *Resolution* was the first to cross the Antarctic circle. Clerke, one of his crew, reported how they passed an ice island as high as the body of St Paul's Cathedral. Cook's *Voyage towards the South Pole and around the World*, published in 1777, gave the first descriptions of the abundant wildlife of Antarctica – the great whales, soaring albatrosses and graceful petrels. Penetrating the thick ice pack that surrounds Antarctica and retreats and advances with the seasons, Cook crossed the circle three times in all during two Antarctic summers. On the third occasion in January 1774, at latitude 71°10´S, his farthest south, Cook was finally halted by unyielding pack ice.

By now the strain was telling on his shipmates and he turned back with some relief. His brush with this hostile frozen world had convinced him that 'this ice extended quite to the Pole' and that 'no continent was to be found in this ocean but what must lie so far south as to be wholly inaccessible for ice'. His view was decided: 'Should anyone possess the resolution and the fortitude to elucidate this point by pushing yet further south than I have done, I shall not envy him the fame of his discovery, but I make bold to declare that the world will derive no benefit from it.'

Almost half a century and the defeat of Napoleon were to pass before anyone followed Cook. Then, in 1819, William Smith, a native of Blyth in Northumberland, rounded Cape Horn on his way from Buenos Aires to Valparaiso. The storms for which the Horn is notorious chased him southwards among islands with snow-capped mountains. He returned the following year to claim them for Britain, naming them the New South Shetlands. The great colonies of seals had impressed him. His accounts also impressed the sealing industry which funded his return as master and pilot to Edward Bransfield to conduct a proper survey of the islands. Bad weather drove them even further south through a thick fog. When it cleared they were surprised to see land lying away to the south-west and were cheered by the hope that this might indeed be the long-sought southern continent. They were right. What they could see was the northern tip of the Antarctic Peninsula.

However, whether they were actually the first to lay eyes on Antarctica became a matter of hot dispute in an age of international rivalry, of claims and counter-claims. Just three days earlier Captain Baron Thaddeus von Bellingshausen of the Imperial Russian Navy, over 3,000 kilometres to the south-east and attempting to circumnavigate Antarctica, had spotted a solid stretch of ice running from east through south to west. Some claim that he was in fact the first human to spy Antarctica, though he did not recognize it as such. Whatever the case he continued his journey, reaching the South Shetland Islands in the happy but misguided belief that he had discovered them.

It was now that British sealers, lured to the islands by the reports of abundant seals and whales, became the explorers of

Antarctica – men like James Weddell, John Biscoe and John Balleny. As Scott himself described admiringly, 'In the smallest and craziest ships they plunged boldly into stormy ice-strewn seas; again and again they narrowly missed disaster; their vessels were wracked and strained and leaked badly, their crews were worn out with unceasing toil and decimated by scurvy.'[3] In 1823 Weddell beat Cook's record for furthest south by 214 miles.

In 1839 James Clark Ross, dashing British naval officer and first at the Magnetic North Pole, sailed in search of the Magnetic South Pole on the greatest Antarctic expedition of the nineteenth century. While preparing in Tasmania he heard disturbing reports of an American expedition under Lieutenant John Wilkes and of the French explorer Dumont d'Urville. Both were apparently busily engaged in the region where the Magnetic South Pole was thought to lie. It was at the very least embarrassing and Ross, while conceding their unquestionable right to select any point they thought proper, was 'impressed with the feeling that England had *ever* led the way of discovery' and decided to 'avoid all inter-ference with their discoveries' and select a more easterly route to the south. This was a far more significant decision than he could have guessed. It was to lead to the most remarkable discoveries yet made in Antarctica and to show the way for the land explorations by Scott, Shackleton and Amundsen.

Ross battered through the pack ice in four days into what is now called the Ross Sea. His two ships, the *Erebus* and *Terror*, had been especially reinforced with giant timbers to enable them to forge their way through the ice pack that could crush a more fragile vessel like a nut. On 10 January 1841 came a startled cry from the officer of the watch. On the horizon, perhaps a hundred miles away, was land – a jagged, mighty row of snow-covered peaks – where no land was thought to be. It moved Ross who wrote a lyrical account of 'a most enchanting view', of 'lofty peaks, perfectly covered with eternal snow'. He began naming the features, calling the impressive northernmost cape after Viscount Adare, MP for Glamorganshire.

Off Cape Adare Ross made another important decision that would affect his successors. He decided to explore the new coast to the south. It was a magical eerie journey of towering mountains and shining glaciers. He carried on with the no doubt politically sensitive and imagination-taxing task of naming feature after feature in this strange new world. He named two mountain ranges, one after the Royal Society and the other after the British Association. Individual mountains in each range were named after illustrious members of the body concerned. Prime Minister Melbourne was also awarded a mountain. A ceremony took place on rocky little Possession Island to claim these new discoveries in the name of young Queen Victoria.

Sailing southward on 28 January 1841, a day of sparkling clarity, Ross sighted two volcanoes which were to become a familiar landmark to Polar explorers and are sited on the island which now bears his name. He called the 12,400-foot active cone Mount Erebus and the 10,900-foot inactive cone Mount Terror. The vastness and remoteness impressed Ross and his men with a sense of awe and of their own insignificance and helplessness. This feeling grew as moving ever south they were confronted by another amazing sight – what Ross called 'a perpendicular cliff of ice between one hundred and fifty and two hundred feet above the level of the sea, perfectly flat and level at the top and without any fissures or promontories on its seaward face'. Now known as the Ross Ice Shelf, or Great Ice Barrier, its surface seemed to him to be quite smooth and like an immense plane of frosted silver. He could only conjecture what lay beyond. His path south was blocked as effectively as if the cliffs of Dover confronted him, he recorded ruefully. Unknowingly, however, he had pointed the way. His explorations had shown that in the Ross Sea the ice cleared more briskly than elsewhere during the Antarctic summer. He had also found Ross Island with its sheltered sound which he named after the senior lieutenant of the *Terror*, Archibald McMurdo.

Ross finally quitted Antarctica in 1843, after setting a new far-thest south of 78°10′ in February 1842, and silence reigned once again. Clearly the only way to penetrate the continent was to land on the ice. It seemed a risky and unattractive prospect and for the next fifty years attention focused on the Arctic. The *Erebus* and *Terror* would soon sail on their fateful search for the north-west passage with Sir John Franklin, never to return to southern waters.

Thus it was not until towards the close of the nineteenth century that interest in the south gathered pace again. In 1895 a young Norwegian and childhood friend of Amundsen, Carsten Borchgrevink, sailed south with an expedition financed by the inventor of the harpoon gun. The purpose was to search for new whaling grounds. On 24 January 1895, he and his companions became the first human beings to make a confirmed landing on the continent. They landed below Cape Adare, where the relatively sheltered position and the abundant supply of penguins to provide a winter larder and fuel suggested to Borchgrevink that it might be possible to winter in this desolate spot.

It took three years for him to raise sufficient funds. In the meantime there had been another significant development. A Belgian expedition led by Lieutenant Adrien de Gerlache in the sealer *Belgica* had explored Graham Land. The ship had become trapped in the icy fastness of the Bellingshausen Sea, and the crew had experienced a dismal and frightening time – some became mentally ill while others fell prey to scurvy. In the end the *Belgica* had to be blasted and sawn free of the ice. She was, however, the first ship to winter in Antarctica and the name of her first mate was Roald Amundsen.

Meanwhile, Sir George Newnes, the wealthy publisher of the weekly *Tit-Bits* and the heavier-weight illustrated *Strand Magazine* had become Borchgrevink's patron and stumped up £35,000 on condition that his venture was called 'The British Antarctic Expedition'. This was the voyage of the whaler *Southern Cross* which arrived at Cape Adare in February 1899 and left ten men and seventy dogs to an uncertain fate. As the seas began to ice over in March the *Southern Cross* made her escape, leaving behind the first men to attempt to winter in Antarctica. It must have felt like being left on the moon. They did not know what to expect and their unease was heightened by the weird light effects in the sky as the Aurora Australis danced high above them. Anxious but determined, they constructed a wooden hut roofed with canvas and seal-skins and weighted down with sacks of coal and set up meteorological and magnetic observatories.

To be condemned to a sunless southern winter of bitter temperatures and wild storms was an immense test of physical and mental stamina. The men soon became depressed and grew impatient of each other's company. 'The silence roars in one's ears. It is centuries of heaped up solitude,' wrote Borchgrevink glumly.[4] Not all survived. By October one of the party, the naturalist Hanson, had died of an intestinal complaint. When the light returned the remaining men went on sledging expeditions, though they could not venture far because of the barrier of mountains and glaciers around the Cape. When the *Southern Cross* returned in January 1900 she carried the party further south to Ross Island and the Ross Ice Shelf and here Borchgrevink sledged over ten miles towards the Pole. He proclaimed: 'I myself accompanied by Lieutenant Colbeck and the Finn Savio, proceeded southwards reaching 78°50′S, the farthest south ever reached by man.'[5] The race for the Pole was on.

All this activity had been watched with growing concern by Sir Clements Markham, the man who was to play such a dominant role in Scott's life and, some would say, in his death. The passion of Markham's life was to bring a British Antarctic expedition into being and he was entirely clear about the form it should take. He did not advocate a dash to the South Pole. Neither did he believe that this was what British science desired. Instead he was convinced that what it wanted was a steady, continuous, laborious and systematic exploration of the whole southern region, with all the appliances of the modern investigator, and that this exploration should be undertaken by the Royal Navy. However, it was implicit that, should there be a scramble for the Pole, Britain should get there first.

Markham was born in 1830, a bare four days after the foundation of the Royal Geographical Society he was to boss, bully and cajole into championing his cause. He became a naval officer. He also became something of an explorer manqué. In 1851, as a young midshipman he sailed on an expedition to discover what had happened to Franklin and struck up an admiring friendship with Lieutenant Leopold McClintock who pioneered the sledging techniques later adopted by Scott. McClintock advocated the establishment of depots of supplies in advance of major sledging trips. He was also a firm believer that fit, well-trained men were more reliable beasts of burden than dogs. Manhauling was best.

The expedition failed to uncover Franklin's grisly fate. This task was left to McClintock to complete a few years later. By

then, however, Markham had quitted the navy to throw himself
into full-time exploration in Peru. He was forced to change his
plans when his father died, leaving him penniless. Undefeated,
he managed to transfer from a dull job clerking in the Inland
Revenue into what was to become the India Office. Here he used
his considerable persuasive powers to convince his seniors that
the Peruvian cinchona tree whose bark produced quinine should
be introduced into India. Soon he was off on his travels again,
smuggling seedlings from Peru to India and helping to establish a
successful quinine industry there.

Next came a spell as a geographer on loan to the British
military expedition which defeated the Emperor of Abyssinia at
Magdala. He was also elected a fellow of the Royal Geographical
Society. This was the perfect playground for a man of his talents and interests. The Society's audiences were eager to hear the
latest travellers' tales and Markham became a dominant figure.
According to the Society's librarian, 'There was a rich fullness
of life in the Royal Geographical Society in the early nineties of
the nineteenth century . . . Sir Clements Markham . . . overflow-
ing with enthusiasm like a boy, used to stage a series of brilliant
evening meetings to commemorate the deeds of Prince Henry the
Navigator, Columbus, Franklin and others . . .'[6]

His romantic infatuation with the heroic exploits of the
Elizabethan voyagers, in particular, masked a steely determination, obstinacy and truculence. Many found this combination
wearing but these qualities helped him to achieve his great aim
– the mounting of a British Antarctic Expedition. In 1893, on his
election as President of the Society, he promptly announced that
the equipping and dispatch of an Antarctic expedition would be
the chief object of his term of office, and appointed an Antarctic
committee which he, naturally, chaired. He had been preparing

for this moment for years and was anxious to lose no time. Delay would only allow foreign rivals to steal Britain's rightful thunder.

Rivals like Borchgrevink for instance. The Norwegian was not noted for either his modesty or his tact and had addressed the International Geographical Congress in London in 1895, proudly laying out the achievements of his first Antarctic voyage and declaring his intention to mount another expedition. To Markham it seemed he had flung down the gauntlet. He had done his best to thwart Borchgrevink's plans for further exploration, including casting doubts on the seaworthiness of the *Southern Cross,* so it had been a severe blow when Sir George Newnes agreed to fund his second 1898 expedition.

However, the 1895 Congress had passed a unanimous resolution demanding that Antarctic exploration should be given the highest priority. Thus encouraged, Markham assailed the Treasury and the Admiralty for funds. When this failed he turned to his own Society and persuaded them to vote £5,000 and to launch a public appeal. An astute operator, Markham had realized for some time that it would take more than patriotic fervour to secure the backing he needed. He had to have the scientific establishment on his side and the Royal Geographical Society was not sufficient. He needed that even more august body the Royal Society. Honeyed words besought the Royal Society to lend its 'great name' to the enterprise and, in February 1898, it graciously agreed.

Gratifying as this was, by March 1899 Markham still only had £14,000. He needed a Sir George Newnes of his own and he found him in the shape of the wealthy businessman Llewellyn Longstaff, who put up £25,000. Markham was delighted. To his even greater pleasure the Treasury then promised £40,000 if an equal sum were raised privately. Markham succeeded and could now turn his attention to the important issue of who should lead the expedition. Markham had firm views. Despite the involvement of the Royal Society, it was axiomatic to him that the leader should not be a scientist but a naval officer with the cool well-disciplined mind only naval training could give. Although the advancement of science was an important part of the enterprise, what really mattered to Markham were geographical exploration and the chance for young naval officers to make their mark.

For the leader must also be young. Sir Clements believed strongly that this was a task requiring not only the physical resourcefulness and courage of youth, but also its intellectual flexibility. 'Elderly men', he wrote, 'are not accessible to new ideas, and have not the energy and capacity necessary to meet emergencies.' Furthermore, they were 'stiff old organisms' hindered, not helped, by experience![7] He may also have found younger men more malleable.

Whom could he find worthy of the challenge? He had always taken a deep, and, it has been alleged latterly, perhaps improper interest in young naval midshipmen and cadets and their careers, sizing them up for his great quest. Captain Wilson Barker, commander of the *Worcester*, the Merchant Navy's training ship, forbade his boys to accept invitations to his home. Whatever Markham's deeper motives, perhaps not even acknowledged fully to himself, he certainly had plenty of opportunity to observe the navy's fledgling stars. Markham tells in his book *The Lands of Silence*, published after Scott's death, how he singled out Scott. His cousin Albert Markham, himself an Arctic explorer, was commodore of the Royal Navy's Training Squadron which, in March 1887, found itself in the sparkling waters of the Caribbean, accompanied by Sir Clements.

In West Indian sunshine a clutch of young midshipmen were

making their final preparations to race their cutters across the Bay of St Kitts. This was just the kind of contest the 57-year-old Sir Clements relished and he watched eagerly from the bridge of *HMS Active*. The challenge for the young officers was to get their cutters under way, make sail and beat up to windward for a mile, round a buoy, then lower mast and sail and row back. It was an exciting race and three young men battled for victory – Tommy Smyth of the *Active*, Hyde Parker of the *Volage* and an 18-year-old from the *Rover*, Robert Falcon Scott. For a time it was touch and go between Scott and Hyde Parker but Scott won, little realizing that this victory was to be one of the defining moments of his life.

The commodore, probably at Sir Clements' prompting, invited Scott to dinner four days later – 'a charming boy' recorded Markham in his diary. Sir Clements talked to the young midshipman and fell under his spell. One of his colleagues was later to remark of Scott that no one could be more charming when he chose. With his intense blue eyes radiating intelligence and energy he made a deep impression on the older man. Markham later wrote in his book that this was the moment when he concluded that Scott was the man destined to command the Antarctic Expedition. However, this was romantic hindsight. Markham had his eye on some other promising young officers as well and the decision was by no means so clear-cut. Fate was to take a hand throwing Scott in Markham's path on two further occasions.

Markham came across Scott again at Vigo. By then Scott was torpedo lieutenant of the *Empress of India*. Markham found his earlier impressions confirmed. He was more than ever impressed by Scott's 'evident vocation' for such a command.[8] However, the critical encounter came in 1899 when Scott was serving as torpedo lieutenant in the *Majestic*. On a warm June day he was on leave in London and 'chancing one day to walk down the Buckingham

Palace Road, I espied Sir Clements on the opposite pavement, and naturally crossed, and as naturally turned and accompanied him to his house. That afternoon I learned for the first time that there was such a thing as a prospective Antarctic Expedition; two days later I wrote applying to command it.'

As Scott himself wrote, at the time he had 'no predilection for Polar exploration'. However, he had other aspirations that this adventure might help him to realize. The melancholy dreamer and the man of action that were two facets of his complex nature might both find fulfilment in the unknown continent. Also, Scott believed in fate.

2

Scott – The Early Days

Each of the five men destined to journey to the South Pole and to die on the Great Ice Barrier was a complex character, but none more so than Robert Falcon Scott. He was not a natural leader. Although he had many inspirational qualities, the responsibility of leading an expedition, of being accountable for so many men's lives, of taking the crucial decisions was a strain. He was haunted by a fear of being 'below par'. He was also one of his own greatest critics, writing, 'The inherited vice from my side of the family is indolence . . . I had to force myself into being strenuous'. In his farewell message to his wife when he knew he was facing death, he warned her to guard their son against the dangers of idleness. It was a warning from the heart and a moving testimony to his struggle to master the conflicting sides of his nature. He confessed to his wife early in their relationship that 'I shall never fit into my round hole'.[1]

Even as a little boy Scott was a curious mixture. His father called him 'Old Mooney' because he was such a dreamer. Physically quite weak, he was a late developer, with a horror of blood and a love of solitude. Yet he was also the first to devise daring games for his brothers and sisters including such alarming tricks as shinning up a porch, over the glass roof and dropping about twelve feet to the ground. A slip could have meant a fatal crash through the glass on to the stone floor below. He could be moody and difficult and given to explosive bursts of temper. He hated losing at any game. Yet he was also warm-hearted and affectionate with a huge capacity to charm and was deeply attached to his large family throughout his life.

Scott was born on 6 June 1868 in Devonport to a middle-class family with a strong naval tradition and, according to family lore, a connection with Sir Walter Scott. It was also rumoured that a great-great grandfather had fought for Bonnie Prince Charlie at Culloden and subsequently fled to France with his wife and baby son. Whatever the case, some thirty years later this son, named Robert, returned to the British Isles, settled in Devon as a school master and told romantic tales of an uncle hanged after Culloden. He married a local girl and had four sons all of whom went into the navy.

The services tradition was still strong by the time of Scott's father John, but he was considered too weak and delicate. He was brought up instead to run the Hoegate Street Brewery in Plymouth which his father and uncle had bought with the prize money won from the Napoleonic wars and which he duly inherited. After a family rumpus he also inherited Outlands, a pretty, rambling house set in a couple of acres just outside Devonport, which had been in the Scott family since 1819. John Scott married Hannah Canning, a handsome, energetic woman whose father was a Lloyd's surveyor, Commissioner of Pilotage and a member of the Plymouth Chamber of Commerce. Two daughters, Ettie and Rose, came first, then Robert Falcon. After him came another daughter Grace, a brother Archie and finally Katherine.

Neatly sandwiched in the middle of this big band of brothers and sisters Scott had a happy, carefree childhood. They made their own amusements because, although they lived in a comfortable house with plenty of servants, there was little ready money to spare. The big annual treat was to go to the pantomime at the Plymouth Theatre. Scott loved the mystery and the drama of the theatre and the magic of those yearly trips to see Robinson Crusoe or the Giant Grumble Grim stayed with him all his life.

One of his sisters left a description of growing up at Outlands which depicts a life out of the pages of E. Nesbitt's stories except they found no psammead in the sandpit! Hannah Scott spent much of her time nursing her elderly parents and John Scott was a fond but not very vigorous parent. As a result the children could largely please themselves, easily outmanoeuvring nurses and governesses. There were daring climbs over high locked gates to the village sweet shop in search of sherbet and humbugs and adventures floating in a tub down a stream that meandered through the shrubbery. At eight Scott apparently appointed himself 'admiral', devised a version of gunpowder and blew his enemy 'the *Terror Of Devon*' (actually a wooden plank) out of the water. 'Con', as his family always called him from his middle name, came to grief one day when his tub overturned, soaking him and his fetching but impractical black velvet suit. His sister recalled how his father seized him by the seat of his trousers in fits of laughter while the young Scott howled his eyes out.

There were other mishaps. Scott cut himself quite badly while playing with his first penknife at the age of seven. Rather than make a fuss he plunged his injured hand into his pocket and wandered off as if nothing had happened. This story is often cited, in the way that 'improving tales' are attached to heroes in their youth, as early evidence of Scott's heroic destiny and linked to the tale of his uncle who, mauled by a tiger, with imperial sang-froid cauterized the wound himself. However, though a remarkable piece of self-control Scott's behaviour was probably practical rather than heroic – if he had made a fuss the knife would have been taken away. Also, the sight of blood made him faint.

There are other insights into life at Outlands – the trips to the nearby parish church of St Mark's with Scott wriggling about in his Eton suit and white collar; his departure every day to school in Stoke Damerel on his pony Beppo when he reached the age of eight and had outgrown his sisters' governess; his affection for animals whether it was stout little Beppo, the family's dogs or the peacock that shrieked and preened on the lawn. One day, as he jogged gently home from school he became distracted by a particular striking view. Dismounting to get a better vantage point he allowed Beppo to wander off. A small disconsolate figure came trudging up the drive with some serious explaining to do. He had, however, stopped to give Beppo's description to every police station he passed, demonstrating that the dreamer had a strongly practical side as well.

Nevertheless young 'Con' began to cause his parents concern. His bouts of dreamy abstraction seemed if anything to grow and he appeared backward at school compared with his younger brother, the energetic and cheerful Archie. He was sent to board at Foster's Naval Preparatory School at Stubbington House, Fareham, to prepare him for competing for a naval cadetship and in the holidays his father made sure that he crammed. What Scott thought of all this can only be guessed. What is known is that he carved his initials in one of the forms, made reasonable but not startling progress, was popular and – initial carving aside – reportedly one of the best-behaved boys the school had ever had.

On the eve of his thirteenth birthday Scott sat successfully for the cadetship exam and on 15 July 1881 left Outlands for the harsh discipline of the naval training ship HMS *Britannia* moored in the River Dart. He quickly knuckled down, recognizing the need to conceal the sensitive, solitary side of his nature. There is photograph of him as a naval cadet – an earnest-featured young boy with hair neatly brushed under his cap gazing at the camera with the faintest suggestion of a smile. Crammed in with 150 other cadets he was subjected to a regime that demanded punctuality, precision and presence of mind. The penalties for those who were lax or failed to concentrate or conform were severe. He learned to sleep in a hammock and was initiated into the mysteries of seamanship, including navigation, astronomy, physics and geometry. There were physical challenges too. First-term boys were expected to climb to the foremast head and by the second term they had to exhibit their daring by climbing a dizzying 120 feet above deck.

Scott found the necessary reserves of concentration and did well, despite the tiresome discovery that, like Nelson and Captain Hornblower, he suffered from seasickness, something that would trouble him all his life. The family was delighted when he passed his exams and was duly rated a midshipman. He joined H.M.S. *Boadicea,* the flagship of the Cape Squadron, in August 1883.

Slight, delicate and reserved – before going to Stubbington House the family doctor had prophesied that he was too narrow-shouldered and -chested for the navy – life aboard the *Boadicea* with her company of nearly 450 was probably rather a strain. It was certainly a rigorous existence. The diet would have comprised such unappetizing items as salt beef, salt pork, pea soup, cabbage and potatoes, plus cocoa and hard biscuit.

As a midshipman most of Scott's time was spent learning the operational duties of running a warship. He kept watch on the quarter deck, helped direct the men during drills and took charge of parties of ratings ashore. He didn't have a natural ability to command and in later life he would lack the easy assurance of his rival Shackleton. As a young officer it must have been hard for him to know how best to assert himself. The picture we have is of an anxious, eager young man masking shyness and uncertainty as best he could. The navy was not a place that tolerated weakness. Cool assurance and decisiveness were the necessities for a successful career and Scott had to conceal the introspective side of his character. Perhaps that is why as a young man he turned to writing a diary. It was a safety valve, allowing him to admit his doubts and fears without laying himself open to ridicule or sympathy, both of which he would have hated and which would have damaged his prospects. There was certainly neither time nor place for dreaming.

Again he overcame the obstacles deep within himself and his captain recorded that he had served 'with sobriety and to my entire satisfaction'. This view was shared by his next commander on the brig H.M.S. *Liberty* who described him as 'zealous and painstaking'. On the battleship HMS *Monarch*, he was rated 'promising' and at the end of 1886, the year he joined HMS *Rover* of the training squadron, the verdict was 'intelligent and capable'. All of this boded well for a solid if not a brilliant career. Yet Scott had to make his mark because he had few family connections to push him up the tree and little private income. An ambitious young man, he knew his career would have to be built on merit.

After the *Rover* – and his encounter with Sir Clements Markham – Scott studied at the Royal Naval College, passed his exams with ease and was commissioned as a sub-lieutenant in 1888. As the year drew to its close he found himself en route to join the cruiser H.M.S. *Amphion* at Esquimault, British Columbia. The last leg of his journey turned into a nightmare but accounts of it show Scott at his very best. In San Francisco he boarded a tramp steamer heading north to Alaska. A ferocious storm blew up which was to last for most of the voyage. Another Englishman, Sir Courtauld-Thompson, a fellow-passenger, later described what happened. The ship was packed with miners and their wives, many of whom were soon sick and terrified. Women lay with their children on the saloon floor, while the men turned to such drinking and quarrelling as the heaving, pitching ship would allow. The crew had other matters to attend to and the young Scott took charge.

> Though at that time still only a boy, he practically took command of the passengers and was at once accepted by them as their Boss during the rest of the trip. With a small body of volunteers he . . . dressed the mothers, washed the children, fed the babies, swabbed down the floors and nursed the sick . . . On deck he settled the quarrels and established order either by his personality, or, if necessary, by his fists.

At the same time he apparently managed to be cheerful – a characteristic he valued in others during his Polar journeys: '. . . by day and night he worked for the common good, never sparing himself, and with his infectious smile gradually made us all feel the whole thing was jolly good fun.'[2]

This account of a confident, competent young man is curiously at odds with an entry in his diary from around that time and may again reflect the improving light of hindsight. Scott wrote in his diary:

> It is only given to us cold slowly wrought natures to feel this dreary deadly tightening at the heart, this slow sickness which holds one for weeks. How can I

31

bear it? I write of the future; of the hopes of being more worthy; but shall I ever be? Can I alone, poor weak wretch that I am bear up against it all? The daily round, the petty annoyance, the ill health, the sickness of heart . . . How, how can one fight against it all? No one will ever see these words, therefore I may freely write – 'what does it all mean?'[3]

Even allowing for the uncertainty that often afflicts people in young adulthood this is a bleak view. Scott was one of those people who was at his best in a crisis because it meant there was something to be done. He needed distractions from the uncertainties inherent in an agnostic like himself. 'Sometimes it seems to me that hard work is the panacea for all ills, moral and physical,' he would later write.[4] Periods of melancholic depression would dog him throughout his life.

Scott duly joined the *Amphion*, a second-class cruiser and in August 1889 was appointed full lieutenant. He was making very respectable progress in his career but years of watch-keeping, of interminable drills and exercises lay ahead before he could reasonably expect his own command. Scott weighed this up and found it unattractive, so he decided to specialize and applied for torpedo training. His captain described him as 'a young officer of good promise who has tact and patience in the handling of men. He is quiet and intelligent and I think likely to develop into a useful torpedo officer'. With this helpful endorsement Scott entered the *Vernon* torpedo schoolship at Portsmouth in 1891.

He enjoyed life on this old wooden hulk and was intrigued by the possibilities of the torpedo. This was not a new weapon but it was only with the development of the self-propelled torpedo that the navy had begun to take it seriously. In the past decade the navy had built up a fleet of over 200 torpedo boats. Scott now learned about torpedoes and also about all the electrical and mechanical equipment of a warship, except that concerned with propulsion. He was also close to his home and family again. Archie had been commissioned into the Royal Artillery and the two brothers were able to take leave together. They played tennis and golf, rode and took their sisters sailing. Scott was working hard too and was able to write to his father that 'I look upon myself now as an authority on the only modern way of working a minefield and such like exercises . . .'[5]

However, he went home to Outlands for Christmas in 1894 to hear disastrous news. His father had sold the brewery some years earlier and had been living off the proceeds, but the money had either been spent or invested badly and the family was ruined. Scott put thoughts of his own career aside to help his sixty-three-year-old father pick up the pieces. Archie played his part as well, abandoning his career as a Royal Artillery Officer and signing up with a Hausa regiment in Nigeria, where the pay was better and the expenses less. Scott, who had never been extravagant, now had to make his meagre lieutenant's pay stretch even further.

Making the best of it, he applied for a transfer to HMS *Defiance*, the second of the navy's two torpedo training ships based at Devonport so he could be even nearer to his family. Outlands was let to a linen draper, and John Scott found a job managing a brewery in Somerset. Although the practical arrangements were soon made it must have been a wrench to part from the family home. Scott visited it in later years and never lost his affection for the old place, carving his initials in a tree. Yet at the same time, this was an opportunity for his family to break out of their confined little world. Three weeks after the crash Rose became a nurse. Ettie, good-looking and vivacious and a star of the local amateur theatricals, decided to go on the stage, joining a touring company whose leading lady was Irene Vanbrugh. Scott, whose artistic side was strongly attracted to the theatre, urged her on, soothing his mother's fears that it was not quite respectable.

Once his family was safely settled Scott applied for a seagoing ship. In 1896 he was appointed torpedo lieutenant of the battleship H.M.S. *Empress of India* and it was now at Vigo that he again met Markham after an interval of nine years. The impression he had made on the older man was confirmed, not that Scott was aware of Markham's close interest. In 1897 he transferred to the battleship H.M.S. *Majestic*. The *Majestic* was only two years old, had cost nearly one million pounds and her armament included four of the new twelve-pounder guns. She was also the flagship of the Channel Fleet and Scott's last naval post before Markham put him on the long, ultimately fatal road south.

It was also his last posting before family tragedy struck. Just four months after Scott had joined the *Majestic* his father died of heart disease and dropsy, leaving barely over £1,500. Scott and Archie each made arrangements with speed and generosity. Archie was able to contribute £200 a year from his Hausa Force pay. Scott's whole salary was little more than that but he managed to find £70 a year towards his mother's upkeep. She moved to London with her daughters Grace and Rose who had set up as dressmakers, taking rooms over a milliner's shop in Chelsea and even more daringly, given their conventional middle-class backgrounds, going to Paris to study the fashions. Again Scott applauded their move and wrote to his mother that 'I honestly think we shall some day be grateful to fortune for lifting us out of the "sleepy hollow" of the old Plymouth life'.[6] His feelings for Hannah verged on veneration – 'If ever children had cause to worship their mother . . .' he once wrote to her.[7]

But the sacrifices he now made for her debarred him from any social pleasures. He had to think carefully about buying even a glass of sherry – or accepting one, given that he could not repay the hospitality. Taking a woman out to dinner was impossible, which must have been galling for a man who had his share of youthful infatuations and liked pretty and intelligent women. It was all he could do to keep his uniform looking reasonably spruce. His friend J.M. Barrie, creator of Peter Pan, was later to suggest that the gold braid on his uniform grew tarnished and that he probably had to darn his socks. Certainly the sheer dreariness of having to worry about money all the time was something that never left him. The dreamer, the enthusiast and the idealist had to take second place to the pragmatist. Doubts had to be put aside, insoluble philosophical questions avoided and uncertainties mastered. And there was more sadness ahead. In 1898 Archie came home on leave 'so absolutely full of life' as Scott wrote to their mother.[8] A month later he went to Hythe to play golf, contracted typhoid and was dead. An even greater burden now fell on Scott, though Ettie had married William Ellison-Macartney, MP for South Antrim, who generously offered to contribute to Hannah's upkeep.

So this was the state of affairs when, just a few months after Archie's death, Scott had his chance encounter with Sir Clements Markham in the Buckingham Palace Road. The succession of blows which had fallen on him since those days of gaily racing cutters under a cloudless sky at St Kitts had made him determined to seize his opportunities. His ambition was if anything more acute, but he had begun to feel 'unlucky', as if a malign fate were pursuing him. He sensed he must fight back or go under. When Sir Clements told him of the expedition he was determined to command it.

3

'Ready, Aye, Ready'

And so the great adventure was on its feet. Sir Clements Markham's dreams were assuming substance and that substance seemed personified in the 31-year-old Scott. Though he was not tall, only five foot nine inches, he was broad and deep-chested with a narrow waist and hips. He exuded calm professionalism.

Furthermore Markham shared Scott's belief in fate and that it was providence which had guided Scott out of Victoria Station and into his path. Scott certainly felt the strangeness of it all: 'How curiously the course of one's life may be turned,' he later wrote. When, two days after their meeting, Scott applied to command the expedition, Markham supported him, though he proceeded cautiously. This was, after all, his life's work, and despite the impression he gave in *The Lands of Silence*, he had actively considered other possible leaders. He consulted Scott's captain on the *Majestic*, George Egerton, a man with experience of Arctic exploration who wholeheartedly endorsed Scott. He also consulted some of the naval grandees including the First Sea Lord of the Admiralty. Their view was equally positive.

Yet there now followed what Markham called 'long and

tedious' wrangles. The problem was the joint committee set up by the Royal Society and the Royal Geographical Society to manage the expedition. The Royal Society members slightly outnumbered their geographical colleagues. More importantly, they had very differing views. The scientists of the Royal Society wanted the primary aim of the expedition to be scientific. Markham's colleagues saw the goal as geographical discovery, while Markham had his young naval officers to promote. Scott soon became the meat in this particular club sandwich. As Markham wrote scathingly: 'The dream of professors and pedants that an undertaking is best managed by a debating society of selected wiseacres has a never ending fascination, but it is a mere dream.'[1]

An increasingly irritable Markham argued that the leader must be a young naval officer in the regular service – a man of action, discipline and resource, as well as a man of tact and discretion. He also reminded his critics that the Royal Navy had played a dominant role in Polar exploration since the days of Cook. The Royal Society, however, was unhappy. Why could a scientist not be in charge? it asked indignantly, reawakening an issue debated just as vigorously in Cook's day. The Admiralty, on the other hand, wanted a naval surveyor to run the show. At one stage the two disgruntled societies joined forces against Markham the common enemy. To Scott, back at sea now with the Channel Squadron as a torpedo lieutenant, his chances were looking slim. However, he was underestimating Markham. Whiskers aquiver with indignation, Markham fought off the plots and counter-plots until, in June 1900, he was at last able to sign Scott's appointment. On 30 June Scott was promoted commander.

There was one last threat. In February 1900, at the height of the wrangling, a distinguished geologist, John Gregory, had been appointed to lead the scientific staff. He was not the type likely to appeal to Markham, being 'a little man with a very low voice, always nervously pulling at his moustache'.[2] He arrived in England in December 1900 from the University of Melbourne under the unfortunate impression that, while Scott might command the ship, he was to be in command of the landing party. Sir Clements quickly disabused him, which led to an unedifying squabble between the country's most distinguished leaders of science and exploration. Needless to say the old campaigner had his way. Gregory was asked to serve under Scott, refused and resigned.

Scott had barely a year from the time of his appointment to make all the preparations before the departure of the expedition which was to be his first independent command. The problems seemed awesome. He needed provisions, clothing and equipment for the most hostile conditions on earth, of which he had no personal experience. He was truly a novice. As *The Times* rather sourly remarked, 'As youth is essential, one without actual Polar experience has had to be selected . . .'. Scott also had to pick his men and learn what he could about Polar travel in general and sledging in particular. By his own admission he was ignorant, and the recent fate of the *Belgica*, trapped and adrift in the ice with some of its sailors going insane, must have weighed on his mind.

He was given a small office in Burlington House which became the heart of his operation and crammed with strange objects from socks made of human hair to wolf skins. In early October he went to Norway to visit the celebrated Arctic explorer and acknowledged expert on sledging, Fridtjof Nansen. Nansen's saucer-shaped vessel the *Fram* had made a journey as audacious as any Viking's. Nansen had allowed her to drift with the Polar current right across the Arctic, thereby proving that the Arctic region was an ocean, not a continent. Nansen – tall, powerful, fair-haired and approaching forty – was impressed with the young commander's earnestness and wry humour and was generous with his advice. In particular he warned Scott that it was vital to take the right supplies and equipment. He also urged him to take sledge dogs, which Scott did, sending to Russia for them.

From Norway Scott travelled to Berlin to consult Professor von Drygalski, who was to lead a German Antarctic expedition. He was shocked to find the Germans very much better prepared and hastened home in considerable alarm, determined to drive his own plans along. To do this he had to have a much freer hand and Markham helped him to get rid of some interfering sub-committees so he could get on with the job.

As well as everything else, Scott had to find time to visit the expedition's ship, the *Discovery*, whose keel had been laid in March 1900 by the Dundee Shipbuilders Company. She was the first vessel in Britain to be purpose-built for scientific exploration since Halley's *Paramore* of 1694. She was also one of the last wooden three-masted sailing ships to be constructed in Britain. The name *Discovery* had a noble pedigree – other explorers like Baffin, Hudson and Cook had sailed in ships of that name and there was a tradition that it was lucky. (Indeed, the name is still used in the space shuttle programme.) Whatever the case, to Scott she was one of the finest craft afloat. The shipbuilders had taken their inspiration from the traditional British whalers which, in the ever-widening quest for their prey, had evolved a design capable of battering through the ice.

The *Discovery* was built of wood – a skill which Scott noted was already passing away – and had a formidable strength. Her frames were of solid English oak and her lining of Riga fir. She had no portholes or sidelights, and daylight filtered into the living spaces through central skylights and small round decklights. Her sides were 26-inches thick and her projecting bow, already eleven feet of solid wood, was further reinforced with steel plates to help her nose her way through the ice-pack and resist pressure. Her stern was rounded and overhanging to give protection to the rudder, an innovation Nansen had pioneered successfully with the *Fram*. Because the uncertainties of voyages of exploration meant she might run out of coal, she was equipped with sail and steam – a combination Scott was familiar with from his naval training days. When completed, the *Discovery* cost just over £50,000, perhaps some £2,500,000 in today's money. She also had a carefully constructed observatory for the taking of magnetic observations. To be effective it was important that there should be no iron or steel within a 30-foot radius of it. The designers managed to achieve this, though on the voyage out consternation was caused by the discovery that someone had hung a parrot in a metal cage within the exclusion zone. The expedition's instruments were lent by the Admiralty and included astronomical, magnetic and meteorological equipment and seismographs as well as sounding gear and dredging nets.

Equally important was the crew. As with so much else this became a fruitful source of argument. The navy had agreed to provide a small naval core. Scott wanted men with the sense of discipline learned in the navy and frankly doubted his ability to deal with any other sorts of men. He was therefore delighted to number three naval officers among his crew. Lieutenant Charles Royds was appointed as Scott's first lieutenant and meteorologist, and Scott was able to welcome two of his messmates from the *Majestic*. Reginald Skelton was appointed engineer lieutenant while the cheerful Michael Barne became second lieutenant and took charge of the deep-sea apparatus.

However, Markham had to turn to the Merchant Navy to find

a deputy leader. He invited 36-year-old Albert Armitage, a P&O officer, to serve in this capacity and as navigator. Armitage had useful experience of Arctic exploration, having been navigator in the Jackson-Harmsworth expedition to Franz-Josef Land in 1894–7, a feat for which the Royal Geographical Society had awarded him a medal. If anything he had expected to be offered the leadership of the British Antarctic expedition and was inclined to turn the offer down. However, the siren voice of Sir Clements wooed him. 'See Scott before you refuse,' he urged.[3]

An evening with Scott in Chelsea, where he was living with his mother and sisters, won him over: 'I was charmed by him from the first. He said to me, "You *will* come with me, won't you? I cannot do without you."'[4] Scott could be irresistible when he chose and Armitage was unable to refuse, though he foresaw a role as a kind of dry-nurse to the less experienced man. He apparently attached certain conditions to his agreement, in particular that his appointment should be independent of Scott, though under his command, and that he would be landed with a team and supplies for two years. He also demanded that his pay should be no more than £50 per year lower than Scott's. In his disillusioned later years he was to claim that only the promise about his pay was kept. He alleged that, arrived in Antarctica, Scott appealed to him to forgo the other promises on the grounds that he could not do without him.

At the time, however, Armitage was concerned to find himself the focus of some Machiavellian activities as the learned societies continued to slog it out. He was approached informally to see whether he would consent to be commander if Scott resigned and to his credit refused. In fact it was he and Sir Clements who joined forces to persuade Scott to stick to his guns in the face of renewed hostility about a naval officer being in absolute command. The crisis duly passed and Armitage was able to give his attention to buying sledging equipment and clothing. However, he was unable to convince Scott and the expedition's advisers that it would be better to take fewer men and more dogs. This lack of 'horse sense' as he called it worried him.[5]

Scott also turned to the Merchant Navy for an executive assistant and an engaging and highly ambitious Anglo-Irishman, Ernest Henry Shackleton, now made his appearance. From Scott's perspective he was to prove something of a Trojan horse but in the *Voyage of the Discovery*, Scott's painstaking and moving account of his first expedition, he described him as 'always brimful of enthusiasm and good fellowship'. Shackleton was educated at Dulwich College, where he found lessons tedious and was usually near the bottom of the class, though adept at avoiding punishment. On leaving school he decided not to follow his father into the medical profession. The sea was the life for him. His father could not afford the cost of entering him as a naval cadet so he instead began his sailing life as apprentice on a merchant vessel bound for Valparaiso. It was hard and dirty work and 'a queer life and a risky one' as he confided to a friend.[6] His captain found him pig-headed and obstinate but he got on well with the men, untroubled by social barriers that might have prevented him, a future officer, from befriending ordinary seamen.

By the age of twenty-five Shackleton was a merchant officer with the Union-Castle line, a confident garrulous man with a love of the poet Browning whom he could quote ad infinitum. His fellow officers liked him though they found him an atypical young officer. Scenting an opportunity for fame and possibly the fortune that might help him win the woman, Emily Dorman, on whom he had set his heart – Shackleton had told his prospective father-in-law that his fortune was all to make, but he intended to make it quickly – he applied for the Antarctic expedition, though he had no special desire to go to the Antarctic and little interest in scientific research. At first he was turned down. However, even more than Scott he possessed the power to charm and became friendly with Cedric Longstaff, the son of the expedition's quiet and pleasant benefactor Llewellyn Longstaff, during a voyage taking troops out to South Africa in March 1900. The result was that Longstaff senior asked whether a place could be found for this charismatic officer. Armitage made some enquiries, the response was universally positive and Shackleton was in. In high glee he took leave from the Union-Castle Line and reported ready for anything.

Shackleton was to play a vital part in the quest for the South Pole but he was never among Scott's inner circle. Not so Edward Adrian Wilson, the man who over a decade later would die next to Scott 'with a comfortable blue look of hope'.[7] Over the years Wilson has probably been the least criticized and most admired of the men who reached the South Pole. He was born in Cheltenham in 1872 to a family with strong Quaker ancestry on his father's side. The family motto was *res non verba*, 'deeds not words', a sentiment of which he wholeheartedly approved. He was a teetotaller with an innate dislike of crudeness or vulgarity but he was no prig. He had a delightful sense of the ridiculous and a quiet power which drew people to him. He was regarded as friend and mentor by many of his companions. Paradoxically, while he loathed self-pity, he always responded with sympathy and understanding to the real problems of others. He was a follower of Ruskin and a decided ascetic reflected, to an extent, in his tall, lean aquiline appearance which a friend compared to that of a thoroughbred horse.

Described by his mother as 'the brightest and jolliest of all our babies', he apparently already showed an extraordinary talent for drawing by the time he was three. At just seven he was designing and drawing Christmas cards, a habit he continued throughout his life. His earliest scrapbook contained pictures of Arctic explorers and he made his own midnight sun out of orange paper. His other passion was for collecting – he hoarded shells and fossils, butterflies and dried flowers and at nine announced that he would be a naturalist. Clutching a sovereign he went out and bought skinning and stuffing tools and invested in lessons in taxidermy.

He delighted in being out of doors and close to nature which induced a kind of spiritual rapture in him. Sometimes he would lie out under the stars in the Cotswold hills wrapped in a horse-blanket and listen to the birdsong. Later, when suffering from snowblindness in the Antarctic wastes, the sound of his skis swishing through the snow would make him think of brushing through fat juicy bluebells in his beloved Gloucestershire. So great was his passion for nature that as a student doctor in London he decked his rooms with branches of willow, hazel, alder, fir and birch. Encouraged by his father he took to observing, noting and sketching everything he saw and his observational powers were acute.

At Cheltenham College he did well at sport because of his remarkably strong legs. Though not a brilliant scholar, he was fascinated by science and did well enough to go as an exhibitioner to Gonville and Caius College, Cambridge, to read for the Natural Sciences Tripos and the medical examinations. Foreshadowing his role on the Antarctic expeditions he often found himself a mediator among the turbulent and troublesome set of undergraduates of his year. The result was that he had little time for himself, yet he was, despite his affection for his friends, a lover of solitude. What he really loathed was 'society' and throughout his life formal occasions, house parties with unknown people, the bland chit-chat of parties and receptions would set his nerves on edge and fill his bright blue eyes with panic. Sometimes he would need to sedate himself in order to face the ordeal. Indeed, he was always keen to master his weaknesses and develop self-control, even resorting to self-mortification. As his biographer George Seaver put it: 'He took out-of-the way means to acquaint himself with the experience of pain, and resolutely set before himself [the] ideal of Christian asceticism . . .'[8] Yet despite this austere side to his nature, Wilson played hard too and, cold sober, was always in the middle of any high jinks. He had a cheerful disregard for minor rules, resulting in him being sent down for a few days after sneaking out of college without leave early one morning to catch a trout.

Wilson took his BA degree in 1894, and in 1895 left what he called his butterfly academic existence to join St George's Hospital in London. Wilson threw himself into his work but he was excited by everything, especially London where he said he felt like a soda-bottle in an oven, primed with enthusiasm for his new life and ready to explode. He still kept close to nature, lying out on Wimbledon Common with supplies of rolls and chocolates listening to the nightingales. He spent as much time as he could working at the Caius College Mission in the slums of Battersea, only to contract TB. He was sent to Switzerland and Norway to recuperate and was so frail that one of his fellow patients later commented that it was the greatest miracle that Wilson managed to reach the South Pole. He was not even considered strong enough to toboggan. Curiously enough his letters showed a distaste for cold conditions. 'Awful, awful, I cannot abide the snow!'[9]

Wilson became engaged to a sensible and well-educated young woman, Oriana Souper, in October 1899 and the following year successfully passed his MB examination. It was at about this time that he learned that a junior surgeon and zoologist was being

45

sought for the National Antarctic Expedition. His natural modesty made him reluctant to apply though he was keenly interested. In 1897 he had heard Nansen speak about the Arctic and had been moved by his account of how the expedition's dogs had had to be shot. Luckily his uncle, Sir Charles Wilson, lobbied Sir Clements Markham, who was impressed by Wilson's remarkable artistic talent. Scott duly met him and accepted him there and then, even though Wilson's arm was in a sling because blood poisoning had given him an abscess in the armpit. At his subsequent interview with the Medical Board he admitted with characteristic honesty that he had had TB and the board predictably rejected him, but Scott now insisted he should come on the expedition. Not only did Wilson have a rare combination of medical and artistic skill but there was something much less tangible which appealed to Scott.

In many ways Wilson was the perfect foil to Scott – optimistic and approachable where Scott was pessimistic and remote; tolerant where Scott could be impatient and critical; cheerful where Scott was quick-tempered and moody. He also believed that things would turn out as they were ordained to, the result of a deep and comforting religious faith. His attitude was live for the day and don't worry about the future. He wrote: 'It is no sin to long to die, the sin is in the failure to submit our wills to God to keep us here as long as He wishes.'[10] This contradicts some interpretations of Wilson as a natural martyr – an almost saintly, rather passive, individual only too ready to embrace death. He had a huge love of life and the clear conviction that it was God not man who should decide when life should end. This became grimly relevant on the return from the South Pole when his desperate companions would force him to hand over his stock of opium tablets so that they could commit suicide if they chose. He was also something of a pacifist. Reports of events in the Boer War made him cry like a baby and he said he would far rather shoot himself than anyone else by a long way. He believed that 'the vilest of sins' were disguised as 'the glories of imperialism'.

Religion was the one area where he and Scott disagreed seriously. Scott was agnostic and suffered grave crises of doubt both about himself and about life in general. Moods of 'black dog', when he doubted any meaning or purpose in life, would suddenly overtake him. Wilson's serenity and sense of purpose were like an anchor in the storm. Scott would later describe him as: 'The life and soul of the party, the organizer of all amusements, the always good-tempered and cheerful one, the ingenious person who could get round all difficulties.' At the same time Wilson was drawn to Scott's sincerity and love of justice. Wilson was delighted by his appointment, announcing cheerfully that it would be a case of kill or cure and was soon enmeshed in preparations, including further lessons in taxidermy at London Zoo.

The expedition's surgeon, Reginald Koettlitz, or 'Cutlets' as he was to be nicknamed, had been appointed before Scott. He was thirty-nine years old, rather tall and gangling and Markham thought him a 'honest good fellow' but humourless and 'exceedingly short of common sense'.[11] Koettlitz's views on scurvy, the curse of Polar expeditions, were the conventional ones of his age – that it was caused by poison from tainted food and that the way to guard against it was to keep food pure and tins airtight. He firmly believed that there were no such things as anti-scorbutics. Like many contemporaries, he did not favour the use of lime juice, long distributed amongst British seamen as an anti-scorbutic and so well known that it had caused Americans to call British seamen and then all their countrymen 'limeys'. Koettlitz also ignored an emerging but as yet unproven view that it was not the presence of a taint but the absence of some essential element that caused the disease. The true cause, the lack of vitamin C, was not to be properly understood for some years. Nevertheless, others, such as Armitage, with Polar experience recognized the importance of fresh meat in both preventing and curing the disease.

The other scientific posts were awarded to the bald and eager Thomas Vere Hodgson, director of the marine biological laboratories in Plymouth, who became the expedition's naturalist. The post of geologist was given to Hartley Ferrar, a twenty-two-year-old Cambridge graduate. The Markham verdict on him was that he was 'very unfledged and rather lazy' but might be 'made into a man'.[12] Louis Bernacchi, at twenty-five another young man, was appointed physicist. Despite his youth, this Tasmanian was the only member of the expedition to have had any Antarctic, as distinct from Arctic, experience having wintered in Borchgrevink's hut on Cape Adare. Markham thought him 'always a grown-up' and was prepared to overlook his association with Borchgrevink.[13]

The petty officers and ratings were drawn from the navy after the Admiralty was pressured not to be niggardly and to release three warrant officers and six petty officers. Among the petty officers was a Welshman of towering physique and robust good humour, Edgar Evans, who with Scott and Wilson would take part in the final, fatal journey. He had served with Scott on the *Majestic* but at this stage Scott little realized the bond which would be forged between them.

Evans had a warm, lively personality and an inexhaustible fund of anecdotes. He enjoyed reading Dumas or 'Dum Ass' as he called him, but definitely not Kipling or Dickens. He was far removed from the shadowy, flawed giant from the lower decks so often depicted. Evans was born at Rhossili in the beautiful Gower in 1876. He was not a Welsh speaker although he knew the soft lilting Gower dialect. His father was a 'Capehorner', a seaman who sailed from Swansea across the Atlantic and round Cape Horn to the west coast of South America for copper ore. His mother was the daughter of the licensee of the Ship Inn at the pretty little hamlet of Middleton.

The family moved to Swansea when Evans was seven and he grew up 'a very venturesome boy' who never complained, according to his mother.[14] A photograph taken in 1893 with his sister Annie shows a strong broad-faced youth with a determined set to his face. He left school at thirteen and for a time worked at the Castle Hotel, frequented by the captains of the copper ore barques. Perhaps it was their stories and his father's tales which sparked his thirst for a life at sea. His mother tried to dissuade him, having seen her husband badly injured when a cargo bale fell on him. His leg was subsequently amputated.

Evans was undeterred. With the impatience of youth he couldn't even wait until he was the right age and tried to enlist at fourteen, only to be sent away. The second time he was nearly rejected because he had one more decayed tooth than officially allowed. He began his training in *HMS Ganges*, a solid old hulk in Falmouth and a year later, in April 1892, was promoted to Boy Ist Class. He progressed well, helped by his outstanding strength and for a while served as a physical training instructor. In 1899 he began two years' service in *HMS Majestic* where Scott spotted him.

So the man who signed on with Scott in July 1901 as one of two second-class petty officers, was an impressive individual, toughened by a decade in the navy. He was nearly six foot tall, weighed a little under thirteen stone and was 'in a hard condition'. At twenty-five he had that great supposed prerequisite for polar travel – youth. His pay was 17s 1d a week at a time when the average wage for a semi-skilled man was around £1 10s 6d and when a live-in maid could be paid no more than 10s a week. Scott by comparison was paid £10 a week and Shackleton £5. These were reasonable salaries – rents at the time were about 10s a week for a six-bedroom house in respectable Clapham and a house with garden in Balham could be bought for £850 and fully furnished for £150, a third-class return rail ticket from London to Newcastle cost £2 5s 3d, a steak and kidney pudding in a cheap restaurant cost 4d, a bottle of whisky 3s 6d and 25 Wild Woodbine cigarettes 5d.

Scott obtained his ratings by writing to his colleagues in the Channel Squadron seeking volunteers and he had no shortage to choose from. Among the stokers he selected was thirty-three-year-old William Lashly, a strong, powerful teetotaller and non-smoker, reserved, even retiring, but always ready to help a comrade and described by Markham as 'the best man in the engine room'.[15] He also picked Frank Wild, later to accompany Shackleton on all his expeditions. All in all he was well pleased. Although the *Discovery* would not be subject to the Naval Discipline Act he wanted to run his ship as closely as possible along naval lines and now he had the men who would help him to maintain those strict standards.

He could also be confident their teeth would withstand the rigours ahead. Markham noted the following in his personal narrative: 'Ship's Company's Teeth. The teeth were examined by dental surgeons from Guy's hospital in July 1901. 178 teeth were stopped, and 92 pulled out. Bill £62.4.5. 41 examinations at the rate of 30s a man.'[16] A not inexpensive business.

On 21 March 1901 Lady Markham snipped a piece of tape with a pair of golden scissors and the *Discovery* slid gracefully into the Tay. Then she was brought back to the dockside to be fitted with her engines and boilers. After sea trials she left her home port in June for the East India Docks in the Thames for loading. This was no trivial matter. She would have to carry provisions for forty-seven men for three years. Ample supplies of roast pheasant, roast turkey, whole roast partridges, jugged hare, duck and green peas and rump steak were carried on board, together with such delicacies of the era as wild cherry sauce, celery seed, blackcurrant vinegar, candied orange peel, Stilton and Double Gloucester cheese. Nor were they to go short of drink with 27 gallons of brandy, the same of whisky, 60 cases of port, 36 of sherry, 28 of champagne. They also took 1,800 pounds of tobacco, a great deal of pemmican (a mixture of dried lean beef and lard), raisins, chocolate and onion powder.

Many companies had been generous with their sponsorship and this was a great help given that money was so tight. Dr Jaeger's Sanitary Woollen System Company Ltd manufactured some special windproof outer garments and gave the expedition a 40 per cent discount, which Scott acknowledged with gratitude. He was quick to recognize the benefits of sponsorship in an age when this was still a relatively new concept. Colman's donated nine tons of flour and plenty of mustard; Cadbury's gave 3,500 pounds of 'excellent cocoa and chocolate' which became one of the greatest treats for hungry sledgers; from Bird's came 800-weight of baking and custard powders and, despite Koettlitz's views on anti-scorbutics, lime juice from Messrs Evans, Lescher and Webb. There were also supplies of Bovril, which became a feature of the sledging journeys. However, the real staple food for sledging was pemmican, with its high fat and calorie content. During the heyday of British Arctic exploration pemmican could be bought in Britain, but now the expedition had to look overseas for supplies. Scott obtained his from a factory in Copenhagen, having found a product made in Chicago unsuitable.

And then there was the equipment to be stowed on board – reindeer sleeping bags, bales of Lapland grass to insulate the feet, seventy pairs of skis and nine nine-foot sledges made to Nansen's design, complete with sledge flags designed by Markham. As if they were knights of old on a quest, their flags resembled medieval pennants. The romantic Markham devised mottos for them – Scott's was 'Ready, Aye, Ready'.

There was also a balloon purchased from the army. Sir James Hooker, the elderly and distinguished botanist who had sailed with Ross in 1839–43 had urged Scott to take one for aerial surveys. There was a growing fascination with the possibilities of air travel at this time. There had even been a premature attempt to reach the North Pole by balloon in 1897 – the ill-fated *Eagle* expedition – but Scott's balloon would be firmly anchored. There was also the array of instruments and other equipment lent by the Admiralty. Given the other necessities – the oil, coal, fresh water, dog food, medical supplies, wooden hut, piano and library and personal possessions like Shackleton's typewriter, make-up box and conjuring tricks for entertainment – it took considerable planning to stow it all in a vessel only 172 feet long and 34 feet wide.

Just before departure Scott received his final instructions. While much was left to his discretion, the expedition was to follow Ross's path along the Great Ice Barrier and winter on the coast of Victoria Land. The main objective was to explore inland, and if possible to explore by sea to the east of the Great Ice Barrier. There was no mention of the South Pole.

On 31 July 1901 the *Discovery* set sail, pausing at Cowes where the glittering royal regatta was in full swing. She was a bit of an ugly duckling with her black hull, stumpy masts and barrel of a crow's nest compared with the elegant vessels around her. King

Edward VII, as yet uncrowned because Victoria had only died in January, came aboard and made a speech and Queen Alexandra tested the bunks. Hannah Scott, bursting with maternal pride, pinned the Royal Victorian Order (fourth class) on Scott's tunic on behalf of their Majesties. There was a moment's panic when the Queen's Pekinese went overboard, to be retrieved by a sailor who dived in to save it. By the next day the memory of the great jamboree, with its glory and farce, was fading as the *Discovery* slipped past the Needles. Her crew wondered what awaited them and when they would see home again.

They went with their nation's blessing, a welcome distraction from the baffling war which was still being fought out with the Boers. As the *Morning Post* put it: 'Even in the last throes of an exhausting struggle, we can yet spare the energy and the men to add to the triumphs we have already won in the peaceful but heroic field of exploration . . .'

4

'Childe Harold
to the Dark Tower Came'

On the afternoon of 2 January 1902 the men of the *Discovery* gazed on their first icebergs, silent ambassadors of the approaching pack. The next day they crossed the Antarctic Circle, earning them the sailors' traditional right to drink a toast with both feet on the table. The *Discovery's* ironclad prow began to nose her way through the honeycombed floes causing the vessel to shudder gently. The world her crew would now inhabit was cold, beautiful and treacherous. No one knew how long the *Discovery* would be in the pack ice. The *Southern Cross* had taken forty-three days to fight her way back into open water. Yet despite the danger and the uncertainty it was a magical sight. Bernacchi was moved by 'the alabaster whiteness of the floes . . . intensified by the exquisite green colouring of the cracks and cavities'.

Scott watched anxiously as the ship forced her way through the grinding floes, relying on the officer of the watch up in the crow's nest or on the bridge to seek out the open pools and channels. Yet there were lighter moments. Bernacchi was on duty one morning and described how a cheerful Shackleton came to relieve him at four a.m. 'full of verses and warmth-giving navy cocoa . . . Shackleton was a poet and that morning poetically very wide awake, and . . . kept me from my waiting bunk reciting endless verses in the voice and manner of an old-time tragedian – "One moment, old son," he wheedled, as I edged towards the gang-way, "have you heard this?"' The cold, yawning young Australian physicist didn't care whether he had or not and, throwing 'polite-ness to the ice-floes', decamped leaving Shackleton to his poetry and the pale Antarctic light.

Meanwhile, Wilson was in heaven, his sketchbook seldom out of his hand. Painting and drawing on board ship had its prob-lems but Wilson found some ingenious solutions: 'For deck work [I] have made a bad weather sketching box which I hang round my neck, and can sketch comfortably in it even when it rains and blows a gale and spray comes all over one. The paper keeps comparatively dry.' The pack was no barren world. As they left the open sea behind them the wheeling albatrosses and delicately swooping oceanic petrels vanished, but other birds took their place. Pugnacious skua gulls flapped past. Giant petrels lumbered by in search of carrion. More appealing were the little snow petrels with their dainty white plumage, black beaks and feet and black beady eyes.

But the strangest, most engaging birds of all were the penguins. Scott described how the squawking of these 'merry little compan-ions' was constantly heard:

> . . . curiosity drew them to the ship, and suddenly their
> small figures appeared on a floe at some distance, only
> to skurry across and leap into the water on the near
> side, when with what seemed extraordinary rapidity

> they bobbed up again, shooting out on to the surface
> of some floe quite close to the ship. Here they paused
> and gazed at us with open-eyed astonishment . . .

What particularly amazed them was when the sailors imitated their call.

Seals were plentiful as well – crab-eaters and Ross seals dozed on the floes. With no natural predators on land they were off their guard and easy to shoot and haul on board for food as well as for research. The deck became awash with gore. Wilson spent a whole day bathed in blood from head to foot. The seal meat, stripped of skin and blubber, was hung in the rigging which served in the cold as a larder.

A late Christmas was celebrated on 5 January and the crew decided to try out their skis. Few had ever skied before and there was much hilarity as they organized races over the ice, crashing and falling about. It seems odd to us, accustomed to modern emphasis on planning and training, that they had not sought an earlier opportunity for practice. Just three days later they were through the pack. Suddenly there was open sea around them and the leaden pall of clouds which had accompanied them dispersed. Later the same day they sighted the peaks of Victoria Land sparkling under the midnight sun. Bernacchi described how the water was a mass of quivering, shifting colour while banks of deep purple clouds caught in the sun's path cast a strange radiance over everything. The men remained on deck until dawn, quite transfixed.

In a sense Bernacchi was coming home, for Scott was steering for Robertson Bay, formed by the long peninsula of Cape Adare, where Bernacchi and Borchgrevink had wintered on the *Southern Cross* expedition. There was a reception party waiting for them. Cape Adare is a breeding ground or rookery for the Adélie penguins, named after the wife of the French explorer Dumont d'Urville, and they nest in the cliff face. Little black figures in white shirt fronts toddled forward to meet the new arrivals and as Bernacchi wrote: 'We saw the ordered communism of their lives.' The noise and the stench were overpowering. The droppings, looking and smelling like anchovy paste, were everywhere. The activity was ceaseless as the parent birds plodded down to the sea and back with food for their obstreperous young.

The hut of the *Southern Cross* expedition was right in the middle of this rookery and contained a letter in English left by the Norwegian for the next explorer. Scott read it out to his companions who fell about with mirth, deriding it for its poor spelling, pomposity and general uselessness. Skelton complained it didn't even have anything helpful to say about stores. Bernacchi seems to have been rather offended by this, though he had not regarded Borchgrevink as the good leader he came to consider Scott. He climbed a nearby hill to visit the grave of his former colleague Nikolai Hanson, the naturalist who had died on the *Southern Cross* expedition, and who was the only human then buried on the Antarctic continent.

Scott sailed on. Luck had been with him so far, but the next day brought the *Discovery* close to disaster. Standing to the south she became caught in the grip of a powerful current. Scott described the horror of it, the feeling of helplessness, made worse by the irony of the tranquil beauty around them:

> Above us the sun shone in a cloudless sky, its rays were reflected from a myriad points of the glistening pack; behind us lay the lofty snow-clad mountains . . . the air about us was almost breathlessly still; crisp, clear and sunlit, it seemed an atmosphere in which all Nature

57

should rejoice; the silence was broken only by the deep
panting of our engines and the slow, measured hush
of the grinding floes; yet beneath all ran this mighty,
relentless tide, bearing us on to possible destruction.
It seemed desperately unreal that danger could exist in
the midst of so fair a scene . . .

Ahead lay a phalanx of icebergs glittering and diamond hard.
It was only at the very last moment that the tide slackened, the
close-locked floes relaxed their grip and the *Discovery* steamed
towards the open sea and safety.

The *Discovery* now headed south along the eastern shore of
Victoria Land, enduring a storm so cold and vicious that, though
it was midsummer, the seawater froze as it lashed the deck. They
were following Ross's course and by mid-January came upon an
inlet in the cliff-face. A scene of such perfect beauty and stillness met their gaze that Wilson swore he would never forget it.
Seals basked beneath the unsetting sun, and the ice around them
was shot through with emerald, azure and aquamarine. However,
once more Wilson the artist had to become Wilson the butcher.
Such a cache of animals was too good to leave and thirty seals and
ten emperor penguins were slain. It was, Wilson wrote, 'a duty
much against the grain'. For Scott it was even worse: 'It seemed a
terrible desecration to come to this quiet spot only to murder its
innocent inhabitants and stain the white snow with blood; but
necessities are often hideous and man must live,' he later wrote.
He and some others went off on their skis to escape the sight and
sound of the carnage.

The value of the penguins and seals was two-fold. To contribute to scientific learning, certainly, but also to contribute to the
larder. Scott feared he had a battle on his hands over the latter.

He knew that fresh food was essential for a healthy diet but he didn't know how his men would react to seal steaks and penguin casserole. Neither did he know how he himself would react, confessing ruefully to a weak stomach in such matters. He could not resort to the stern measures taken by Cook, who had flogged his men for not eating sauerkraut and so was delighted when most of his crew displayed a healthy appetite for the local fare. Seal liver in particular was soon looked on as a real delicacy when fried in pemmican or bacon fat.

Swinging eastward the *Discovery* began to explore the Great Ice Barrier. There was tremendous excitement when what looked like the print of some large land mammal was spotted on a floe covered with soft snow. Cameras were soon hanging over the side, but it was quickly seen that the footprint was webbed and probably left by a giant petrel as it half ran, half flew to become airborne. On 22 January they managed to force a whaleboat 'somewhat crowded with sixteen persons' through the surf to land on Cape Crozier on the north-eastern edge of Ross Island. The decision to land was taken by Scott without consulting his crew. Wilson, Hodgson and Royds all noted this characteristic of taking sudden action without discussion. It was the old boyhood habit, perhaps, of going off into a reverie and then suddenly realizing there was something to be done. That old bugbear of abstraction was certainly still with him– his young steward Clarence Hare later told how Scott sprinkled milk and sugar over a plate of curry.[1]

Scott, Wilson and Royds climbed up a 1,350-foot volcanic cone to look down on the Barrier. Scott's description captured a feeling of macabre grandeur: '. . . the barrier edge, in shadow, looked like a long narrowing black ribbon as it ran with slight windings to the eastern horizon . . . the very vastness . . . seemed to add to our own sense of its mystery.'

They turned their back on this extraordinary sight to find themselves dealing with a rather more immediate problem. They were in the midst of another vast Adélie penguin rookery. The young chicks ran hither and thither in alarm as Scott and his companions tried to weave their way through the mass of downy small bodies. This panic roused the parent birds. Scott described how they rushed at them with hoarse cries of rage: 'After beating wildly at our shins with their beaks and flippers they would fall back growling and cursing in the most abominable manner.'

The *Discovery* now steamed eastwards along the Barrier. On 30 January they passed the extreme eastern position reached by Ross in 1842. Shackleton was overcome with the strangeness of looking on lands never before seen by the human eye. Scott named this new region King Edward VII land. He charted 150 miles of its coast but was tantalized by glimpses of distant hills that there was no time to explore. The moment was approaching when they must seek winter quarters and they turned westward again.

However, there was still time on 4 February to unpack the balloon, nicknamed *Eva*, and send it aloft. What happened next caused Wilson to express his feelings with unusual asperity. Scott decided to be the first up and at 500 feet threw all the sandbags overboard. He nearly shot straight into the heavens and was saved only by the balloon's secure mooring. 'As I swayed about in what appeared a very inadequate basket and gazed down on the rapidly diminishing figures below I felt some doubt as to whether I had been wise in my choice,' he later wrote laconically. Shackleton, undeterred by his commander's erratic ascent, went next, clutching a camera. All they could see was the surface of the Barrier. Wilson described the episode as perfect madness: 'If some of these experts don't come to grief over it out here, it will only be because God has pity on the foolish.' In fact, that was that as far as ballooning was concerned. *Eva* sprang a leak and never ascended again to Wilson's profound satisfaction.

As the *Discovery* sailed west the temperature began to drop rapidly. Scott found a winter home in McMurdo Sound which he had decided would be a good base for sledging exploration when the spring came. By 8 February the *Discovery* was secured to an ice-foot* off Mount Erebus. Stoker Lashly recorded glumly that it looked 'a dreary place',[2] but there was a plateau of volcanic rubble level enough for the erection of the large hut brought from Australia. This was 'a fairly spacious bungalow of a design used by the outlying settlers in that country' called 'Gregory Lodge' after Professor Gregory who had designed it. Hardly, at first glance, ideal for Antarctica, Armitage described it as more suitable for a colonial shooting lodge than a Polar dwelling. However, it was not to be their winter home. Although the original intention had been that the *Discovery* should land a small party and then turn north before the season closed, Scott hoped that McMurdo Sound would be a safe haven where she could ride out the winter months and provide the main living quarters although she would, inevitably, be iced in. He was, however, taking a gamble and had no evidence on which to base his decision.

The hut was still important as a shelter for returning sledging parties in case the ship had to put out to sea. It was also to serve as the 'Royal Terror Theatre' when, during the dreary Antarctic winter, the men turned to amateur theatricals and concerts. Two smaller asbestos-covered huts had also been brought to house the magnetic instruments, and there were kennels for the twenty-three Siberian dogs which had been taken on board during a last stop-over in New Zealand. The crew were heartily glad to get these snapping snarling

* An ice-foot is a strip of frozen sea or blocks of ice along the shore-line.

creatures ashore so they would stop fouling the decks. The dogs spurned their kennels, preferring to curl up in the snow.

Lashly tried to erect a windmill to drive a dynamo for electric lighting, but its success was short-lived. The winds were too strong and an acetylene plant was used instead. In between their labours they played football on the ice and there was always ski practice. Scott described how 'figure after figure can be seen flying down the hillside, all struggling hard to keep their balance . . .' and usually coming a cropper. Tobogganing, using a contraption artfully fashioned out of a pair of skis and a packing case, soon became the craze while Ferrar, feeling full of energy, was the first to climb the nearby 'Observation Hill' and discover that they were in fact on an island. Named after Ross, it became one of the great landmarks in Antarctic exploration.

The dogs provided another diversion. Scott and his men, nearly all inexperienced, began experimenting to see whether dogs could pull loads but while some worked well, others were so timid they grovelled at any attempt to drive them. They all fought 'whenever and wherever they could', Scott noted. What was the best way to handle dogs? Bernacchi, from his *Southern Cross* experience, was sure that all that was needed was kindness. Armitage, from his Arctic knowledge, argued that the only thing to do was to apply the whip. They decided to put their theories to the test and each selected a team of dogs. At first neither team could be persuaded to start. After a period of wild confusion with twisted traces and some vicious fights, Bernacchi eventually managed to coax his animals into a trot which became a wild career up a steep snow-slope leaving him panting behind. The other team declined to move at all. It seemed that gentle persuasion was the best approach, but if the incident proved anything it was that Scott and all his men had a great deal to learn about working with dogs.

Life settled into an ordered routine but there remained a profound sense of the strangeness and the beauty of it all. The sun was now circling so low that a soft pink light tinged the snow and ice, fading into the purple outline of the distant mountains. The surrounding peaks seemed to turn to gold in the pure shafts of sunlight. The closer winter approached, the more spectacular were the effects – the diaries describe saffron tints deepening to crimson, fleecy clouds with bright gilded edges. But on 11 March the magic fled. Scott was forced to record one of their blackest days in the Antarctic. A sledge party had departed for Cape Crozier, some fifty miles away, under Royds. Scott had intended to lead it himself but had injured his knee skiing. He watched it depart in some despair, conscious of the very limited experience of his men – they did not know – and he had not arranged for them to learn – how to allocate their rations, how to put up their tents, how to use their cookers, how to run their dogs or even how to dress for the conditions. His misgivings were confirmed by the news, brought back by the distraught and wild-eyed survivors, of a tragedy out on the ice.

Royds had decided to send most of the party, dogs included, back to the ship because of bad conditions and inadequate equipment. There were only three pairs of skis between them all. However, some of the returning party, which included Edgar Evans, found themselves in a driving blizzard on a steep icy slope some 1,000 feet high. This was their first real experience of an Antarctic blizzard, often caused by the wind whipping up snow crystals on the ground rather than by falls of new snow. They slithered, struggling for a purchase on mirror-smooth ice and suddenly saw a precipice beneath their feet and below it the open sea. They managed to stop themselves with one exception. Able seaman George Vince, an obliging and cheerful character, was unable to get a grip on the ice because of the fur boots he was wearing. What followed was over in an instant. Before his horror-stricken companions had time to react, Vince flashed past and disappeared. When news of the tragedy reached the ship the siren was sounded and Shackleton went out in a whaler to search forlornly among the floes, but everyone knew Vince was dead.

For the first time since they had arrived at McMurdo Sound their new environment had shown the treachery lurking beneath the beauty. Some of the men became so overwrought at this loss to their small community that they thought they could see a figure crawling down the hillside, only to find it was an illusion. The accident brought reality back into what had been a *Boy's Own* adventure. It also emphasized their isolation. There was no way of relaying the news to the outside world and to Vince's family. Meanwhile another member of the party was still missing. There was great relief, not to say astonishment, when Clarence Hare the steward, also believed to have perished, was seen descending the hillside and staggering towards the ship having spent forty-eight hours exposed to wind and snow. He was not even frostbitten and was strong enough to complain to Wilson, his doctor, about being given invalids' fare.

Vince's death was, in fact, the second to have occurred since the *Discovery* had sailed from England in 1901. As she left the New Zealand port of Lyttelton on her way southwards, another young seaman, Charles Bonner, had, in his excitement, shinned up to the top of the mainmast with a bottle of whisky to wave farewell, lost his balance and crashed to the deck. Able seaman Thomas Crean, an Irishman from County Kerry who was to achieve such a name for himself on Scott's final expedition, had replaced him. Scott felt these deaths keenly and must have brooded over his own responsibility for them. He attributed the death of Vince to the expedition's lack of experience and prefaced one of the chapters in the *Voyage of the Discovery* paraphrasing Shakespeare's words, 'Experience be a jewel that we have purchased at an infinite rate.' In his heart of hearts Scott had been troubled from the beginning by the knowledge that he and his team were just amateurs. He might know about the navy and how to run a ship but he was no seasoned explorer.

The community was now kept busy by the numerous tasks which had to be accomplished before the sun set for the last time. There was plenty to occupy them. The dogs fought suddenly and savagely for no apparent reason, having lulled their masters into a false sense of security – '. . . alas for dog morals!' Scott wrote. Gradually he and his companions learned that when one dog was shown particular favour, or separated from the rest of the pack, it immediately became an object of suspicion to the rest. Yet despite these insights Scott remained genuinely shocked at their behaviour, talking anthropomorphically of 'murderers' and 'victims' and finding the dog mind quite inscrutable.

In mid-March Royds and his companions returned safely from their sledging trip to learn of the death of Vince. They brought tales of hardship of their own: the difficulty of handling the dogs, of extraordinarily localized extremes of weather and terrifying, all-engulfing blizzards, of cramp and frostbite and the inadequacy of night suits made out of thin wolf-skin. They had had to turn back without reaching Cape Crozier.

There was now the worry of what the full winter would bring. They were nearly 500 miles further south than where the *Southern Cross* had wintered. Would they be able to cope with the cold, and dark and isolation? Scott took his mind off such thoughts by organizing a further sledging trip, ostensibly to lay depots for journeys south when the spring came, but in reality to gain more experience for himself and his men. He waited until the sea was sufficiently frozen to allow them to take the best route south over the ice of the bay. The sea duly froze over on Good Friday. To Lashly, however, this was less important than what the cook was up to. He glumly recorded: '. . . had hot cross buns or bricks, could not tell hardly which.'[3]

The final sledging trip brought further problems with the dogs and Scott wished heartily that he had left them behind. Not only did they refuse to pull properly but they began to shed their coats. They were, after all, dogs from the northern hemisphere. In Siberia, their home, summer would be beginning. All in all there was nothing but hard graft, discomfort and frustration. After three days the party was only nine miles from the ship and Scott decided to bring the autumn sledging to an end. There would be time through the long dark winter to analyse the hard lessons learned and plan to do better. However, one lesson he did not absorb in time was that the ship's boats, which had been moved to the sea-ice to allow a canvas deck-covering to be fitted snugly over the *Discovery*, would become completely frozen in. On the basis of his past experience, Bernacchi warned what would happen, but Scott told the physicist sharply to mind his own business. It was Bernacchi's 'one and only experience with what seemed an unreasonable side of his nature'. Over the winter the boats became embedded in the solid floe and it was indeed a colossal task to free them.

On 23 April the sun sank for the last time, not to reappear until late August. However, sombre thoughts were banished by an extra ration of grog and much hilarity as the men drank to the speedy passage of the long night. Scott was careful to establish a routine to give life some appearance of normality. The home of the eleven officers, including Scott, was the *Discovery's* comfortable wood-panelled wardroom. This was 30 feet by 20 feet with a huge stove at one end, a table down the middle and a piano which only Royds could play well. It was a communal life but without the degree of boredom and irritation that Bernacchi had experienced at Cape Adare. Each officer had the sanctum of his own cabin while the crew's quarters, called the mess-deck, were separate which eliminated what Bernacchi called 'the friction of conflicting tastes' and made it easier to run things along naval lines. The crew's quarters were also larger and warmer as they were situated over the provision rooms and hold, which provided good insulation against the cold.

Meals were always at the same time and the fare was wholesome and simple. The only problems were caused by the inefficiency, dirtiness and insubordination of the cook, a sulky Antipodean named Brett whose ability to tell tall stories far exceeded his culinary skills. At one stage Scott clapped him in irons and on his next expedition he paid rather more attention to the recruitment of his cook, recognizing the vital link between good food and morale during the long Antarctic winter.

Breakfast was a large bowl of porridge with bread, butter, marmalade and jam and sometimes seal liver. The midday meal was soup, seal or tinned meat and either a jam or a fruit tart. Supper was the remains of the day's meat dishes or bread, butter and tea, perhaps with some jam or cheese. Although the men and the officers ate separately and had their main meals at different times, Scott was adamant that the fare should be the same, except for luxuries sent by friends, wines and such 'few delicate but indigestible trifles' that were produced for special dinners in the wardroom. Out sledging on the ice, officers and men would be alike in every respect so there was no reason to make unnecessary distinctions on board ship. When a merchant seaman complained about the quality of a cake that had been served, Scott was able to prove that exactly the same cake had been served in the wardroom and to punish the complainer for whingeing. The same individual was plainly unhappy with more than just the cuisine and on sledging trips had been known to sit up and exclaim, 'Fancy *me* from bloody Poplar, on the bloody Ice Barrier, in a bloody sleeping-bag!'[4]

In the wardroom it was a regulation that each member should take his turn as president of the mess, keeping order with a little wooden mallet and imposing fines of 'port all round' on anyone who swore or gambled. Shackleton was fined five times in one meal for offering to bet that someone was wrong.[5]

During the day there was plenty to keep them all occupied. There was the sledging equipment to be seen to – sleeping bags to be made or repaired, as well as sledges, tents and cookers to be checked. Outside there was always work to be done – digging and clearing, making holes in the sea-ice for fish-traps, freeing the paths to and from the huts where the scientific observations were carried out, and a constant programme of repairs to put right the damage inflicted by the heavy winter gales. In the evenings other more relaxing tasks took over – the seamen occupied themselves with wood-carving, netting, mat-making, whist, draughts, 'and even chess' as Scott observed patronizingly and in apparent surprise. He also recorded that much time was beguiled by 'a peculiar but simple game called "shove-ha'penny"' and he explained to the uninitiated how it was played. The officers concentrated on chess, bridge and once a week, at Bernacchi's suggestion, there were debates in the wardroom where such topics as women's rights or the rival merits of Browning versus Tennyson were vigorously discussed.

Books on Arctic travel were in demand on the mess-deck; so were such stirring tales as *Fights for the Flag* and *Deeds that Won the*

Empire. One man was deeply immersed in *The Origin of Species.* However, both officers and men had something home-grown to read. One of the products of the long winter was the *South Polar Times,* edited by Shackleton. As Scott described '. . . he is also printer, manager, type-setter, and office-boy'. He plainly relished the task and produced five issues during that long dark winter of 1902, often sitting in conclave with Wilson who contributed fluid sketches of sea leopards pursuing emperor penguins and squads of evil-eyed killer whales hunting among the ice floes.

The two constructed an 'editor's office' in one of the holds and the men of the *Discovery* – from the mess-deck as well as the wardroom – submitted material anonymously or under a *nom de plume.* 'Fitz-Clarence' alias Michael Barne was delighted to find his 'Ode to a Penguin' considered worthy of publication:

O creature which in Southern waters roam,
To know some more about you I would wish.
Though I have seen you in your limpid home,
I don't think I can rightly call you 'fish'.

To taste your body I did not decline
From dainty skinner's fingers coming fresh,
'Twas like shoe leather steeped in turpentine,
But I should hardly like to call it 'Flesh'.

The *South Polar Times* was also an excuse for some terrible jokes: 'Why did the Weddle waddle? Because the Crab'it'er (Crabeater)'. There was even a sports page. However, it was intended to be educational as well as amusing so there were erudite articles by the scientific staff. It certainly produced a sense of comradeship and helped morale over a difficult period when for hours if not days weather conditions pinned the men to the ship and sunshine seemed just a distant memory. Sometimes the squalls were so severe that, even though the *Discovery* was iced in, the men could feel her 'give' or flex.

The issue which described Midwinter's Day was determinedly buoyant in tone: 'Everything and everyone was bright and cheerful; the dark demon of Depression finds no home here; "Depression" can be taken out of our Polar Dictionary, and the phrase "white silence" will not suit a place where the hills re-echo the voices of busy men.' Certainly there was nothing depressing about the dinner of mutton, plum pudding, mince pies, jellies and 'excellent dry champagne' followed by crystallized fruits, almonds and raisins, nuts, port and liqueurs. The *Discovery* was decorated in honour of the coming return of the sun – the mess-deck was made particularly gorgeous with chains and ropes of coloured paper and Japanese lanterns, while the stokers' mess surpassed everything with a magnificent carved ice-head of Neptune.

Royds had been throwing his surplus energies into organizing amateur theatricals. It could be hazardous trying to return to the ship after rehearsing in the hut. Blizzards could blow up so suddenly that the troupe had to join hands and sweep forward until someone was able to grab the guide rope leading to the gangway.

However, the shows for which the mess-deck supplied most of the performers were a triumph. The 'Royal Terror Theatre' was set out with chairs for the officers and benches for the men – (the general egalitarianism did not apparently extend as far as the theatre). In the flickering glow of a large oil lamp the audience was treated to a performance containing such delights as songs, with Royds at the piano and 'singers in true concert attitude' and a 'screaming comedy' in one act. The *South Polar Times* graciously reviewed this as one of the most successful entertainments ever given within the Polar Circle. The next performance was the 'Dishcover Minstrel Troupe', which gave its all in temperatures of -40°F. Songs like 'Marching through Georgia' and 'Swanee River' had probably never been sung in stranger surroundings. And there were more schoolboy jokes – Mistah Johnson apparently asked of Mistah Bones, 'What am de worst vegetable us took from England?' to which the reply was 'The Dundee Leak' – a punning reference to the mysterious and persistent leak that had plagued the *Discovery* on her outward voyage.

As the winter progressed all the officers including Scott took it in turns on night duty to make the two-hourly observations required for the scientific research. Scott also recorded how he used the opportunity to do his laundry though he feared he made a poor job of it. But there were compensations. The night watchman was allowed the luxury of cooking himself a box of sardines. As the toothsome smells penetrated, 'a small company of gourmets' would rouse each other to devour a small finger of buttered toast with two sardines 'done to a turn' with a grunt of satisfaction and go back to sleep. There is something redolent of midnight feasts in the dorm here. Of course, they were a young crew. The average age of the forty-four men on board was only twenty-five. The New Zealand ladies had christened them 'The Babes in the Wood' in view of their youth and their wooden ship.[6] Their youth also showed in their inexperience in their respective fields. Wilson wrote that 'With the single exception of Hodgson we are all intensely ignorant of anything but the elementary knowledge of our several jobs.'[7]

Wilson's own modesty and high standards made him unduly severe – the men had at least the eagerness to learn and enthusiasm of youth so revered by Markham. Armitage was to be seen out on the ice undertaking the chilly task of taking star observations with the large theodolite. Thermometers had been placed in strategic positions on the shore, towards Mount Erebus or on Crater Hill and they needed to be read. Hodgson the naturalist spent his time dredging and digging. Occasionally he bore a frozen mass in triumph back to the ship's wardroom where it was allowed to thaw out and disclose 'the queer creatures that crawl and swim on the floor of our Polar sea'.[8] Royds looked after the meteorological records. Bernacchi tended his magnetic instruments and the electrometer and made auroral, seismic and gravity observations. Barne led a sort of 'picnic life' journeying with just a few sticks of chocolate in his pocket to some distant seal-hole where with the help of a flickering lantern he let down strings of thermometers.[9] It was chilly and laborious work and in his darker moments Scott wondered, whether it even possessed the advantage of being useful.

Koettlitz had little in the way of real sickness to deal with, though he did carry out the first operation in Antarctica, removing a cyst from Royds' cheek. The knives and pincers and scissors were assembled in the wardroom and 'Cutlets' attracted quite an audience for, as Bernacchi described, 'the general reaction was one of pleasurable interest rather than sympathy for the unfortunate victim'. Scott's own reaction is not recorded. However, given that he was highly strung enough to faint while awaiting news of whether his sister had safely given birth, it is unlikely he was one of the curious onlookers.

Wilson was always at work, checking that the food and milk for breakfast were fresh, taking meteorological observations, directing teams of bird-skinners, writing up his zoological notes and of course working on his paintings. His technique was to make several sketches from different locations to work up at a later date. He worried, unnecessarily in the event, that the colours he used in his art which had to be completed under the harsh glare of acetylene or flickering candlelight would look strange when seen in daylight.

At this early stage in their relationship Scott was already writing about Wilson with real warmth and affection, detecting and appreciating the qualities that would draw them yet closer. These qualities were recognized by others as well. Ford, one of the *Discovery*'s stewards, left this perceptive pen-portrait of Wilson:

> Dr Wilson combined with an essential manliness a sweetness of character unusual amongst men. Full of constant thoughtfulness for others, always sensitive to their peculiarities, never harsh to their weaknesses; temperamentally nervous himself, yet always setting an example of the highest courage; he was the bravest and most unselfish man I have ever known.[10]

Bravery and selflessness were among the most essential qualities for survival on long sledging trips. As Scott observed, sledging drew men into a closer relationship than any other mode of life. He wrote that 'In its light the fraud must be quickly exposed, but in its light also the true man stands out in all his natural strength'. During the winter months as he had pored over calculations of weights and measures and read everything he could find about Polar travel (though, as he himself noted, he had not actually brought many books on the subject) Scott had also been mentally reviewing who should accompany him south when daylight returned.

He had originally contemplated taking Barne but decided against it because Barne's hands had not recovered fully from frostbite. On deeper reflection Wilson seemed best fitted to endure the strains of such a journey. Though not physically the strongest, his medical expertise would be invaluable as would his intellect and capacity for work. Even more than that, Scott knew he would find comfortable companionship in a man who, like him, was at heart retiring and sensitive. It was therefore to Wilson that Scott turned on 12 June. Summoning him to his cabin he outlined his plans for the summer sledging parties, going over practical details like weights and rations. Then came the surprise. He wanted Wilson to accompany him on the journey south towards the Pole. He also wanted Wilson's views on whether he should take a third. Nansen had travelled in the Arctic with just one companion, Johansen, in the interest of efficiency and simplicity. He proposed to do the same.

Wilson was astonished and delighted to have been singled out. However, he urged Scott to take a third member of the party. What would happen if one man fell ill or had an accident? The other would never be able to cope alone and both would probably perish. Scott acknowledged this sound good sense and changed his mind. Knowing Wilson's friendship for Shackleton, he picked the silver-tongued Irishman with the love of Browning. He did it to please Wilson, proof of the bond forming between them, but it was a decision he would regret.

5

'Poor Old Shackleton'

On 22 August Scott and his men greeted the sun with an almost pagan enthusiasm: 'We seemed to bathe in that brilliant flood of light, and from its flashing rays to drink in new life, new strength and new hope.' It was a symbol of their mental and physical survival through the months of darkness. The mood was now one of excitement and energy as the ship's sewing machine hummed incessantly, sledges were assembled, provisions weighed, dog-harnesses untangled, fur clothing overhauled. Yet, although they had come through the winter quite well, Scott remained painfully aware that he and his colleagues were novices. Vince's death had shown the dangers of inexperience. It was Scott's responsibility to make sure that from now on there were as few mistakes as possible and this weighed on him. The early sledging trips had proved that 'sledging is not such an easy matter as might be imagined' and that they had made many mistakes: 'food, clothing, everything was wrong, the whole system was bad.'

However, as he planned his campaign and calculated provisions, Scott had cause to believe that he had stamped his mark on the enterprise and his fellow explorers. There had inevitably been tensions, some of them stemming from the contradictions in his character, his reserve, highly strung and impatient temperament and occasional outbursts of temper. Clarence Hare later described how Scott could be 'over sensitive and got wound up if things did not go as planned' and that 'being used to having his orders obeyed at the double in navy ships, the easygoing response of the Merchant Shipping men was the cause of ... temper'.[1] Fortunately, Wilson had shown a remarkable ability to smooth away the frictions inevitable when a group of men are cooped up in difficult conditions. Although not 'clubbable' like Shackleton, he had become the one to whom the others turned instinctively. Talking to 'Uncle Bill', as Wilson became known, was a safety valve for anyone with a worry or a problem. While the men of the *Discovery* on the whole admired Scott, they did not feel able to confide in him, perhaps fearing that he would take their problems as signs of weakness. He was hard on himself and so unlikely to be softer on others.

Wilson's view of Scott had clearly developed over the winter. In the early days Wilson had found him quick-tempered and impatient, but during the voyage down to Antarctica he had begun to understand the complex but admirable qualities of his leader, writing to his parents:

> He is thoughtful for each individual and does little kindnesses which show it. He is ready to listen to everyone too, and joins heartily in all the humbug that goes on. I have a great admiration for him, and he is in no Service rut but is always anxious to see both sides of every question, and I have never known him to be unfair. One of the best points about him too is that he is very definite about everything; nothing is left vague

or indeterminate. In every argument he goes straight for the main point, and always knows exactly what he is driving at. There will be no fear of our wandering about aimlessly in the Southern regions.[2]

Wilson was particularly gratified that Scott took his advice: 'He has adopted every one of my suggestions. It's a great help to have one's ideas appreciated by a man who is always trying new and knacky things on his own . . .'[3] An interesting comment given that Scott, in particular on his final expedition, has often been criticized for being autocratic and not innovative enough. Wilson also believed that over the winter he and Scott had come to understand each other better than anyone else on board despite one profound difference that would remain throughout their lives – the question of religious faith. Where Wilson believed and was serene, Scott doubted. He was still tormented by that old question, 'What does it all mean?', but he found Wilson's certainty comforting. In the danger and uncertainty ahead Wilson's inner peace would be a welcome resource.

At this stage, though, Wilson would have described Shackleton rather than Scott as his friend. During the months of darkness Wilson had found himself increasingly drawn to Shackleton or 'Shackles'. The Irishman's charm and roguish good humour were irresistible to the quieter man. The two of them would climb Crater Hill to check the thermometer and they had spent hours in conclave over the pages of the *South Polar Times*. They had watched the return of the sun together, rejoicing in the 'very grand golden sky'.[4] However, Wilson worried about taking his friend on the Polar journey, doubting whether he was physically strong enough. 'Shackleton hasn't the legs the job wants,' he wrote, but loyalty prevented him from confiding in Scott.[5] He knew it was

Shackleton's one ambition to go on the southern journey. Perhaps at the same time he was conscious that he had hardly been in top condition himself when Scott had agreed to take him on the expedition and that Shackleton should also be given the benefit of the doubt.

Before the southern journey could begin there were many preparations to be made, including some trial runs with the sledges and the dogs. Scott made several journeys which if anything highlighted the problems they would face rather than provided any solutions. But there was a more immediate difficulty. Returning from one expedition in early October he found that three men who had been sledging on a reconnaissance trip westwards with Armitage were in a state of collapse due to scurvy. The symptoms were frightening and unmistakable – discoloured swollen limbs and spongy gums. Scott insisted the entire crew be examined and almost everyone displayed some signs of the disease. He noted approvingly that Armitage had consulted the doctors and, using his own previous Arctic experience as a guide, taken steps to remedy the situation by serving fresh seal meat, increasing the allowance of bottled fruits and taking the cook in hand. 'I don't know whether he threatened to hang him at the yardarm or used more persuasive measures, but whatever it was, there is a marked improvement in the cooking.'

Armitage was later to claim that much of the fault lay at Scott's door for relying too much on tinned food, largely because of 'a sentimental objection to slaughtering seals in anything like the number requisite for the winter's supply'.[6] Whatever the case initially, Scott was now convinced that the answer lay in fresh food. A party 'girt about with knives and other murderous implements' went off to slaughter seals.[7]

The change of diet did the trick and the southern journey

was able to start on schedule. On 30 October Michael Barne led the supporting party of twelve men southward, manhauling. One of his sledges sported the message 'No Dogs Admitted' – the dog teams were being held back for the main party. Bad weather delayed the departure of Scott and his companions but they found solace in a plate of mustard and cress provided by Dr Koettlitz and grown to fight scurvy. On 2 November, a cold and windy day, they finally set out, cheered by a glass of champagne. Scott described how 'every soul was gathered on the floe to bid us farewell . . .'

Their little party of three men, nineteen dogs and five sledges was departing on the most daring journey yet made in Antarctica. For all its failings it would place Scott and Shackleton in the ranks of experienced Polar explorers. It would also show the dangers and uncertainties of travelling in this terrain and confirm Scott in a number of views, most of them shared by Shackleton, and some of which would ultimately prove fatal to him.

The men knew that they might not return. All left letters of farewell – Scott to his mother, Shackleton to Emily Dorman and Wilson to his beloved Oriana. Wilson seems to have viewed the journey with mixed feelings. He hoped it would be more than 'monotonous hard work on an icy desert' and that he would find something worth sketching. Reflecting on the challenge ahead he wrote that when the day came when Polar exploration could be achieved by motor transport or flying machines it would lose its attraction for men like himself and his companions.

At first they made good progress, flying over the ice like three Polar knights with their sledge pennants fluttering bravely and quickly catching Barne. The dogs cracked along at a fine pace, chasing away across the snow so that the three men had a struggle to keep up, but the weather soon began to play tricks. The snow became sticky, making the sledges harder to pull and blizzards held them captive in their tents. Shackleton found it irksome 'to lie here using up our provisions and not getting on at all'.[8] He would learn that this was a common experience in Polar travel. They were quite comfortable in their separate sleeping bags of reindeer skin, which gave them an important degree of privacy. As Wilson described: 'Once inside your bag and toggled up with the flap over head and all, you feel quite comfortably apart from your companions.' They read Darwin's *Origin of Species* to pass the time. However, Wilson had something else to distract him. On just the fourth day out Shackleton started what the doctor described as 'a most persistent and annoying cough' – an ominous sign so early in the game.

Travelling on they began to realize the psychological effect of travelling in a featureless terrain. The scenery became depressing – they emerged onto a great open plain on which they felt insignificant as ants. Scott remarked the terrible monotony of this monochrome world – grey skies, grey terrain, grey thoughts. Yet by 12 November their spirits were buoyed up by the fact that they had penetrated further south than Borchgrevink. On 15 November, when Barne and the supporting party turned back, the sunshine had returned and the photographs show them all posing cheerfully before parting.

What was in Scott's mind as he and his two companions now set out alone? He wrote: 'We can but feel elated with the prospect that is before us,' but it is uncertain exactly what Scott believed that prospect to be. He did not refer directly to the South Pole but it must have been tantalizing to know that if he reached it he would be made for life. The days of worrying about money and of having to 'make do' would be over and his career assured. Shackleton too must have speculated. Even more ambitious and less financially secure than Scott, perhaps, and certainly more optimistic and improvident, he must have calculated as he trudged southwards that victory at the Pole would secure him the wife he wanted and a vast deal more besides. During the winter he had acted the role of a successful traveller to the Pole being received by the crowned heads of Europe before an enthusiastic audience in the Royal Terror Theatre. Curiously, though, it was Wilson who made one of the most overt references to the ultimate goal, writing: 'Our object is to get as far south in a straight line on the Barrier ice as we can, reach the Pole if possible, or find some new land . . .' However, far too little was known about the conditions to predict with accuracy what would happen. Scott believed that the Barrier might run straight on to the Pole without coming to land, but who could tell?

Problems began almost immediately. The dogs lost their initial burst of energy and were tiring rapidly. They had to be coaxed and bullied along, confirming Scott's original view of their useful-ness. Progress became so difficult that Scott decided to lighten the sledges by carrying the supplies forward in relays. In practice this meant that each sledge would now only carry half a load. When this had been deposited the men and dogs would return for the other half so that the number of miles they travelled was tripled. Relaying was very hard on the men – Shackleton complained that 'the travelling is awful'[9] and did not seem to help the dogs who continued to weaken. Scott and his companions were distressed that the only thing which had any effect on them was beating. Nansen had found it hard too, admitting that exploration in such harsh conditions demanded a 'hard-hearted egotism'. The difference was that Nansen beat his dogs relentlessly while Scott was inconsistent, only 'occasionally bringing the lash down with a crack on the snow or across the back of some laggard'. The dogs were almost human to him and he drew engaging pen portraits of them: 'The general opinion of "Spud" was that he was daft – there was something wanting in the upper storey.' Jim, on the other hand, was 'a sleek, lazy, greedy villain, up to all the tricks of the trade'.

In fact, the problems they were experiencing stemmed largely from something which could have been prevented – the dogs' food. Scott had intended to take dog biscuits for them but had been persuaded, possibly by Nansen, that the best food was dried stockfish. However, on the long voyage out the fish had rotted. It was poisoning the dogs, who began suffering acute diarrhoea and passing blood. The progressive failure of the dogs put all three men under pressure. Shackleton was nominally in charge of them and it may have been his perceived failure that fuelled the resentment which seems to have built up between him and Scott during the journey. The extreme conditions, the cold and the isolation, encourage men to brood and nurse grievances and Scott may have begun to wonder whether Shackleton was all talk and no substance. There is certainly evidence that their relationship deteriorated during the journey, exacerbated by their very different personalities.

Wilson may have needed all his peacemaking skills to maintain a balance between his reserved and determined leader and the volatile Irishman. According to a story told twenty years later by a disillusioned Armitage, which he claimed came from Wilson but which is not recorded anywhere direct by any of the three participants:

Wilson and Shackleton were packing the sledges after breakfast one morning. Suddenly they heard Scott shout to them 'Come here you B.F.s.' They went to him, and Wilson quietly said 'were you speaking to me'. 'No Billy' said Scott. 'Then it must have been me' said Shackleton. He received no answer. Shackleton then said 'Right, you are the worst B.F. of the lot, and every time that you dare to speak to me like that you will get it back.'[10]

However, there were also moments of euphoria. On 25 November they crossed the 80th parallel and Scott wrote with prosaic understatement: 'This compensates for a lot of trouble.' Shackleton wrote in his diary of the delight of 'finding out the secrets of this wonderful place', while Wilson was enthralled by the magical light effects, the mock suns and snow crystals sparkling like gems, a pleasure which he shared with Scott whose own accounts are sometimes lyrical. Each man was in his own way falling under the Antarctic spell despite the hardships and the eerie silence when as Wilson wrote: 'One could imagine oneself on a dead planet. Everything was so still and cold and dead and unearthly.'

Their journey was taking them over the Barrier towards the Western Mountains, as they are now called, that lie between the Barrier and the high inland ice sheet and which form part of the Transantarctic Mountains linking the Ross and Weddell Seas. But hunger, rather than the beauty of their surroundings, began to dominate their thoughts. The accounts reveal a dogged fatalism: 'We cannot stop, we cannot go back, we must go on,' Scott wrote. It was soon clear that their rations were inadequate for the physical work they were doing. Breakfast was usually bacon fried with biscuit, two cups of tea and a dry biscuit. Lunch was a modest further biscuit with two cups of Bovril, some chocolate and four lumps of sugar. Supper, which they dreamed about as they trudged along, was a boiled-up hoosh of pemmican, red ration (pea meal and bacon powder), biscuit, a square of dried soup and powdered cheese with a comforting cup of cocoa to finish off. Yet as they journeyed on, the food failed to satisfy appetites which had grown immense. Scott had seriously underestimated the amount of highly calorific fatty pemmican they should have been consuming, allowing about half the correct amount according to current theories. The waking and sleeping moments of all three became dominated by thoughts and dreams of food – the richer the better – roast duck, sirloins of beef, juicy dripping, jugs of fresh milk.

They were also learning the other discomforts of sledging – their faces were so sore and chapped from the sun that it hurt to touch them. The harsh glare caused snowblindness – the burning of the cornea by sunlight reflected back off Antarctica's shining white surfaces. It felt like hot sand in the eyes. The dogs began to die and Wilson tried the experiment of feeding the dead ones to their companions. The flesh was devoured instantly by the starving dogs, who showed no scruples about cannibalism. Wilson graduated to killing the weaker dogs to feed the stronger, referring to this as his 'butcher's work'. Scott with his aversion to blood and feelings of guilt about the dogs could play no part in this though he despised himself for his weakness.

Struggling on Scott decided to depot the dog food and most of their own remaining supplies for the return journey and to travel on without relaying. However, the pattern was set. The men were too hungry to have very much pulling power and continued to be tormented by snowblindness. To add to their worries Wilson believed that Shackleton and Scott were showing signs of scurvy as he was himself. They forgot their woes on Christmas day, which was celebrated with extravagant fare. The travellers feasted on a breakfast of biscuit and seal-liver fried in bacon and pemmican fat, and blackberry jam. Lunch was cocoa, a whole biscuit and more jam. Supper was a hoosh consisting of a double whack of everything and more cocoa. Shackleton then produced the *pièce de résistance* – a Christmas pudding the size of a cricket ball he had 'stowed away in my socks (clean ones) in my sleeping bag'.[11] They boiled it in cocoa and decorated it with a piece of artificial holly.*

Yet this was only temporary comfort. Wilson was suffering horribly from snowblindness caused by taking off his goggles to sketch. His painful eyes watered so much he could not see. He anointed them with liquid cocaine and had to dose himself with morphine to help him both to sleep and to continue to haul his sledge. While he pulled, he wore a blindfold and fantasized about walking through woods of beech or fir. The swish of the skis made him think of brushing through heather or succulent bluebells in his native Gloucestershire. Scott became his eyes, describing the magnificent new ranges of mountains coming into view to the south-west. Wilson managed to open one eye long enough to sketch the scene. They named the highest, a glorious twin-peaked mountain, after Sir Clements Markham. On 30 December 1902 they reached their farthest south – 82° 17′S, over 410 miles from the Pole but over 250 miles further south than any other human being before them. Later that day Scott took Wilson with him on skis to chart the mountain chain visible southwards. Modestly, he named a distant cape after Wilson and a nearby inlet for Shackleton but nothing after himself. 'We have almost shot our bolt,' Scott wrote. Had they but known it they were almost within sight of the ascent to the Polar plateau which Shackleton would

* This piece of artificial holly was auctioned at Christie's in April 1997, and sold for over £4,000.

discover in six years' time. The three men tried to push on by ski to reach land and take some geological samples but found their way barred by a crevasse. Shackleton took a photograph showing Scott, a small resolute figure dwarfed by the grandeur around him. Then they turned back.

To head north again must have been both a relief and a frustration, but the realities of the return journey soon became clear. It became a finely balanced race to reach the various depots before supplies ran out and was predicated on the men remaining fit. However, their rations had had to be progressively reduced during the journey, leaving them starving and susceptible to scurvy. They were physically weak and mentally depressed and the situation with the dogs did not help. They were literally on their last legs, so feeble that Scott and his companions loaded them onto the sledges which the men helped to pull. Others had to be killed or just died in their tracks. Scott found it appalling and again left the killing to Wilson and Shackleton, an abdication of responsibility as he admitted. When one of his favourites, Kid, finally collapsed he wrote: 'He has pulled like a Trojan throughout and his stout little heart bore him up till his legs failed beneath him . . .' It brought him close to tears. Clearly they could no longer expect the surviving dogs to pull the sledges and they released them. For the first time they were able to converse freely instead of having to shout at the dogs. They were also relieved to be free of the moral burden of driving reluctant, exhausted animals even if it meant hauling the sledges themselves – a view that would seem insane to explorers like Amundsen but which had a profound influence on Scott and Shackleton.

Perhaps the situation did begin to seem a little insane to them as they pushed on. The weather had turned mild, making the snow wet and soggy so that it clung to the runners and made the three men perspire, leaving them perpetually damp and clammy. They managed to reach their depot and rewarded themselves with a generous hoosh, but they were in a miserable condition, all suffering from scurvy and with Shackleton deteriorating fast. His gums were inflamed, he found it hard to breathe and he was spitting blood, yet they still had about 150 miles to go. A sick companion was one of the worst dilemmas a Polar commander could face. Scott listened carefully to Wilson's diagnosis of Shackleton's condition and decided there was nothing for it but to give up any idea of further exploration, kill the two remaining dogs and make a dash for the *Discovery*. It never occurred to these sentimental Britons to eat the dogs, as Amundsen was to do. Had they done so they would have alleviated their scurvy. As it was, the death of the dogs affected Scott deeply in his weakened and emotional state. He described how: 'This was the saddest scene of all; I think we could all have wept. And so this is the last of our dog team, the finale to a tale of tragedy; I scarcely like to write of it.' The dogs had become like personal friends. Wilson's poignant sketch 'the Last of the Dogs' was testimony to his own feelings about the dogs' fate. When the explorers eventually returned to the ship the dead dogs would be toasted for their gallant contribution to the cause of science.

Scott and Wilson now pulled the sledges, which each had a weight of over 260 lbs, while Shackleton tottered dizzily alongside. Wilson described how hard it was to make the excitable Irishman take things quietly. A change of diet with more dried seal meat and no bacon seemed to help combat the scurvy, but Shackleton remained desperately ill. At one stage he sat on the sledge. The going was good and his task was to help slow the pace on downward gradients using a ski stick. There was later to be ill-feeling between Shackleton and Scott over whether he had ridden on the sledge partly through weakness or simply to act as a brake, but Scott was to pay public tribute to his 'most extraordinary pluck and endurance'.[12]

They pushed on as best they could, Scott and Wilson sharing the main burden and cementing their relationship in the midst of the hardship. Wilson's heroic efforts bore out Scott's view that sledging is 'a sure test of a man's character'. Wilson described how he and Scott discussed every conceivable subject and he recorded that 'indeed he is a most interesting talker when he starts', an interesting sidelight both on Scott's reserve and their growing bond. It is also noteworthy that at one stage Wilson felt it necessary to have 'had it out with Scott'.[13] What they discussed, and why, is unclear but if – and it is only if – Wilson raised Scott's failings – his outbursts of temper and sometimes autocratic behaviour and his attitude towards Shackleton – he must have done it very tactfully. If anything the dialogue only heightened the respect and affection of each man for the other. Wilson had set out as Shackleton's friend but was returning as Scott's. Somewhere along the line the chemistry between the three men had altered.

Scott's first great Antarctic journey finally ended on 3 February. Distant specks on the ice turned out to be not penguins but Skelton and Bernacchi who had come out to look for them. Wilson described them as 'clean tidy looking people'. They were certainly in stark contrast to the three travellers who were skeletally thin with faces the colour of brown boots except where lamp soot had blackened them, hair, beards and moustaches that were long and wild, lips that were blistered and raw. Scott's ankles were swollen, Wilson was limping badly and Shackleton was on the brink of complete collapse. They had travelled some 850 miles, including relays, and been away from the *Discovery* for ninety-three days.

As they marched the final half dozen miles to a *Discovery* freshly painted and decked with bunting, Skelton and Bernacchi were eager to tell them everything that had happened while they had been away. The most important piece of news was that a relief ship, the *Morning*, had arrived bringing post and parcels. It had been part of the original plan that a relief ship should be sent down to Antarctica after a year to bring supplies, take back news and invalids or even rescue the whole expedition. There was great psychological comfort in the thought of this contact with the outside world.

The *Morning* brought orders instructing Scott to take what he needed from the relief ship and sail the *Discovery* to Lyttelton. However, despite attempts to free her, the *Discovery* remained locked in the ice and Scott concluded that she would have to pass another year in McMurdo Sound. He was later to be accused of not trying hard enough to release her. *The Times* suggested that like another famous naval man he had chosen to turn a blind eye to his orders. He was certainly tenacious and, having now experienced Antarctic exploration, was not sorry to be able to stay, although it was probably the weather conditions that actually clinched matters.

Scott now faced some important decisions. He knew he would have to cut back on crew members if he was to remain. He called for volunteers to return on the *Morning* and received eight including Brett, the highly unsatisfactory cook. Scott later congratulated himself that they were exactly the eight men he would have wished to send back. However, it is highly likely that he had exercised some persuasion behind the scenes. He also suggested to Armitage that he might like to return. Not only had his wife recently had a baby but in one of the letters brought to him by the *Morning* Scott had learned that she had been involved in some unsavoury scandal. Scott was therefore trying to be tactful and compassionate but Armitage reacted angrily. He interpreted this as evidence that Scott believed that the expedition should be the preserve of the Royal Navy and that he had a prejudice against the Merchant Navy, noting that several merchant seaman were among those returning on the *Morning*. He may also have believed there was a more personal dimension. He suspected that Scott considered Antarctica peculiarly his own after these first endeavours and feared Armitage as his greatest potential rival. Armitage accordingly resisted Scott's suggestion on the grounds that his command was independent of Scott and stored this up as a further source of grievance.

Scott was, however, adamant that Shackleton, the man who was to prove his real rival, must return on the grounds that 'He ought not to risk further hardships in his present state of health'. Koettlitz seems to have been in two minds about his fitness and Armitage later claimed that the doctor believed Shackleton was as capable of remaining as Scott. He also claimed that Scott threatened that 'If he does not go back sick he will go back in disgrace'.[14] However, these were the accusations made after the death of Shackleton, as well as Wilson and Scott, by an embittered man whose career had not prospered and whose wife, 'a hell of a woman' as Skelton called her, had ruined him financially.

Wilson recorded in his diary that 'Poor old Shackleton has been sent home as the result of his break down on our southern sledge journey, a thing which has upset him a great deal as he was very keen indeed to stop and see the thing through. It is certainly wiser for him to go home though.' Wilson had been concerned about his friend's health from the very beginning and these comments on the wisdom of sending him home ring true. Michael Barne who escorted Shackleton to the *Morning* noted that they made very slow progress 'as poor old Shackles is still very shaky'.[15] Whether Scott had deeper motives is difficult to judge. His experience of sledging with Shackleton had revealed not just the other man's physical weakness but a propensity to argue and to resist authority running counter to the spirit of naval discipline which Scott valued so highly. So while there were sound medical reasons for sending Shackleton home, it may also be true that Scott was not sorry to see him go. However, one story sheds a more human light on the relationship between these two men who had experienced so much together. Safely back on the *Discovery* they had found it hard to satisfy their hunger in spite of the great feast to which they were treated. An officer from the *Morning* related how he heard Scott rousing Shackleton, whose cabin was next door. "'Shackles," I heard him call, "I say Shackles, how would you fancy some sardines on toast?"'[16]

On 2 March the *Morning* stood out to sea on course for Lyttelton in New Zealand. Shackleton was on the deck apparently in tears as the small figures waving from the ice disappeared from view. This was a defining moment for the future of all three men who had made the southern journey together. Scott wrote in the spirit of the age, 'If we had not achieved such great results as at one time we had hoped for we knew at least that we had striven and endured with all our might.' They had, however, surveyed some 300 miles of new coastline, added to knowledge about the Barrier and set the scene for the quest for the South Pole, even if they had not fulfilled their own and others' expectations.

6

'Little Human Insects'

As the air grew chillier and the winter darkness returned, Scott reflected on what he had learned. He had gained a new assurance, born of experience. In many ways the southern journey had been a revelation, showing him that he had the mental and physical strength to lead an expedition and helping him to overcome his persistent self-doubt. The narrow-chested dreamy child had turned into a tough and purposeful leader. He remained therefore in an optimistic mood as, some months later, the new sledging season dawned and his enthusiasm communicated itself to the rest of the crew. 'To judge by the laughter and excitement, we might be boys escaping from school,' he wrote. The winter had passed much as the previous one. For example, Michael Barne, a great jokester, had dreamt up such pranks as dressing in furs and jumping out at the nervous Koettlitz, pretending to be a bear. Others had written up their diaries and scientific notes and got up plays, and further editions of the *South Polar Times* had appeared. A feast on Midwinter's Day had been a jolly affair, leaving the normally abstemious Scott 'quite as much excited as was necessary for his dignity'.[1]

Scott was determined to improve the technique of sledging and initiated the method of supporting parties which he was to use on the way to the Pole. This meant taking a large party and shedding men along the way thus enabling the many to carry and depot supplies for the few. A dozen men left the *Discovery* on 12 October 1903 – an advance party of six including Scott, Evans and Lashly, and two other groups of three but no dogs. The plan was to explore to the west and probe the interior of Victoria Land of which Armitage had broached the periphery the previous year. The geological specimens he had brought back suggested that the area was of considerable scientific interest. Conscious of the criticisms of the men of the Royal Society, who according to his mother Hannah were still behaving like underbred schoolboys, Scott was determined to show that an expedition led by a naval officer could achieve as much scientifically as one led by a professional scientist.

There was a false start when three of their four sledges became damaged. The runners, made of German silver, had split and the wood beneath was deeply scored forcing them to return to the *Discovery* for repairs. On 26 October the party set out again, this time consisting of only nine men. Continuing to learn from hard experience Scott was horrified to discover that the lid of the instrument box on the one good sledge, which they had depoted and left behind, had blown open in a gale with the result that Skelton's goggles had gone whirling down the hillside together with *Hints to Travellers*, an invaluable little publication from the Royal Geographical Society containing logarithmic tables which Scott needed to work out his sights and gauge his party's position once on the Polar plateau and beyond the mountains.

Scott was desperately anxious not to have to return again and was heartened by his companions' willingness to go on despite 'the risk of marching away into the unknown without exactly knowing where we were or how to get back'. It is hard to know whether this was brave or simply foolhardy, but it was certainly the answer Scott expected from his men. At the same time, though, it seems unlikely that a man of Scott's caution and sense of responsibility would have marched casually into the unknown if he had truly believed there to be a significant risk. Perhaps he exaggerated his ignorance in the interests of dramatic effect when his journals were published. Anyway, he knew himself to be resourceful – during this trip he improvised a method of calculating the daily change in the sun's declination to allow him to fix his latitude with reasonable accuracy when out of sight of geographical features and therefore to navigate.

The party struggled up the Ferrar Glacier to an altitude of some 7,000 feet to pitch their tents in a place they aptly named 'Desolation Camp'. Here they endured a week of blizzards where Scott's frustration was not assuaged by reading soothing passages from Darwin's *Cruise of the Beagle*. At the time he called this the most miserable experience of his life. Getting away at last they climbed a further 2,000 feet to the summit. Their reward was to find themselves on a great Polar plateau with Mount Lister and the Royal Society Range away to the south-east. It was a cheerless prospect but it offered the fascination of the unknown. The geological party led by young Ferrar now turned aside to carry out research, leaving Scott with Evans, Lashly and three others, Skelton, Feather and Handsley, to struggle westward across the plateau in the teeth of a bitter wind.

The surface was so bad they had to resort to relaying, which Scott hated. By 22 November he had decided that the latter three, though 'lion-hearted', were not pulling as hard as was necessary and he sent them back. Skelton's diary revealed how demanding

Scott could be, impatient at delay and determined to push himself and his men to their physical and mental limits. Skelton wrote: 'I can't agree with forcing men to such work, all the time one is at the highest strain, & it is that, that I don't like to see, – something might snap.'[2]

Scott was now alone with two men whose names would also become synonymous with his Polar journeys. Leading Stoker William Lashly would be one of the Last Supporting Party who would watch Scott set off on the final leg to the South Pole, while Petty Officer Edgar Evans would be marching with him. Both men had remained supremely fit (or 'hard' in Scott's terminology) since arriving in Antarctica, and Scott was convinced that they had the character and spirit for successful sledging. They now manhauled across the vast lifeless plateau facing temperatures which dropped at night to the -40s and which seldom rose above -25 degrees Fahrenheit in the day. They found it hard to catch their breath in the rarefied air. The plain was uneven and the surface varied from silkily smooth to the treacherous corrugations of 'sastrugi' or frozen snow waves that capsized the sledge. Scott felt they were like a small boat at sea 'at one moment appearing to stand still to climb some wave, and at the next diving down into a hollow'. He reflected with satisfaction on the strength of his two companions, describing how with them behind him 'our sledge seemed to become a living thing, and the days of slow progress were numbered'.

However, they found no end to the desolate plateau. In his diaries Scott wrote of the daily difficulties of sledging and camp life: 'The worst time for sledging is the coldest time . . . the human body is always giving off moisture . . . much issuing through the pores of the skin . . . a small quantity will remain as ice on one's garments . . . accumulating until one is completely enclosed in it . . .

all these things which on board the ship were so caressingly soft to the touch will have become as hard as boards. Worse still, this ice will be found plastered as thickly on everything that makes for comfort at night: sleeping-bag . . . night foot-gear will have grown equally hard and chill.' The only way of unthawing frozen sleeping bags at night and frozen boots in the morning was by inserting limbs into them until they thawed a little with body warmth and as they did so, pushing the limbs, often painfully sensitive from frostbite, progressively further into them while occasionally pulling them out and rubbing them to prevent them getting too frozen.

Scott had resolved to turn back by the end of November and their final march westward took them up a slope steeper than usual. He was optimistic, hoping they would glimpse some new and exciting feature after the monotony of the plateau, perhaps a range of mountains forming a western coast of Victoria Land, but there was nothing but the plain, 'a scene so wildly and awfully desolate that it cannot fail to impress one with gloomy thoughts . . .' Scott described how they had reached the end of their tether – '. . . all we have done is to show the immensity of this vast plain'. It was an awful desert over which 'we, little human insects . . . are now bent on crawling back again'. He needed the 'unfailing courage and cheerfulness' of his companions to pull him through what he would remember as 'some vivid but evil dream'.

Their behaviour during the journey had convinced Scott that there was 'no class of men so eminently adapted by training to cope with the troubles and tricks of sledging life as sailors'. Not only were they tough, resourceful and brave but they obeyed orders, knew their place, and adhered to strict naval discipline. Scott, shy and introspective, felt at ease and unthreatened in their company and drew comfort from it. 'Few of our camping hours go by without a laugh from Evans and a song from Lashly. I have not quite penetrated the latter yet; there is only one verse, which is about the plucking of a rose. It can scarcely be called a finished musical performance, but I should miss it much if it ceased.' What innuendos lay behind that verse for men devoid of women's company for so many months can only be guessed at.

Yet despite this companionship, the responsibilities of leadership and navigation, and thus of their safety, rested squarely on Scott and it must have been a psychological burden. He could not let them guess his anxiety. They in turn probably made it a point of honour to show him a brave face. All alone on the great ice sheet they discussed who would follow in their footsteps. In fact it was to be three men making for the South Magnetic Pole during Shackleton's Nimrod expedition of 1907–9.

On 1 December 1903 they turned and began their long journey back to the *Discovery* under a leaden sky. Within a few days Scott was worrying about the perennial problem of running out of food if they were delayed. He had been feeling guilty for some time that he was eating the same rations as Lashly and Evans, though considerably lighter, but knew that he could not help himself. He was also still worrying about how to find the way. The optimism of his companions became even more necessary to him – he noted that they could always find something to joke about. 'Taff' Evans was known for his fund of anecdotes and picturesque curses such as 'May the Curse of the Seven Blind Witches of Egypt be upon you!'

Of course, their mutual affection for the navy provided an inexhaustible topic of conversation – 'In the evenings we have long arguments about naval matters, and generally agree that we could rule that Service a great deal better than any Board of Admiralty.' The other dominant topic was food. Edgar Evans rhapsodized about pork while Lashly talked of vegetables and apples and Scott of Devonshire cream. Despite the discomforts and the dangers it was an example of true comradeship. Discipline, respect and obedience remained but at the end of a hard day's sledging they could laugh and all squeeze companionably into their three-man sleeping bag. Scott always used 'we' in his writings about this journey in tribute to the remarkable team spirit.

The conditions remained atrocious. A sharp wind bit at them and the surface was so heavy they felt as if they were dragging the sledge through sand. They could only manage a mile an hour and it was back-breaking work for men who were increasingly hungry and plagued by frostbite. Evans was suffering particularly badly with his nose. Scott discovered they were short of fuel oil partly due to seepage – a problem that he failed to investigate fully and discover the cause of and which he would face again on his Polar journey with far more serious consequences – and so increased their daily marching time. On 10 December Evans's sharp eyes espied land beyond the edge of the plateau, but the question now was how to find their way back down. Could they identify the Ferrar Glacier up which they had toiled from the many which flowed down from the plateau? The mountain tops which would have given them a clue were shrouded in mist. By his own admission Scott was travelling 'by rule of thumb'. Slowly, carefully, they began to descend trusting to luck, as Scott often seemed to do, as much as to their own sense of direction.

14 December brought them close to disaster. Manoeuvring the sledge around hummocks of ice and across evil-looking crevasses, they emerged onto a smooth slope. Scott was guiding the sledge in front, with Evans and Lashly holding it at the rear when Lashly lost his footing. In an instant he went hurtling down on his back. Evans was similarly thrown off his feet and before Scott realized what was happening the two men and the

sledge had shot past him. Scott braced himself to stop them but might just as well have tried to stop an express train. Whipped off his legs he joined the mad career. He described 'a sort of vague wonder as to what would happen next' and then became aware that they had stopped sliding smoothly and were now bouncing over a much rougher surface. He was sure they were going to break their arms and legs when suddenly they flew right up into the air and landed with an almighty thump on a patch of hard snow. They were badly bruised and shaken but to their great surprise no one was seriously injured. Looking upwards they saw that they had tumbled some 300 feet down one of the ice cascades of the very glacier they had been searching for. In the distance was the comforting sight of the smoke-capped summit of Mount Erebus. This was either luck again or else their improvised methods of navigating had been remarkably successful.

However, the danger was not over yet. Further down the glacier both Scott and Evans suddenly fell the full length of their harness down a crevasse with walls of icy blue. Lashly was left on the top with the task of trying to rescue his companions while preventing the sledge, precariously balanced over the abyss, from following them. Slowly and carefully he secured the sledge with two skis over the crevasse. Meanwhile Scott removed his goggles and by dint of swinging backwards and forwards in his harness managed to find a spur of ice to stand on. He then helped Evans, who had responded to his call 'in his usual calm, matter-of-fact tones', to manoeuvre into a similar position. At least they were no longer dangling over the chasm but they were some twelve feet beneath the surface. The cold from the surrounding ice was intense, numbing their faces and fingers. While Lashly held grimly on to the sledge Scott struggled up out of the abyss to be greeted by a heartfelt 'Thank God!' from Lashly. Then he and Lashly helped Evans scramble to the surface.

The loquacious Welshman was rather lost for words. As Scott described: 'For a minute or two we could only look at one another, then Evans said, "Well I'm blowed"; it was the first sign of astonishment he had shown.' Later that day at their camp he kept referring to their narrow squeak. 'With his sock half on he would . . . say suddenly, "Well, sir, but what about that snow bridge?" or if so-and-so hadn't happened "where should we be now?" and then the soliloquy would end with "My word, but it was a close call!"' Scott found it touching and amusing. He was also more than ever convinced that he had chosen the right sledging companions. They had shown neither fear nor panic but had acted coolly. That night as Evans continued to shake his head in amazement Lashly sang a cheerful ditty over the cooking pot. Events had also shown Scott the utter unpredictability of Antarctic travel. All the planning in the world could not protect a sledging team from tumbling into a crevasse or down a glacier. He and his companions had been very lucky to survive. Scott's belief in fate was reinforced.

Arriving back at the *Discovery* on Christmas Eve Scott was disappointed to find her still fast in the ice. However, he now gave his time to writing up the achievements of the western journey. He calculated that they had averaged nearly fourteen and a half miles a day during their fifty-nine-day journey, sledging some 700 miles. This confirmed Scott's view that men were better than dogs. The distances compared well with the agonizingly slow progress made on the journey south when the average was only around ten miles a day. Scott was also able to record a number of important geological discoveries arising from his journey, including one of the glacier's tributaries where they found a deep moraine of mud that struck the vegetable-loving Lashly as 'a splendid place for growing spuds' and a steep dry valley, one of the three forming the McMurdo oasis, the largest ice-free area in Antarctica.

During his absence a number of other trips had gone well. Scott knew that the expedition would be returning to England with some useful scientific information under its belt. Royds, Bernacchi and a party had sledged for thirty-one days south-east over the Barrier proving that it continued level and Bernacchi had made a number of observations yielding useful data about the region's magnetic conditions. He also left a more down-to-earth account of sledging, describing some of the problems not addressed in Scott's loftier and more dignified accounts. In particular he described 'one of the nightmares of sledging in Antarctica' – going to the loo in sub-zero temperatures. Explaining that there was no room for facilities in the tiny tents, that latrines took too long to dig and that temporary shelters were an impossibility in the whirling snow, he described how:

> Feeling like a ham in a sack, you go through various preparatory antics of loosening garments – preferably within the tent, and prowl around some distance away facing always the biting wind, and watchfully awaiting a temporary lull. The rest is a matter of speed and dexterity, but invariably the nether garments are filled instantly with masses of surface-drifting snow, which you must take along with you and suffer the discomforts of extreme wetness for hours.

Later less inhibited explorers have also commented that few Polar travellers avoid piles, the agony of which can all too easily be imagined in a rushed evacuation.

Mulock, who had joined the *Discovery* from the *Morning* in place of Shackleton, had fixed the position and heights of over 200 mountains. Armitage, Wilson and Heald had surveyed the Koettlitz Glacier to the south-west. Armitage had wanted to sledge south but Scott, after consulting Wilson, had ruled that there was no point going over old ground. It would be more productive to explore somewhere new. A reasonable proposition, but Armitage interpreted it as Scott's desire to keep the record for farthest south for himself. Wilson had been able to make another visit to the emperor penguin rookery at Cape Crozier, and had solved the mystery of how the young birds, still downy and unable to swim, were able to leave the Cape. He had watched them float serenely out to sea with their parents on the ice floes.

However, all the parties were now safely back on board the *Discovery* in relative warmth and security. Lashly and Evans were tucking into some fine dishes created by Ford, who had taken over as cook and took his inspiration from a copy of Mrs Beeton, and were fast regaining their strength and lost weight. Indeed Scott observed that Evans was assuming gigantic proportions. He himself was suffering from his recurring problem of dyspepsia, perhaps stress-related, and could not indulge quite so freely. His condition was not helped by worry over whether the *Discovery* could be freed from the ice in time to sail from McMurdo Sound when the relief vessel joined them. Psychologically and emotionally the *Discovery* meant a great deal to Scott. She was the symbol of everything that had been achieved during their stay in Antarctica and she had been their home and their refuge. She was also his first independent command and abandoning her would be very difficult for him.

By early January twenty miles of solid ice still separated the *Discovery* from the open sea. The sawing camp which Armitage had set up on Scott's orders to try and cut a channel was achieving little and Scott ordered the work to stop. He faced a real possibility of yet another winter in McMurdo Sound and ordered his men to lay in a stock of penguin meat. Meanwhile he and Wilson made a journey northwards. Scott was watching for signs that the ice was breaking up. Wilson was studying penguins. They enjoyed a relaxed couple of days breakfasting off fried penguin liver and seal kidneys and resting and chatting in their tent. Then Scott looked out and saw the relief ship *Morning* barely three miles out to sea. And she was not alone. 'Lo and behold, there before us lay a second ship . . .' This was the whaler *Terra Nova*. Scott and Wilson were looking at the ship that would take them back to Antarctica for their race to the Pole.

For the moment Scott's chief concern was to understand what was going on. 'Sun scorched, unwashed, unshaven and in rags',[3] Wilson and Scott hurried on board the *Morning* to learn that, because of the wranglings of the two societies, the government had felt obliged to undertake the relief of the *Discovery* itself. The Admiralty had accordingly despatched the *Morning* and the *Terra Nova*, considered a more powerful ship. Shackleton, by then fit and well again, had been asked to go as chief officer of the *Terra Nova* but had, perhaps wisely, refused. The orders brought for Scott were unequivocal. If the *Discovery* could not be freed in time to leave with the relief ships she must be abandoned.

Scott was deeply upset at being put in 'a very cruel position' and his men shared his sentiments, greeting the Admiralty's orders with a 'stony silence'. However, he had to obey. There seemed a real prospect that the ice would not break up in time and so he began to arrange the transfer of equipment from the *Discovery* across the ice to the relief ships. He had not abandoned all hope and ordered the ice to be blasted at various strategic points but this

103

had only limited success. If the ice broke up it would be of its own volition and at last this began to happen. By 12 February there was only two and a half miles of solid ice between the *Discovery* and freedom. Would it break up in time?

14 February brought what might have seemed to a religious man to be a miracle but to the agnostic, fatalistic Scott may have seemed the smile of fortune. A combination of sea swell and firing charges finally broke open the way. Captain Colbeck of the *Morning* left an astute description of Scott's joy: 'Scott was terribly excited. He came on board as soon as I got alongside the ice face and could scarcely speak. It meant all the difference of complete and comparative success to him and there was not a happier man living than Scott on that night.'[4] The news had been broken on the *Discovery* by a shout of 'The ships are coming, Sir!' during dinner. In a moment the men were racing for Hut Point from where they could see the ice breaking up. Scott described how no sooner was one great floe borne away when a dark streak cut its way into the solid sheet which remained and carved out another: 'Our small community in their nondescript, tattered garments stood breathlessly watching this wonderful scene. For long intervals we remained almost spellbound, and then a burst of frenzied cheering broke out . . .' The *Terra Nova* and the *Morning* raced for the distinction of being the first to reach the *Discovery* and at about half past ten the *Terra Nova* broke through amid scenes of huge excitement. The men on Hut Point ran up their silken Union Jack in celebration.

The last of the ice around the *Discovery* was dislodged two days later by explosive charges. The final blast shook the vessel from end to end but it did the trick. Scott wrote thankfully that 'our good ship was spared to take us homeward'. On 16 February 1904 a sombre ceremony took place. The company of the *Discovery* gathered bare-headed around the cross erected to George Vince while Scott read prayers. Nine years later another cross would be erected nearby to mark another tragedy.

The next day brought near disaster. As if a malicious southern spirit was reluctant to give her up, a gale forced the *Discovery* headlong onto a shoal. For a few hours 'truly the most dreadful I have ever spent', Scott wrote, it looked as if she might not survive. The engines would not function and she was trapped in the gale, being pounded against the shoal. However, during the evening the current turned, running south rather than north, and the *Discovery* began to work astern. The crew managed to get the engines running again and were relieved to find that the ship had sustained little damage. She was ready to begin her long journey home.

As the *Discovery* set sail for New Zealand and the now familiar landmarks of McMurdo Sound faded from view, Scott must have wondered what kind of reception his expedition would receive when he reached England. He could look back on some remarkable achievements but he was wise enough to realize that he faced enemies as well as allies in the establishment and that his reception might not be all he wished.

7

The Reluctant Celebrity

On 10 September 1904 a spruce and gleaming *Discovery* steamed into Portsmouth Harbour. Friends and relatives packing the quayside were delighted to see that the crew looked 'wonderfully well'. These fit bronzed men, with skins 'like seasoned mahogany' according to the *Daily Express*, were the antithesis of the wasted and exhausted figures that some had expected to return. Sir Clements Markham bore some of the responsibility for stirring up anxieties about the men's condition because he had wanted to ensure that a relief expedition was sent. The horrors of the Franklin Expedition had made a deep impression on him in his youth and he was determined there should be no similar tragedy in the South. In fact the figures standing proudly on the deck were not only in the rudest of health, they had actually put on weight. The only sign of their ordeal was that they appeared to talk rather slowly and to move ponderously as if still shrouded in their heavy weather-proof garments.

A few days later the *Discovery* sailed for London where she tied up in the East India Docks. However, there was no official reception – the only dignitary to greet the returning heroes was the

Mayor of Gravesend. The following day a lunch was given by the Royal and Geographical Societies but it was in a warehouse. The *Daily Express* condemned the shabbiness of this 'luncheon in a shed' and asserted that the City of London should have offered the intrepid explorers a Guildhall banquet. It was noted that none of the Lords of the Admiralty were present while 'The Lord Mayor sent a sheriff to say a few words'. A guest at the lunch wrote with eerie foresight and a true understanding of human nature:

> I cannot help feeling that there still ought to remain some sort of ceremony of a national character to show that we as a nation realize and appreciate the sacrifice these men have made for science and to the credit of their country. Had the ship's crew perished in the Antarctic, we doubtless should have raised a national memorial to them. It seems to me a pity that we should suffer their deeds to pass to oblivion because they have returned safe and sound.

Scott had been worrying about how the expedition would be judged by the Admiralty and the waspish scientific establishment. He knew some would blame him for allowing the *Discovery* to be frozen in, thereby necessitating a second winter, but a more pressing concern was gnawing at him. In New Zealand the press had been quick to report that he had criticized the Admiralty for sending down the *Terra Nova*. He had been quoted as asserting that the men of the *Discovery* had been very well able to take care of themselves and that a single ship, the *Morning*, would have been quite sufficient for their relief. Indeed, that was what he genuinely believed. Like the rest of the crew he had felt humili-ated by the scale of the relief expedition which had smacked of overkill and melodrama. He prided himself on his self-sufficiency and resented being portrayed as vulnerable and in need of rescue. However, he had far too much common sense to have expressed these views publicly and had hastily issued a rebuttal to *The Times* and to Reuters and telegraphed the Admiralty and the Secretary of the Royal Geographical Society. He feared, correctly, that it would be hard to convince them of his innocence and he was afraid that his chances of promotion would suffer. Therefore it was a relief to learn that he had been promoted captain with effect from the day of his arrival.

Scott was also gratified by the generally positive reaction to the *Discovery*'s achievements. The accusation that he was not fit to lead a scientific expedition had rankled from the early days when the scientific establishment turned their noses up at him. Sir Clements Markham, of course, was quick to claim that splendid things had been achieved, pronouncing that 'Never has any Polar expedition returned with so great a harvest of scientific results'.[1] Yet Scott was aware that Sir Clements was regarded as tiresomely opinionated and thoroughly partisan.

Far more significant, therefore, was the endorsement of the scientific results by Chief Hydrographer to the Admiralty, Rear-Admiral Sir William Wharton, who had at one stage caballed with the scientists against Scott, but who now wrote that: 'Commander Scott and his staff have most magnificently maintained the high standard of efficiency of former Polar explorers.'[2] The press took note of the growing swell of approval and began to lionize Scott. 'True to the spirit of his instructions he has done what he set out to do, and even more,' applauded *The Times*. A contributory factor was that by 1904 explorers were back in fashion. Scott had sailed away at a time when the country was struggling to come to terms with a disturbing and unsatisfactory war in South Africa and interest in an adventure like his had been muted. However, by the time the *Discovery* returned, the Boer War had been won and people had regained their appetite for tales of romance and derring-do. There was a sufficient flavour of heroic recklessness about the *Discovery* expedition to excite the public. The other news sensation of the year was the Younghusband expedition to Tibet.

Scott could reflect that the plaudits were justified – he had indeed told a good story in his formal report to the Admiralty. The expedition had identified a coastline where it was possible to land, revealed much about the general geographical nature of Antarctica and shown that it was possible to survive the bleakest of conditions on this frozen continent and to travel over it. The expedition had made a total of twenty-eight sledge journeys and Scott, Wilson and Shackleton had advanced over 250 miles further south into Antarctica than any man before them. Important magnetic, meteorological, geological, zoological research had also been completed, including Wilson's pioneering work to unravel the mysterious life cycle of the emperor penguin.

In his report to the Admiralty Scott praised the 'exemplary behaviour' of all his men but among those marked out for special commendation were Evans and Lashly, his companions on 'the terrible plateau'. Lashly was immediately promoted to chief stoker – Scott reported that he had 'undoubtedly saved our lives by his presence of mind when Evans and I had fallen into a crevasse'. Evans was promoted petty officer 1st class and went off to the gunnery school at Portsmouth to train. Scott's praise of the men of the mess-deck also shows how thoroughly he was a man of his time.

> Both in New Zealand and at home they have been
> feted, and made much of, and fully exposed to all the

temptations which so frequently demoralize men of their class ... they have come through such an ordeal unscathed and have preserved their good name to the end ... The Officers will be the last to forget how much they owe to the rank and file.

His new-found celebrity made Scott anxious. Though ambitious, he was not someone who courted the limelight and he had a natural modesty. From the very beginning he was quick to emphasize that: 'An Antarctic expedition is not a one-man show, not a two-man show, nor a ten-men show. It means the co-operation of all ... There has been nothing but a common desire to work for the common good.'[3] (Scott's later rivalry with Shackleton shows that this generous and genuine view did not prevent him from believing that, as leader, he had personal claims on the area he had explored.) He was intensely proud of his success at welding a team out of the young and inexperienced Antarctic novices, himself included, who had sailed out together three years earlier. The fact that so many would be eager to return with him suggests that for all his faults he had succeeded as a leader and was not the cold-blooded egocentric, jealously preserving the best opportunities for himself that an embittered Armitage would depict.

Scott could now turn his attention to more domestic matters, taking satisfaction in his ability to afford to move his mother and sisters from their lodgings over the shop to somewhere more comfortable. He also treated himself for the first time to a really well-cut suit from a good tailor. If he was to become a lion he knew he needed to be a well-groomed one. He had been able to make his naval uniform last, disguising its shabbiness, but he now needed clothes that would pass muster in the eyes of that cruel and observant entity 'society'. In fact, he had received an invitation to Balmoral. Edward VII had been delighted to have a newly discovered area of Antarctica named after him and had sent Scott a congratulatory telegram. He now wanted to meet the young explorer.

Scott described his visit in a letter to his mother, but only after first encouraging her to go ahead with her move and urging her not to worry about money. He wrote that on the first evening the King appointed him a Commander of the Victorian Order – the only official honour he was, in fact, given as the press indignantly pointed out. On the second evening he lectured to the 'King, Princess of Wales, some of the Connaughts, Prime Minister, and many others'. His talk had only been intended to last an hour but went on for nearly two because the King asked so many questions. Apparently 'all sorts of nice things' were said afterwards. Disconcertingly, the Prime Minister Balfour, announced that he himself was 'Father of the Expedition!!!' (The exclamation marks are Scott's.) The next day the King took Scott on a grouse drive. It was all clearly something of an ordeal although Scott was gratified by the honour. His letter concluded 'P.S. I never had to wear knee breeches or a frock coat.'[4] It's hard to tell whether he was wistful or relieved.

A week before his visit to Balmoral, Scott had written to the First Sea Lord asking for six months' leave in which 'to undertake a narrative of our voyage', to be published in the spring. He was careful to express himself in suitably modest language, saying that he would be very sorry to do anything which the Admiralty might think unbecoming to a naval officer and that apart from writing the book he was 'trying to keep as quiet as possible'. However, this was difficult. Markham arranged an exhibition at the Bruton Galleries which opened on 4 November amid extraordinary scenes. The fashionable world alighted from their carriages, horseless or otherwise, confidently bearing their cards only to be told by the patient policemen that they would have to queue like anybody else. It was a new experience for the great and the good to have to stand in line and perhaps a sign of the changing times. The exhibition, which featured several hundreds of Wilson's inspirational sketches, Skelton's photographs, a model of *Discovery* and sledging equipment, drew about 10,000 visitors.

Three days later Scott found himself addressing 7,000 members and guests of the two societies in the Royal Albert Hall. It must have been daunting, even though his *Discovery* comrades were on the stage with him. He was so flustered that he forgot to pay tribute to Armitage and other colleagues. The response from the audience was rather cool – a muted clapping echoed around the huge hall. In fact just a few days before the lecture Markham had been furious to receive what he thought 'a very nasty letter' from the secretary of the Royal Society effectively demanding that the men of the *Discovery* should neither lecture nor deliver papers. The next night Scott got a very different reception when he gave his first public lecture entitled 'Farthest South' to an audience which had paid anything from a shilling to ten and sixpence (the standard rates for West End theatre tickets) to hear him and applauded loudly.

The need to raise funds to pay off the expedition's debts put Scott on the treadmill of the lecture circuit. He was soon in great demand, traversing the country and honing his lecturing skills. Shackleton arranged for him to address the Scottish Royal Geographical Society in Edinburgh where he was awarded the Livingstone medal. In fact he and Shackleton were quite close during the period after his return, the trauma of 'Shackles's' departure home forgotten in the excitement of reunion. Shackleton was one of the first to surge aboard the *Discovery* and had stayed until the early hours talking excitedly and quizzing Scott. Markham had helped him win his appointment as Secretary to the Scottish Royal Geographical Society. Though the pay was poor, only £200 a year, Emily Dorman's father had died, leaving her mistress of an income of £700 a year, quite enough for them to marry and live in middle-class comfort. Shackleton was also enjoying himself, shaking the fusty members of the society by introducing such technological devilry as electric light and a typewriter.

Scott soon developed skill and confidence as a speaker, learning such tricks as running a hand in mock despair through his hair when a slide failed to come up on the screen at the right time and delighting his audiences with very English understatements and humorous asides about the savage conditions he and his comrades had endured. According to the newspaper reports of the day he was a very rapid speaker, but clear and compelling. He had no need of notes. The *Manchester Guardian* pronounced that 'if he is as efficient an explorer as he is a lecturer, then he stands in the front rank'. As so often in his life he had to exercise economy, travelling third class, which caused embarrassment when a group of city dignitaries came to greet him in the Midlands expecting the hero to emerge triumphant from a first-class compartment.

However, Scott worried that he was making only slow progress with his book. Despite his passion in his early youth to express himself in writing he felt intimidated by the scale of the task and the fear of failing. He wrote that 'Of all things I dread having to write a narrative and am wholly doubtful of my capacity; in any event if I have to do it, it will take me a long time.'[5] By early 1905 Scott was close to despair and asked the Admiralty to spare him for a further three months to complete the book. To force himself to progress he went every day to the Markhams' house where Royds was staying while he completed his study on meteorology. Sir Clements enjoyed the company of the two young men, strolling with them, and Minna his wife, in Eccleston Square in the evenings. There are two interpretations of his interest in them – the traditional one that they were substitutes for the sons he had never had or the more modern and cynical one that he had a homosexual fascination with young men. Whatever the reason he was certainly fond of them and rather possessive.

Scott probably found the old gentleman a bit overpowering. By the spring he knew he needed greater solitude and moved to Ashdown where, with the help of Reginald Smith, senior partner in the publishers Smith, Elder and Co and editor of the *Cornhill Magazine* who became a lifelong friend, the book at last took substance. Scott dedicated it to Sir Clements Markham as 'the Father of the Expedition and its Most Constant Friend' as Markham no doubt expected. Published in October 1905 in two volumes it immediately sold out and the accolades poured in – the *Times Literary Supplement* called it 'a masterly work'.

However, the question facing Scott was what to do next. The publication of *The Voyage of the Discovery* marked a watershed in his career as an explorer. Receiving a gold medal from the American Geographical Society in April 1906 he gave his audience to understand that in all probability he had finished with exploring. A factor in this was that he had become exasperated with being a celebrity, confiding to a relation that he had had enough notoriety to last him a lifetime. He returned to sea in August 1906 to serve as flag captain to Rear-Admiral Egerton in HMS *Victorious*. However, within a bare month he had apparently had a change of heart. In September his friend J.M. Barrie, the tiny playwright then enjoying huge success with *Peter Pan*, was writing to express his delight that all the old hankerings were coming back to Scott and promising to keep an eye out for a likely millionaire to fund the expedition.

What had changed? Whatever Scott may have said publicly, the siren call of the South had never really gone away. At the very least he knew he had not finished the job and that the public had expectations of him. On his return, *The Times* had asked the question: 'Will the problem of the Antarctic be left where it stands?' To a man of Scott's persistence and ambition this was galling. If he could reach the Pole the security which had so far eluded him would be his for life. A knighthood, official honours, fame would all follow. If he did not make the attempt, his career would progress but would be unlikely to bring him the great prizes. However, something deeper than personal pride and ambition was at work here. During the very speech in which he had announced he was unlikely to return to Antarctica, he had described the sparkling frozen landscapes with an emotion that bordered on longing. That beautiful solitary world held a special place in his heart, appealing to the romantic in him while the excitement it represented could never be matched by anything the peacetime navy could offer. The challenge of adventuring into the unknown was fundamentally more attractive than the prospect of a conventional naval career and 'the whirl of this modern life'.[6]

Barrie had recognized this romantic side of Scott's nature. On the night of their first meeting he had walked through the streets of London quite enchanted with Scott and unwilling to part from him. He observed the extraordinary contradictions in him: 'Scott was naturally a strange mixture of the dreamy and the practical, and never more practical than immediately after he had been dreamy. He forgot place and time altogether when thus abstracted.'[7] Here we have an elegant and insightful updating of the 'Old Mooney' of Scott's childhood which was clearly still a dominant part of Scott's psychological make-up. It would not have surprised Barrie that Scott presented himself at a smart dinner party in white tie and waistcoat but no dinner jacket – a fact he only realized when handing his overcoat to a scandalized footman. Unlikely as an alliance between the diminutive playwright and the toughened young explorer might have seemed, there was a common bond. Each of them found aspects of modern adult life sad, unpalatable and inexplicable. Barrie found his comfort in the creation of his never-never land. Scott had Antarctica as his escapist kingdom of the imagination.

In January 1907 Scott quietly began to put his plans into action, writing to the Secretary of the Royal Geographical Society that he reckoned he could mount an expedition for £30,000. However, something then happened which Scott had not foreseen. He had been worrying about the possibility of foreign rivals but had not anticipated a serious challenger much closer to home. In February 1907 Shackleton announced his own intention to lead a 'British Antarctic Expedition' to conquer the South Pole. To Scott this seemed an act of treachery and it did not bring out the best in him. Shackleton claimed that he had only learned of Scott's plans when he wrote to Mulock, the man who had replaced him on the *Discovery* expedition when he was sent home, inviting him to join his expedition to find that he was already committed to Scott. Characteristically Wilson now resumed his role as peacemaker. Shackleton had also written to him, begging him to be his number two, an offer that Wilson felt obliged to turn down because of his work researching the cause of disease in grouse. However, on the very next day he received an agitated letter from Scott asking him what he thought Shackleton was playing at. Wilson did his best to defend his old friend, replying soothingly that Shackleton had been ignorant of his intentions and adding that he himself had had no idea that Scott meant to return.

This mollified Scott a little, and he was prepared to proclaim publicly that what really mattered was that Britain should reach the Pole before any foreigner intervened. However, behind the scenes the wrangling continued. Scott was angry that Shackleton planned to make his base at McMurdo Sound, feeling this was not the act of a man of honour. Scott seemed, perversely, to see it as a personal fief. A man less anxious about position might have shown greater magnanimity. The problem from Shackleton's point of view was that he had promised his sponsors, notably the Clydeside industrialist William Beardmore, that he would be starting out from Scott's former base. A change of plan would look like sharp practice.

However, Wilson, acting as a go-between, told him firmly that Scott had a prior claim. Shackleton listened to his gentle friend and accepted *force majeure*. In March he telegraphed to Scott that he would meet his wishes regarding the base. In May he met his erstwhile leader at Wilson's instigation and drew up a memorandum renouncing the use of McMurdo Sound. It was very formal and more in tune with Scott's disciplined, cautious way of doing business than the lively Irishman's. He promised Scott that he was 'leaving the McMurdo Sound base to you, and will land either at the place known as the Barrier Inlet or at King Edward VII Land, whichever is the most suitable. If I land at either of these places I will not work to the westward of the 170 meridian W. and shall not make any sledge journey going W . . .' He concluded politely that 'I hope this letter meets you on the points that you desire. – Yours very sincerely, E.H. SHACKLETON.'[8]

Scott's response was frigid and formal. He wrote that so long as Shackleton stuck to the arrangement they had agreed, 'I do not think our plans will clash . . .'[9] The dispute marked a profound shift in their relationship from the days of the *Discovery* expedition when a kindly Scott had tried to tempt his erstwhile sledging companion 'Shackles' with sardines and their camaraderie on Scott's return. Scott now regarded Shackleton with suspicion bordering contempt. Shackleton on the other hand had been bitterly offended by the account in *The Voyage of the Discovery* of how he had had to be carried on the sledge, asserting he had only ridden on it to act as a brake, and this had soured his view of Scott.

With so much at stake all of a sudden, the tension must have been unbearable for Scott as he tried to pull his own plans together. He had the comfort of knowing that Wilson would be going with him. In March the doctor had accepted his offer, adding that his wife Oriana was one hundred per cent behind him. Yet in July Scott had to endure the send-off given to Shackleton as he set sail aboard the rundown old sealer *Nimrod*, taking with him a motor vehicle – indeed, he was the first man to land a car in Antarctica – and two seamen from the *Discovery* expedition, Frank Wild and Ernest Joyce. At least the jealous and proprietorial Scott had the satisfaction of knowing that none of the *Discovery*'s officers had joined the venture.

However, the year 1907 had not yet done with Scott. Other traumatic times awaited him because he was now in love. The woman who had caught his heart was at first glance the very antithesis of Scott. She challenged his middle-class ideas and insecurities. She was an artist, a free spirit, and fearless. Scott recognized that here at last was the being to whom he could reveal his doubts and his aspirations. Yet the prospect of marriage brought his insecurities to the fore. He had the courage to be a Polar explorer but could he take on the challenge of such an unconventional wife?

8

Captain Scott in Love

At first glance Kathleen Bruce was an extraordinary mate for Scott. Artistic and cosmopolitan, she had a knack of getting away with things that would have sunk lesser women, from junketing across Europe with Isadora Duncan and camping out on the thyme-covered slopes of Mount Hymettus to making midnight calls in Chelsea with the district maternity nurse and touring the doss houses and opium dens of the East End. She also had considerable talent as a sculptress.

Scott first met her at a lunch party given by Mabel Beardsley, sister of Aubrey, in December 1906. Scott's actress sister Ettie Ellison-Macartney had toured with Mabel, who had taken a fancy to Scott. Indeed, her possessiveness about him was a standing joke. Scott, in turn, enjoyed these forays into the bohemian artistic world. This seemingly unfettered existence had attractions for a man who from an early age had struggled with the weight of family responsibilities and whose career was in thrall to that inflexible machine, the navy. Kathleen was sitting between Barrie and Max Beerbohm but glancing down the table she spied Scott and something about him arrested her attention. As she later described: 'He was not very young, perhaps forty, nor very good-looking, but he looked very healthy and alert, and I glowed rather foolishly and suddenly when I clearly saw him ask his neighbour who I was.' She was introduced to him after lunch and he asked her how she had acquired her 'wonderful sunburn'. She told him she had been 'vagabonding in Greece, and he thought how entrancing to vagabond like that'.

That was that for the time being because Kathleen had to leave to catch a train. She later wrote that Scott had hurried after her 'but he saw me just ahead carrying a rather large suitcase, and his "English gentlemen don't carry large objects in the street" upbringing was too much for him. He did not catch me up.' In those few words she captured some of the essence of Scott – his shyness, his middle-classness and his fears about what other people thought.

It was ten months before their paths crossed again. Then in October 1907 Scott cajoled Mabel Beardsley into inviting them both to tea. Kathleen took unusual care with her wardrobe, hacking two hats into one and cutting up a handkerchief to make a new collar and cuffs. She was excited and curious but also aware of a certain incongruity – writing that 'the like of him should not go to tea parties'. She left a vivid account of their meeting. At one moment she was being entertained by Ernest Thesiger and Henry James, but then:

> . . . all of a sudden, and I did not know how, I was sitting in a stiff, uncomfortable chair with an ill-balanced cup of tea, being trivially chaffed by this very well-dressed, rather ugly and celebrated explorer. He was standing over me. He was of medium height, with broad shoulders, very small waist, and dull hair beginning to thin, but with a rare smile and with eyes

of a quite unusually dark blue, almost purple. I had noticed those eyes ten months before. I noticed them again now, although by electric light. I had never seen their like. He suggested taking me home.

His photographs show that her impression of Scott as 'rather ugly' is surprising – perhaps there was a loving touch of irony at his vanity, perhaps she was comparing him with the dazzling young men who were her regular companions, but she certainly did not think him unattractive.

Kathleen had expected Scott to do the conventional thing and hail a hansom cab, but instead they walked to her little flat in Cheyne Walk 'laughing, talking, jostling each other'. This horse-play seems unlikely public behaviour for a mature naval officer, but Kathleen's exuberant love of life liberated and excited Scott. From that day onwards he wrote or called constantly and his notes were intimate and tender and in the high-flown language of the day – 'Uncontrollable footsteps carried me along the Embankment to find no light – yet I knew you were there dear heart – I saw the open window and, in fancy, a sweetly tangled head of hair upon the pillow within . . .'[1] Within just a few days of that merry and bois-terous promenade through Chelsea he was thinking of marriage.

This was by no means Scott's first romantic foray. He had always been attracted to pretty, lively, intelligent women but lack of time, money and opportunity had been powerful obstacles. His sister believed that 'The sailor's life and his romantic nature caused him to idealize women. His affections were easily caught though not easily held.'[2] According to Bernacchi he particularly admired women who could 'do a job of work successfully'.[3] In her biography of Scott, Elspeth Huxley cites evidence that during 1907 he suffered the pangs of disappointed love. The object of his adoration was Marie-Carola, a wealthy young society widow and daughter of an Irish baronet. Scott was entranced by this clever, sophisticated, cosmopolitan woman who divided her life between the drawing rooms of fashionable London and the Paris salons. Yet it came to nothing and there is a story that after she rejected him they met unexpectedly at a dinner party and Scott was so overcome with emotion that his linen napkin was found torn to shreds beneath the table.

He had also been attracted to the actress Pauline Chase, the toast of London for her boyish portrayal of Peter Pan, evidence again that he liked women from outside his own rather restricted milieu. Barrie acted as go-between and, when he could, Scott used to take her to supper after the performance and away for weekends in the country. The photographs show a slight girl with a charming, regular-featured face, very different from Kathleen Bruce's strong, striking Mediterranean looks.

Kathleen derived these from her unusual ancestry. Her father was the Reverend Lloyd Stewart Bruce, Canon of York and son of Sir James Bruce, Baronet of Downhill, Londonderry, but her mother was the granddaughter of a Greek prince. Nearly ten years Scott's junior, Kathleen was born in March 1878 in her father's rectory, the youngest of eleven children. She was orphaned young – Canon Bruce died in 1886 and his wife expired six years earlier, apparently of Bright's Disease, but also worn out, no doubt, by all that childbearing. Kathleen's childhood was spent in the household of her childless Episcopalian great uncle William Forbes Skene, an eccentric though fond old gentleman who was Historiographer Royal of Scotland. However, he was no substitute for a mother. Kathleen grew up restless and attention-seeking.

She and her siblings were clearly a handful. Her older sister Podge later recalled how parents were 'warned not to let their children associate with those dreadful Bruce girls!!' after a row at Kathleen's school.[4] When her great uncle died Kathleen was left with just £72 a year and life became a succession of boarding schools interspersed with living with her sister Elma and her husband Canon Keating, a gloomy and eccentric couple. It was a dreary and spartan existence for this bright-eyed exuberant girl anxious to be noticed and hungry for affection. The ping-pong existence of her early years contributed to her feeling that she was a gypsy who could afford to travel light through life. She never attached much importance to possessions or appearances.

After studying at the Slade School of Fine Art in London Kathleen chose a life as a near-penniless art student in Paris. She enrolled as a pupil at a popular studio, the Academie Colarossi, learning the skill of drawing but soon finding her greatest satisfaction in sculpting. Like many girls of her class and time she was very innocent. The sight of a naked male model posing for a life class apparently made her physically sick. However, she soon adapted to a bohemian way of life that came to suit her admirably. Because she had never known real maternal affection and had been a tomboy she had little time for members of her own sex, unless they were exceptional. She quickly abandoned classes for women only – *dames seules*, nicknamed 'damned souls' – a soubriquet she agreed with. She joined mixed classes where she was popular with the male students who were attracted by her striking looks and zest for life. She had a mass of dark hair, vivid blue eyes and an athletic figure.

Her attraction had nothing to do with how she dressed. She had no interest in clothes. In later life she was described as one of the worst-dressed women in London with a 'sort of aggressive no-taste'.[5] However, she had undeniable sex appeal and enjoyed the power it gave her over men. She admitted she found their admiration 'so exciting, so stimulating, so sunshiny'. In modern parlance she would probably be called a 'tease'. Aleister Crowley, who met her in 1902, described her as 'strangely seductive' and insinuated that her chastity, or as she called it 'my determined, my masterful virginity', was a device with which to torture men. Whatever the case, one frustrated young Swede became so enraged that he lay in wait for her with a revolver.

Her behaviour was at least partly the result of a need for attention and admiration unfulfilled from childhood and a determination to preserve her independence and to be in no one's power. She was shrewd enough to know that plenty of men would be only too eager to take advantage of a young *ingénue*. An incident in her youth may also have had an influence. While she was still a little girl a drunk tried to abduct Kathleen in the street in Edinburgh. She bit him hard and managed to escape.[6] She later described how the incident had given her a horror of drink. It also made her nervous of men but as she grew up she came to look on them 'as fairly ordinary mortals' according to Podge.[7] Her diaries suggest that by the time she met Scott in her late twenties she was still a virgin. She claimed that she had been saving herself for a man worthy of siring the son on whom she had set her heart. This was certainly true – she scrutinized any man she was interested in with the coolness of a genetic scientist – but there may have been something deeper behind this determined chastity.

Kathleen studied in Paris for five years and it could hardly have been a headier, more conducive environment. She was soon on easy terms with some of the foremost artists of the day, including Picasso and Rodin, who taught and encouraged her. Rodin also introduced her to the American dancer Isadora Duncan and told them to help each other. They became friends and Isadora asked Kathleen to be with her during the birth of her child. The pregnancy was supposed to be a secret and to put the press off the scent, Isadora asked Kathleen to dress in her clothes and dance about on the beach. She later accompanied Isadora and her family or 'the dancing vagabonds' as she called them, to Greece where they slept out of doors and danced to greet the dawn.

It was shortly after this back-to-nature existence that Kathleen returned to London to begin her life as a sculptress, met Scott for the first time and dazzled him with her tales of vagabonding and her marvellous golden suntan. She must have seemed like a being from another world to this shy, restrained naval officer. Certainly from the time of their second meeting he was caught. Kathleen in turn was touched by his obvious sterling qualities. There was something reassuring about him. Her own world was peppered with admirers, talented, good-looking and amusing but also raff-ish, volatile, egocentric and unpredictable. As she recognized, they could not offer the stability she sought as she approached the end of her twenties, and none of them was fit to give her the son she yearned for – 'this healthy, fresh, decent, honest, rock-like naval officer was just exactly what I had been setting up in my mind as a contrast to my artist friends, as the thing I had been looking for.' She did not want an ordinary man. Her mate must be remarkable but he must also be reliable and someone she could look up to. He must be father figure and potential father. In Scott she believed she had found him.

Within just a few weeks they had decided unofficially to marry and Kathleen met Hannah Scott. This was a crucial step. Like other men of his era Scott had a deeply reverential attitude towards his mother and he wanted Kathleen 'to know and love that dear mother'.[8] This was alien to Kathleen but she indulged him. Scott's mother, in turn, did her best to respond to her disconcertingly exotic future daughter-in-law. Scott wrote to Kathleen: 'You're in a fair way to capture my mother's head, she was full of you today. What did you say to her, do or say you little witch?'[9] But, whatever Scott chose to believe, the relationship was never to be an easy one. Hannah Scott did her best but she would perhaps have preferred a more conventional woman and preferably one who had some money.

Of course, money was an important consideration. Could they actually afford to marry? At least a quarter of Scott's modest income of some £800 a year (reduced by a half when he was between naval appointments) was spent supporting his mother. Kathleen had very little money of her own. She could make money from sculpting, which she enjoyed, but Scott was anxious that she should not commercialize her art for profit. It also wounded his pride to think that he could not keep a wife and he made calculations with all the precision of planning equipment and rations for a sledging trip. He sent Kathleen an 'Estimate for 2 persons living in a small house in London in this year of grace'[10] and it was very detailed, showing the depths of his anxiety – he allowed 10 shillings a head per week for food, and an annual expenditure of £25 for laundry, £15 for coal, £6 for stationery, papers and other necessaries and £45 for a servant. The total came out at £329 a year.

Scott knew he should not let such considerations prevail and he took comfort from Wilson's happy marriage, which he admired as 'a glaring example of how happiness may be achieved without a large share of worldly gear . . .'[11] However, his family's past was against him. He tried to explain it to Kathleen: 'Yet oh my dear, there is another side to me, born of hereditary instinct of caution and fostered by the circumstances which have made the struggle for existence an especially hard one for me. Can you understand? I review a past – a real fight – from an almost desperate position to the bare right to live as my fellows.'[12] He was afraid she would think him a feeble, spineless being – her maxim was 'Reality is in the present, not in the past or future', and it was not in her nature to fuss and fret over what had been or might be.[13]

The correspondence between the lovers shows how their thoughts and emotions ebbed and flowed. Sometimes one was downcast only to be rallied by the other. At other times both were in despair. In early January 1908 Kathleen had written 'Dearest Con. Don't let's get married ... I have always really wanted to marry for the one reason, and now that very thing seems as though it would only be an encumbrance we could scarcely cope with.' She also touched on the more fundamental problem. 'We're horribly different you and I, the fact is I've been hideously spoilt ... let's abandon the idea of getting married ...'[14] Scott's response was pensive and very honest – 'I want to marry you very badly, but it is absurd to pretend I can do so without facing a great difficulty and risking a great deal for others as well as for myself.'[15] He begged her to work with him, not against him.

On 25 January 1908, Scott took command of *HMS Essex*. Worries about his relationship with Kathleen mingled with worries about assembling his own new Antarctic expedition. In March he was preoccupied with testing motor sledges in France. An engineer called Belton Hamilton had designed a motor sledge for Polar travel with financial backing from Lord Howard de Walden. The French explorer, Jean-Baptiste Charcot, had also developed a prototype and the idea was to test the two designs, together with a third invented by Michael Barne. The tests were only partly successful and there was clearly more to be done. However, of greater concern to Scott was the news which reached him while he was in Paris that Shackleton had reneged on his agreement. Unable to find a way through the pack ice to Edward VII Land he had turned back and had landed in McMurdo Sound, making his base close to Scott's hut. According to Shackleton this had been his only option and had caused him much soul-searching. Scott saw it as a breach of an agreement and a downright dishonourable action – a view shared by Edward Wilson – and, of course, Sir Clements Markham was furious.

Kathleen, meanwhile, continued to procrastinate. At the end of March she was writing to Scott again to break off the marriage, though adding: 'Goodbye, dearest. I love you very very much.'[16] Her brother Rosslyn thought it was strange behaviour: 'She's frighteningly in love with him I should think but tells me that she never writes to him without saying let's put it off again and forget and forgive!'[17] Scott continued to steady and reassure her, perhaps what she was seeking through her wild correspondence, but he was feeling desperately insecure himself. In May he wrote: 'Darling. I don't know what to think. Another post has come and not a word from you . . . what does it mean?'[18]

Their relationship was at a critical point. Kathleen was being wooed by a former acquaintance, the young writer and lawyer Gilbert Cannan, described by Henry James in 1910 as one of the most promising young writers in England in company with D.H. Lawrence, Hugh Walpole and Compton MacKenzie. He had an attractive crooked smile and bright corn-coloured hair. He was also to spend the last thirty years of his life in a lunatic asylum suffering from delusions, one of which was that he was Captain Scott the great explorer. However, Kathleen, on the brink of stepping into an unknown world, was attracted by this reminder of her old bohemian life and she allowed him to pay court to her. In April she also allowed him to meet Scott, who was home from sea and who was disturbed and upset to find this man intruding on the scene. Cannan seems to have been contemplating a *ménage à trois*, hardly likely to appeal to a man like Scott, who was confused and hurt but still desperate to marry Kathleen.

When Kathleen decided to go on a walking holiday to Italy

with her cousin's husband, outwardly at least, Scott took the news stoically saying simply 'Write to me often, and don't stay too long.' She was delighted calling him '. . . a grand man; no self-pity, no suspicions, no querulousness, no recriminations. Perfect man!'[19] She did write to him – of the freedom and irresponsibility of 'vagabonding' and of how precious it was to her. This struck a deep chord in Scott and he responded with some of his most revealing comments:

> Knock a few conventional shackles off me, you find as
> great a vagabond as you but perhaps that won't do. I
> shall never fit in my round hole. The part of a machine
> has got to fit – yet how I hate it sometimes . . . I love
> the open air, the trees, the fields and the seas, the open
> spaces of life and thought. You are the spirit of all this
> to me . . . I want you to be with me when the sun
> shines free of fog.[20]

Scott knew he was too 'buttoned up' and it was an appeal to Kathleen to help him break free.

In Venice Kathleen met Isadora again and her description of the encounter prompted another agonized response. Could he ever satisfy her? He believed he could, but it would require an enormous act of faith from her: 'Do you realize that you will have to change me . . . infuse something of the joyous pure spirit within you? A year or two hence it would have been too late. I should have been too set to admit the principle of change . . . oh the grinding effects of a mechanical existence – in the end, I am half fearful. Shall I satisfy you?'[21]

Kathleen saw the absurdity of Scott's abasing himself like this. Perhaps the evidence of weakness and vulnerability worried her. Her man must be a champion, a dragon-slayer – she had had enough of tortured, sensitive men and she responded in suitably rallying tones: 'Here am I a little ass of a girl who's never done a thing in her life allowing a real man to talk to her of superiority. My sense of humour can't be doing with it.' She also provided a spur to his ambition. 'You shall go to the Pole. Oh dear me what's the use of having energy and enterprise if a little thing like that can't be done. It's got to be done so hurry up and don't leave a stone unturned.'[22] The young Norwegian Tryggve Gran, who was with Scott's final expedition, later described Kathleen as 'a very, very clever woman very very pushing . . . very ambitious . . . I don't think Scott would have gone to the Antarctic if it hadn't been for her.'[23]

They decided to make their engagement public at last and the months of painful indecision ended. Practical problems such as where to live after they were married took over. They purchased the lease of a Georgian House in Buckingham Palace Road where Victoria Coach Station now stands for £50 a year. It had eight rooms and a garden studio where Kathleen could sculpt. However Scott continued to worry, writing: 'Girl, I'm a little frightened, vaguely. You're so uncommon and I conventionalized.' It was, he admitted, self doubt, not doubt of her. She was free-thinking, he was crippled by 'the reserve of a lifetime . . . not easily broken'. He confessed that he had once been a dreamer, an enthusiast, an idealist but that the memory of this made him feel he was growing old. In a particularly poignant admission he wrote that 'the dreaming part of me was and is a failure.'[24] Now it was Kathleen who reassured and steadied him. It was a paradox that this man of action had an almost feminine sensitivity – Cherry-Garrard was to remark that he 'never knew a man who cried so easily' – while several of Kathleen's contemporaries commented that she had a masculine turn of mind and outlook on life.

It was decided that the wedding would be at Hampton Court where one of Kathleen's aunts, the widow of an Archbishop of York, had a grace and favour apartment. Scott wrote to Kathleen's brother Rosslyn that 'from male man's point of view it seems as pleasant a place as can be chosen for a trying ceremony' but he was no doubt pleased to have such a prestigious venue.[25] He wrote careful instructions to Kathleen about the invitations reminding her that 'single cards can be sent to husband and wife plus daughters but sons have separate cards – also sisters and brothers living together separate cards – Look out to get details right as regards titles and forms in general.'[26] He also appears to have been anxious about the wedding cake, writing to her that 'Mother says it wouldn't do *not* to have a wedding cake. People would think it odd.'[27] Kathleen was obviously indifferent to such proprieties.

It was also typical of Kathleen that she was totally unconcerned about wedding clothes and trousseau and the other appurtenances of marriage considered indispensable in polite society. Even Rosslyn was surprised by her indifference. He was himself something of an eccentric, rumoured to have kept an elephant at Oxford because the college rules stipulated no dogs. He also devoted a large part of his life to breeding mice of exotic hue from lavender to bright green. But even he now wrote that 'Kiddie', as he had called Kathleen since childhood, was going too far: 'She won't let him give her any jewellery not even a ring nor will she submit to the usual veil and orange blossom.'[28]

However, Scott knew exactly how to appeal to his bride: 'The serious consideration is that when we are married you mustn't only look nice (which you can't help), but you must look as though there wasn't any poverty . . . just think of my feelings when I am so to speak "expensively" dressed whilst your costume shows a saving spirit . . . am I dreadfully sensitive to appearances?'[29] The incident again brought into sharp relief the differences between them. At root it was a question of confidence and Kathleen was by far the most self-confident. But of course she weakened. As the press reported she was married on 5 September 1908 in a white satin dress trimmed with Limerick lace with a chiffon bodice and a tulle veil. Rosslyn conducted the service, choristers warbled and the 150-strong congregation included Rodin and his wife. As the service proceeded a violent storm thundered overhead but the skies soon cleared and as the congregation streamed out, one of the guests, Admiral Sir Lewis Beaumont, exclaimed: 'Gad, what a salute from heaven,' which would have amused Kathleen.[30]

The brief honeymoon was spent in France. Kathleen described that it passed 'as confusedly and insecurely as most honeymoons', presumably a reference to the sexual side. However, it was soon clear to curious onlookers that this marriage of opposites was a success. In Kathleen, Scott had found 'the only woman to whom I can tell things'.[31] At last he had someone to whom he could confide his faults. He knew for example that he was bad-tempered and irritable and made her promise that she would never compromise her own ideas just to humour him. He continued to worry that he was unworthy of her. 'I've a personality myself, a small mean thing besides yours . . . I'm obstinate, despondent, pigheaded, dejected, there's something growing bigger inside that keeps shouting the greatness of you . . . You're so exalted, I somehow can't reach up.'[32] She in turn had found a man she could trust, respect and love 'desperately, deeply, violently and wholly', though she was not yet truly 'in love' with him. That was to come later. She certainly understood him. When a Miss Madeleine Morrison told his fortune at tea and commented on his laziness, untidiness, touchiness and tendency to look on the gloomy side,

Kathleen cheerfully remarked that Miss Morrison must have been married to him for years instead of just reading his palm.

Scott returned to sea to captain *HMS Bulwark* and Kathleen resumed a life perhaps not so different from before. She went out to dinner, parties, plays, danced a lot and pursued her sculpture vigorously. She was delighted when she sold a mask for 18 guineas and wrote triumphantly to her more equivocal husband that she loved making money not because she did not wish to spend his, but because she did not wish them to have to think about money. Her private correspondence with Scott at this time provides some further insights into their lives, characters and motivation. She cajoles him to further his career, to make himself indispensable: 'You must have the first ship in the Fleet or what's the use of you?' He is sometimes melancholy or depressed and regrets what were clearly arguments when they last met. 'Girl, I can't describe what comes over me. It's too indefinite . . . I'm obsessed with the view of life as a struggle for existence. I seem to be marking time, impotent to command circumstances. The outward signs are the black moods that come and go with such apparent disregard for the feelings of those dear to me . . . Wife dear, my own wife, for every lapse believe there is repentance.' A few weeks later he wrote 'I think you hurt me unintentionally and then perhaps meanly. I strike back with vague intention to hurt. My sweetheart . . . try to understand – I want someone to anchor to, someone sweet and sound and sure like yourself and how I long to be up and achieving things for your sake.'[33]

Kathleen too wrote of such tiffs. 'Oh my darling, I'm so sorry, how persistently and brutally we do hurt each other and would it hurt so each time if we were not all important to each other?' Their letters are also full of their wish to meet more frequently to 'make a baby' and of their disappointment when each month

Kathleen proved not to be pregnant but in January 1909 Kathleen learned that she was indeed expecting a baby, to be born in the autumn. Scott's reaction when he heard the news was to roll a fellow officer to the floor in jubilant horseplay. Shortly afterwards he was delighted to be told that he was to be given a desk job in the Admiralty. His pay would be increased and he could live at home.

In March 1909 news came that Shackleton had made an astoundingly successful journey south but that he had not reached the South Pole. Scott saw the newspaper headlines at a railway station and came running along the platform, paper in hand, to say excitedly to Crean, then his coxswain, 'I think we'd better have a shot next.'[34]

In June Shackleton returned to a hero's welcome. His achievements were inspiring. Though he had failed the final hurdle he had crossed the Ice Barrier, found a way up the mighty Beardmore Glacier, named for his sponsor, and got within ninety-seven geographical miles of the Pole. However, here he had deemed it wiser to turn back, commenting that he assumed his wife would rather have a live donkey for a husband than a dead lion. He had accomplished his great odyssey using ponies, not dogs, a fact not lost on Scott.

Scott agonized about how he should greet his fellow explorer. In the end common sense and generosity got the better of animosity – although Shackleton's broken promise was not forgotten – and he joined the crowds thronging Charing Cross Station to greet the returning hero. It was a far cry from the *Discovery*'s muted reception and of course Shackleton revelled in it. He was as keen to court publicity as Scott had been to avoid it, reflecting the profound difference in their temperaments – one of them the flamboyant showman, the other the reserved naval officer. Scott added his voice to the chorus of praise. At a dinner he referred to 'these great works of Mr Shackleton'.[35] He also promised to profit from Shackleton's discoveries before some other country intervened. However he took the precaution of writing to Shackleton explaining his intention to return to the Ross Sea and there was more than a little irony in his letter: '. . . of course I should be glad to have your assurance that I am not disconcerting any plans of your own.'[36]

On 13 September 1909 the Antarctic Expedition was formally announced. Scott told an eager public that 'The main object of the expedition is to reach the South Pole and to secure for The British Empire the honour of this achievement'. He declared that the journey would be made with motor sledges, Manchurian ponies and dogs. The very next day, and it must have seemed like an omen, his son was born. Kathleen had spent the latter stages of her pregnancy on the south-west coast, bathing by moonlight and sleeping on the beach, determined that her child would love the nights and the sea. It was a defining moment for both husband and wife, but particularly for Kathleen who later wrote: 'Very large, very healthy, quite perfect was my boy baby; and then a strange thing happened to me. I fell for the first time gloriously, passionately, wildly in love with my husband. I did not know I had not been so before but I knew now. He became my god; the father of my son and my god. Until now he had been a probationer, a means to an end.' The object of this passionate joy was named Peter Markham, after that perpetual little boy Peter Pan, and Sir Clements Markham, who, with Barrie, was one of his godparents.

As the year drew to a close each of the Scotts now had a grand purpose. Kathleen to nurture the child she had dreamed of for so long and Scott to return south and finish what he had begun.

9

A Matter of Honour

And so the die was cast. The coming months were to introduce new characters and reunite former comrades. As far as Scott was concerned, Wilson was the cornerstone of the expedition so he was delighted by his agreement to serve as chief of the scientific staff and official artist. Wilson's motivation was complex. He wrote to his wife about his fear that 'I am getting more and more soft and dependent upon comforts, and this I hate. I want to endure hardness and instead of that I enjoy hotel dinners and prefer hot water to cold and so on – all bad signs and something must be done to stop it'. He also believed he would survive to write and publish all the things in his head. 'This conviction makes me absolutely fearless as to another journey South, for whatever happened I know I should come back to you.' Most powerful of all, though, were his feelings for Scott. He confessed that 'I should not feel it was right now to desert Scott if he goes . . .'[1] His task was to pull together the largest, best-equipped scientific team ever sent to Antarctica.

Another prime mover during the early stages was the super-energetic twenty-eight-year-old Lieutenant Teddy Evans who had been second officer on the relief ship *Morning*. His loud rumbustious nature was the antithesis of Scott's quiet reserve. As a boy he had been expelled from one school and sent to another specializing in dealing with problem boys. It seems to have succeeded because in 1895 he joined the *Worcester* where he won a naval cadetship. He loved horseplay and such ludicrous feats of strength as picking his fellow officers up by the seat of their trousers with his teeth or ripping packs of playing cards in half. He abandoned plans of his own for an expedition in return for appointment as second-in-command and responsibility for helping Scott select the officers and men. In the months ahead, and particularly once they had reached Antarctica, Scott would come to question his abilities writing 'I cannot consider him fitted for a superior position.' Other expedition members would question Evans's competence on non-naval matters and also his loyalty to Scott. His appointment was also a severe embarrassment to Scott, who had at least half promised the position of second-in-command to Reginald Skelton, who had done so well on the first trip and had been helping Scott to develop the motor sledges. Skelton wrote to Scott, 'Hang it all, judge the case fairly',[2] but on this occasion Scott seems to have sacrificed loyalty to expediency.

The news of the expedition attracted over 8,000 eager volunteers. They included Captain Oates whose cool self-sacrifice on the retreat from the Pole would capture the public's imagination as a perfect encapsulation of the values of the day. The fuss would have embarrassed this horse-loving, upper-class cavalry officer known as 'Titus' by his comrades. He was a quiet man with well-defined views on duty and honour, but not the 'stiff upper lip', unimaginative, conventional representative of his caste sometimes painted. He was certainly reserved but those he liked found him good company and enjoyed his wry very English sense of humour. Like Scott he had a close relationship with his mother. Caroline Oates was a woman of powerful personality who, rather ominously from a psychologist's point of view, called him 'Baby Boy' for years, despite the subsequent birth of another son. She was a wealthy and generous woman but was careful to control Oates's purse strings and hence his actions throughout his adult life.

Like Wilson, Oates had been a delicate child. At one stage Caroline feared that he might have tuberculosis and took him to South Africa for a while. The local people near the family seat at Gestingthorpe in Essex remarked on this frail little boy. One later described how 'He looked as if a good meat pudden would've done him more good than going to the South Pole'.[3] However, he grew more robust and at Eton distinguished himself as a sportsman rather than as a scholar. He became a good middle-weight boxer, but his career at Eton was terminated by severe pneumonia and he completed his education at a crammer's specializing in preparing boys for the army exams.

Oates wanted to gain his commission through going to Oxford, but the entrance exams proved too much for him. He probably lacked application rather more than intelligence and much preferred hunting to studying. One phrase sums it up – 'so bored am I with exams'.[4] You can almost hear the yawns of a young man who simply could not see the relevance of Greek unseens and Latin prose, the statutory subjects of the day. Neither did he have any time or gift for mathematics as Scott would later discover – 'I had intended Oates to superintend the forage arrangements but rows of figures, however simply expressed, are too much for him.'[5] He was also a poor speller and quite possibly dyslexic.

Oates joined the 2nd Volunteer Battalion of the Suffolk

Regiment which provided an outlet while he continued to wrestle with academia. However, in the event it also provided his route into the regular army. In 1900, at the height of the Boer War, all qualified militia officers were offered commissions without examinations. A cockahoop and relieved Oates was gazetted into the 6th Inniskilling Dragoons on 6 April. His correspondence at the time shows his love of fine horse flesh with eloquent appeals to his mother for money to buy good horses. However, his over-riding ambition was to join his regiment in South Africa and fight in the Boer War. He worried that it would end before he had his chance of glory, but in November 1900 he was on his way. His youth and inexperience did not inhibit him from criticizing his commanders as he would one day criticize Scott. Oates wrote scathingly of one officer that 'I only hope that I am not under him if I go to the front, he is one of those fussy people who are I believe perfectly hopeless on service'.[6‡]

When the news of Queen Victoria's death reached the troops in South Africa, Oates's reaction exemplified the general mood of gloom and foreboding as Britain squared up to the new century. 'We heard about the Queen's death while on the march, and were all very much cut up. It is awfully sad and the worst thing that could happen to England.'[7] His reaction was entirely in tune with an era which took an exalted view of motherhood and had now lost its imperial mother figure. As Henry James put it, 'We all feel motherless today.'[8] However, Oates's reaction also exemplified

‡According to Michael Smith's recent biography of Oates, pp. 263-270, in 1899 Oates also fathered an illegitimate daughter by a young girl named Etta McKendrick. The child is said to have been born in March 1900 when Etta was only twelve years old but the evidence is insufficient to substantiate that Etta even knew Oates, despite the story having circulated for some time.

a natural pessimism and uncertainty about the meaning of life which he would seek to assuage in Antarctica. Like Scott, he needed a sense of purpose to galvanize him.

Shortly after the news of the Queen's death, Oates saw action at last when the fifteen-man patrol he was commanding came under attack. Outnumbered and surrounded on all sides by the Boers, he refused to surrender, managed to send most of his men to safety and earned himself the name 'Never-say-die Oates' and a mention in despatches for conspicuous bravery. His left thigh was shattered by a bullet but he continued to hold the position for eight and a half hours until a rescue party reached him. According to the senior medical officer he never uttered a murmur, though he must have been in great pain with the bone protruding through his skin.[9] It took Oates months to recover and his mother insisted that he consult a specialist, whose verdict was that the injured leg would always be an inch shorter than the other and that he would have a permanent limp. In fact the wound gave him permanent trouble which he concealed with his usual stoicism.

Oates spent the post-Boer War years indulging his passion for 'the only thing that makes this life endurable' – horses and hunting. His military career took him to Ireland, a huntsman's dream, and then to Egypt where he took up polo, not altogether successfully, and on to India where he devoted himself to his pack of hounds. However, these activities hid a restlessness. There are echoes here of Scott's own agnostic anxiety about 'what is it all for?' Oates contemplated leaving the army, irritated by what he saw as the inefficiency and stupidity of others and frustrated by the difficulty of getting on. He also felt that life was not sufficiently challenging and that Antarctic exploration would suit him better than soldiering on in India. A fellow officer later analysed his motives: 'He wanted something that would require a good deal of sacrifice on his part. I think he wanted adventure and he wanted something that would be a tough proposition.'[10]

In January 1910 Oates wrote to his mother from base hospital in Delhi, where he was recovering from eating a bad tin of fish while on manoeuvres:

> I have now a great confession to make. I offered my services to the Antarctic expedition which starts this summer from home under Scott. They wrote and told me to produce my references which I did and they appear to have been so flattering that I have been prac- tically accepted. Now I don't know whether you will approve or not but I feel that I ought to have consulted you before I sent in my name. I did not do so as I thought there was very little chance of my being taken (as cavalry officers are not generally taken for these shows) ... Scott however appears to be a man who can make up his mind and having decided he told me so at once which was the first intimation I had I was likely to go.

What Oates had actually offered was £1,000 to the expedition's coffers and his services for free. He added in naïve mitigation that: 'The climate is very healthy although inclined to be cold.'[11] Apart from worrying about Caroline Oates's reaction he was also concerned to find 'a decent chap' to take his hounds. He hoped they would not have to go to 'some native prince, they hate the sight of a black man'.[12]

The War Office agreed to release Oates and so, after a great deal of stubbornness from Oates, did his regiment. Teddy Evans's description of the young man who presented himself captures his charm and his eccentricity:

> We had pictured a smartly-turned-out young cavalry officer ... Our future companion turned up with a bowler characteristically on the back of his head and a very worn 'Aquascutum' buttoned closely round his neck, hiding his collar, and showing a strong, clean-shaven, weather-beaten face with kindly brown eyes indicative of his fine personality. 'I'm Oates,' he said.[13]

His job was to look after the ponies which, on the basis of Shackleton's less than fully successful experience, Scott had decided somewhat quixotically would be the core of his transport plans. It was, however, a decision which puzzled his great rival. Amundsen later wrote: 'We had heard that Scott, relying on his own experience, and that of Shackleton, had come to the conclusion that Manchurian ponies were superior to dogs on the Barrier. Among those who were acquainted with the Eskimo dog, I do not suppose I was the only one who was startled on first hearing this.'[14]

Oates showed such a capacity for hard work that Evans persuaded Scott to enrol him as a midshipman so he could stay aboard the expedition's vessel rather than going to Siberia to select the expedition's dogs and ponies. Scott agreed but it was a foolish decision he would have cause to regret and perhaps made in a moment's weakness to appease the overpowering Evans. Oates knew far more about horseflesh than the man to whom the task was entrusted, Cecil Meares. However, Oates duly signed on as a midshipman at a salary of one shilling a month at the West India Docks and presented such a strange appearance that the seamen 'never for a moment thought he was an officer for they were usually so smart! . . . but oh! he was a gentleman, quite a gentleman, and always a gentleman!'[15] The appearance he usually presented was of a 'stableman with unusual good manners'.[16]

Oates soon made the acquaintance of another of his future comrades – as short and ugly as he was tall and handsome, as quick at figures as he was slow – indeed he chaffed Oates that his thoughts were as slow as snails climbing up a cabbage stalk. This was Henry Bowers of the Royal Indian Marine who was quickly to be nicknamed 'Birdie' by his friends because of his huge and distinctive beak-like nose. In a letter to his mother he complained, 'I was of course the first to pick up a nickname. Why, I don't know – it has always been the same. I was "Polly" at Sidcup, "Beakie" at Streatham . . . "Nosy" on the *Fox* and now I am "Birdie".'[17] One of his expedition colleagues, Frank Debenham, left this endearing description: 'Imagine a fat little man with a perfectly immense nose and red bristly hair, unquenchable spirits and energy, and marvellous endurance.' Born in 1883 he was just three years younger than Oates and came of old Scottish seafaring stock. His father died while he was still a child, leaving Birdie to be brought up by his kind and deeply religious mother to whom he was always devoted. Though he was somewhat troubled by reading Darwin's *The Descent of Man*, he shared his mother's fundamentalist evangelical faith, was a keen reader of the *Watchtower* and regarded the liberal Church of England as 'the daughter of the harlot'. Bowers grew up with a passion for butterflies and a very real terror of spiders. During the voyage to the Antarctic, he would write of an encounter in his bunk with a spider. 'I would rather dive on the back of a sixteen-foot shark than face that awful thing.' He was also, like so many boys of his day, captivated by stories of faraway places. When he was just seven he wrote a letter to an Eskimo: 'Dear Eskimo, Please write and tell me about your land. I want to go there some day. Your friend Henry.'[18] His fascination with the unknown remained with him all his life.

Unlike Oates's, Birdie's school reports were peppered with praise about his hard work and conscientiousness. In September 1897 his mother allowed him to enrol as a cadet in the *Worcester* and he went into the Merchant Navy. In 1905 he left it for the Royal India Marine Service as a sub lieutenant. Such a transfer was a rare privilege – the Indian Marine was second only to the Royal Navy – but Bowers had worked hard for it, submitting his application very soon after leaving the *Worcester*. As he once wrote to his sister, 'I leave no stone unturned, and I leave nothing to chance.'[19] He was a very purposeful young man and one of his driving forces was, rather like Scott, the desire to ensure a degree of security for his mother, who had little money.

Bowers learned to navigate the tortuous Irrawaddy River and did so well in the Marine that at just twenty-three years old he found himself in temporary command of a ship. His comrades commented on his seemingly perennial good fortune, but one of them predicted accurately enough, 'Your bad luck will come all at once.'[20] However, at this stage in his life his good luck also extended to his health. In a notoriously unhealthy part of the world he remained untouched by malaria or any serious ailment. His only worry was that he could not get his weight below about twelve stones which he felt was too much for his five-foot-four-inch frame. However, he was immensely fit, boasting that he had more energy than he knew what to do with. His passion for physical fitness probably resulted, at least in part, from a desire to compensate for his size and looks. Though short, he was determined to show that he was strong.

Birdie's experiences in Burma and India confirmed his

imperialist views. In 1907 he wrote to his mother about a prophecy that the British would lose India 'They [The Indians] will never conquer us unless we degenerate at a greater rate of speed than we are at present disintegrating' and then added prophetically himself 'perhaps a "Labour" government will get into power and give them self-government'. Imbued with the xenophobic as well as religious prejudices of his age, he believed his country had given 'peace, famine relief, protection and a degree of happiness thrown in' to 'the coolie' and he loved it profoundly, expressing the sentiments that just four years later would send millions of young men to face the guns in France and Flanders:

> I love my country, and trust that I shall not be found
> wanting when the day comes to act. That dear old
> country – I wonder if a fraction of its inhabitants
> appreciate its worth, or does it require a probation
> of long absences to show one that that little island
> is – under *any* circumstances of weather or anything
> else – the best, the very best place on God's earth.[21]

He regarded Germans as 'sausage machines' and dismissed the French as 'Froggies' – 'the most gay, over-dressed, pleasure-sodden animals ever made in the image of God' who at the forthcoming end of the world would see 'their hopelessly flimsy castles and hopes dashed from them finally'. Another thing he wrote was 'their food . . . all their dishes exude oil'.

Although he was enjoying life in the East his mind returned again and again to thoughts of the south. At one stage in his career, he had sailed within 3° of the Antarctic Circle and felt the lure: '. . . I have thought – as I thought then – that's my mark! The Southern Continent. Reading Capt. Scott's two volumes on the '*Discovery*' Expedition made me as keen as mustard. Perhaps my chance will come later.'[22] He eagerly read the newspaper accounts of the departure of Shackleton's expedition aboard the *Nimrod*. When his sister criticized him for having such foolhardy and vainglorious aspirations he rebuked her as a man of his age: 'How can anyone in conjecture say it will be of no use to mankind to penetrate North or South to the Pole? ... apart from all the magnetic or meteorological interest, is it nothing to a nation to produce men willing to undergo hardships and privation with practically no gain to themselves?'[23]

For the time being, though, Bowers had to content himself with pursuing smugglers in the Persian Gulf and playing intricate games of bluff and double bluff. However, luck again played its part. He met Sir Clements Markham, who agreed to recommend him for the expedition and managed to persuade his former commander on the *Worcester* to second the recommendation. As a result Birdie was offered a place without interview. Picked out of thousands of applicants, he felt that destiny had taken a hand. He wrote to his mother: 'I am going to do a man's work, which only a strong man could do ...'[24]

Bowers's prejudices, racial and religious, were of a theoretical sort and he was kind and considerate to all on a personal basis. His dependability, meticulous planning, cheerfulness and endless appetite for work soon impressed his new comrades. Teddy Evans described the incident which quickly became a legend:

> Lieut. Bowers came home from the Indian Marine
> to begin his duties as Stores Officer [on the exped-
> ition's ship] by falling down the main hatch on to the
> pig iron ballast. I did not witness this accident, and
> when Campbell reported the matter I am reported

to have said, "What a silly ass!" This may have been true, for coming all the way from Bombay to join us and then immediately falling down the hatch did seem a bit careless. However, when Campbell added that Bowers had not hurt himself my enthusiasm returned and I said "What a splendid fellow!". Bowers fell nineteen feet without injuring himself in the slightest. This was only one of his narrow escapes and he proved himself to be about the toughest man amongst us.[25]

The other officers all came from the Royal Navy. They included the camera-shy naval surgeon Atkinson or 'Atch' who was soon 'very thick' with Oates and almost as laconic. Oates's verdict on him was 'He is an extraordinarily quiet man, he hardly ever speaks but is a capital chap and a first-rate boxer.' Praise indeed. Teddy Evans marvelled that two such silent men managed to have a relationship at all. A second naval surgeon, G. Murray Levick, was also lent by the navy and the two of them were to be responsible for studying bacteriology and parasitology in addition to their medical duties. There were also two naval lieutenants. Harry Pennell, a lively energetic character, was appointed navigator and took charge of the ship's magnetic work. Henry Rennick was made responsible for the hydrographical survey work and deep-sea sounding. Victor Campbell, a recently retired naval officer, was appointed chief officer and his mission was to lead a second party to Edward VII Land while Scott went for the Pole. In fact Campbell's story was to be as remarkable as anything which befell Scott's men.

The ship's company included twenty-six naval petty officers and men. Five of the twelve who were to be in the shore parties were old 'Discoverys' as Markham called the men who had sailed with Scott in 1901. They included William Lashly and Edgar Evans with whom Scott had shared a sleeping bag on 'the terrible plateau' and Thomas Crean, his coxswain who had been with him on the railway station platform when he heard the news of Shackleton's failure to reach the Pole. Scott had been particularly determined to take Edgar Evans, writing to him in March 1910 that he had asked for his services and that 'I expect you will be appointed in about a fortnight's time, and I shall want you at the ship to help fitting her out.'[26] Evans was no less eager to go. Apart from loyalty to Scott, it was an opportunity for him to make something of himself. Since the *Discovery* expedition Evans had married a local girl from the Gower, become a father and was now a highly competent naval gunnery instructor with a reputation for being a strict disciplinarian who had no time for shirkers but gave credit where it was due.

Edgar Evans reported as soon as he could to the expedition's headquarters where his magnificent physique caused a sensation. There was no doubt that he was the dominant personality on the mess-deck. Scott had tried hard to persuade another old *Discovery* seaman, Frank Wild, who had accompanied Shackleton on his farthest south, to join him but Wild declined.

Wilson had picked the scientific team with care, looking for first-class expertise. However he also valued enthusiasm and commitment, as in the case of Apsley Cherry-Garrard, like Oates a member of the landed gentry, who had recently graduated from Oxford where he had read Classics and Modern History. He was appointed assistant zoologist, though his claims to any zoological skills were at the least tenuous. He was so short-sighted that people on the other side of the street appeared to him only as 'vague blobs walking'. Inexperienced but eager, he was to write some of the most evocative and moving accounts of the final expedition. He understood what drove men to take terrible risks, writing that exploration was the physical expression of the intellectual passion. He was to be marked by his own experiences to the end of his days. He also had a wry sense of humour illustrated by his famous observation that 'Polar exploration is at once the cleanest and most isolated way of having a bad time which has been devised'.[27]

Cherry-Garrard had been desperate to go since meeting Wilson at a house in Scotland belonging to his cousin Reginald Smith, the publisher who had assisted Scott with *The Voyage of the Discovery*. Wilson had so inspired him that, like Oates, he had offered £1,000 to the expedition as well as his services. When his application was initially turned down by Scott he asked that his donation should stand. This was exactly the sort of gesture that appealed to Scott who agreed to see the young man again. Wilson wrote revealingly about Scott to his protégé: 'I have known him now for ten years and I believe in him so firmly that I am often sorry when he lays himself open to misunderstanding. I am sure you will come to know him and believe in him as I do, and none the less because he is sometimes difficult.'[28] Scott eventually agreed to accept him.

There were to be three geologists this time, compared with one on the *Discovery* expedition. These included the Australians Griffith Taylor – who in true Antipodean style referred to 'his mates' and to his satisfaction with his 'tucker' in his subsequent accounts – and Frank Debenham. The third, Raymond Priestley, who had been on Shackleton's expedition and was an Englishman from Tewkesbury, was in fact recruited later and joined the expedition in Australia. The somewhat dry and acerbic but highly competent Dr George Simpson, of the Indian Weather Bureau Simla, was appointed meteorologist. The biologists were Edward

Nelson of the Plymouth Marine Laboratory, a rich and rather idle man with 'a taste for gin and bridge',[29] albeit a professional scientist, and Denis Lillie, an acknowledged expert on marine mammals and in Scott's view a bit cranky – he believed in reincarnation and thought that he had been a Persian and a Roman in earlier lives. One of his colleagues wrote gleefully that: 'Much fun can be got from him if handled properly.'[30] The young Canadian Charles Wright from Toronto was chosen as physicist.

Taylor and some of the other scientists decided to demonstrate their fitness. Fuelled by a dozen hard-boiled eggs and some chocolate bars, they walked the fifty miles from Cambridge to London in twenty-four hours. Taylor described the scene on their arrival in the expedition's London offices: 'The offices were . . . in Westminster, situated in a district peculiarly devoted to the Empire's interests . . . In a large room occasionally sat Captain Scott but he was usually busy [elsewhere] with some ingenious food stuffs or patent appliance . . . Adjacent was the secretary's office, and there [Scott] was seen wading through some of the 8,000 applications from eager souls anxious to get out of the rut by joining the expedition . . . Another room was almost filled with a huge petty officer who was sorting gear for the sledges . . . An old 1902 sledge was lying in the passage . . .'

Bernard Day, who had been with Shackleton, was put in charge of the motor sledges. He also bought a bicycle, which several of the party used in Antarctica. On one occasion Griffith Taylor went so far across the ice that he got lost and it was only the providential arrival of Wright that saved him. The man appointed to look after the dogs and who had been dispatched to Siberia to arrange the purchase of dogs and ponies was Cecil Meares, an intriguing individual of somewhat wild and unkempt appearance. He was rumoured to have been a secret agent, playing a hand in the 'great game' – the intrigues between Britain and Russia in the far north of India – and he could certainly speak Hindustani and Russian. He had been a fur-trader in Kamchatka and Okotz in north-eastern Siberia and claimed to have seen the fall of Peking and to have fought in the Russo-Japanese War and the Boer War. He also told an extraordinary tale of a great journey he had made into Tibet where his companion, an army officer named Brooke, was killed by Lolo tribesmen and he brought the body back to civilization. Wilson, the pacifist, was fascinated by Meares whom he considered a man of action, a most entertaining messmate and full of fun. However, Meares was to find his relationship with Scott difficult. As a freewheeling adventurer he did not respond well to what he regarded as interference and regimentation. Scott did not respond well to what he saw as insubordination and slackness.

However, that lay in the future. Meares now made an exotic journey by Trans-Siberian railway, horse and sleigh to Nikolievsk in Siberia where he chose his dogs carefully. However, he was much less knowledgeable about ponies and took the advice of a four-foot-ten-inch Moscow jockey, Anton Omelchenko. Meares's commission from Scott was a bizarre one – to buy only white ponies, because Shackleton had noted that his dark ponies had died before the white ones. This significantly reduced Meares's scope for choice and according to Anton produced 'a plenty big smile' from a no doubt incredulous but extremely cheerful horse dealer at a fair in Mukden.[31] Oates was to be horrified by the sight of the broken down old crocks when they eventually came aboard in New Zealand, gloomily cataloguing such deficiencies as 'Narrow chest. Knock knees . . . Aged. Windsucker . . .'[32]

His buying completed, Meares persuaded Anton and a Russian dog-driver, Dimitri Gerov, to help him transport the animals to

151

New Zealand to meet the expedition. It was a difficult task and Kathleen Bruce's brother Wilfred, 'broad, beaming, always with a weather eye for the girls', was sent out to assist this Noah's Ark.[33] They managed to convey their menagerie across the Pacific to Lyttelton without losing a single animal but were no longer on speaking terms. Meares considered Bruce 'too "kid glovey" for this job'.[34]

Finally, there was the experienced and talented Herbert Ponting, who joined as the expedition's official 'camera artist'. He was so devoted to his art that he had abandoned his wife and children, claiming they interfered with his photography. His wonderful pictures would capture the compelling beauty of Antarctica and he was also the expedition's 'cinematographer'. His poignant footage of Captain Scott and his colleagues departing for the Pole, small determined figures plodding away across a great white infinity, is as powerful now as it was in 1912. Ponting was writing a book about Japan when Scott approached him. Scott tempted him with word pictures: '. . . he talked with such fervour of his forthcoming journey; of the lure of the southernmost seas; of the mystery of the Great Ice Barrier; of the grandeur of Erebus and the Western Mountains, and of the marvels of the animal life around the Pole, that I warmed to his enthusiasm . . .' Ponting also fell under Scott's personal spell: 'The determined face; the clear blue eyes, with their sincere, searching gaze; the simple, direct speech, and earnest manner; the quiet *force* of the man – all drew me to him irresistibly.'[35] Scott reciprocated describing his photographer as 'a very charming character, generous, highly strung, nervous and artistic'.

Ponting completed the team that was to go south. However, there is a story, later told by Kathleen Scott to Nancy Mitford, that the birth control pioneer Marie Stopes had wanted to go on the expedition and that 'Scott had to use all his willpower to stop her!'[36]

There was also the all-important question of a ship. Scott tried to get hold of the *Discovery*, to which he had a strong sentimental attachment, but she was now owned by the Hudson Bay Company which refused to give her up. Instead he negotiated for the *Terra Nova*, the relief ship whose appearance in McMurdo Sound had so startled him and Wilson. She was old with an extravagant consumption of coal, but, as Teddy Evans described, she had a worthy pedigree: 'She was the largest and strongest of the old Scotch whalers, had proved herself in the Antarctic pack-ice and acquitted herself magnificently in the Northern ice-fields in whaling and sealing voyages extending over a period of twenty years. In spite of her age she had considerable power . . .' Her hull was constructed of massive oak beams 14 inches thick while her bow was a solid bulkhead of timber, 9 feet thick and clad in iron plating. Scott secured her for a down payment of £5,000 which he had great difficulty in finding, leaving the balance of £7,500 to be paid later. She was handed over in November 1909.

While the *Terra Nova* was indeed a suitable vessel, she was also filthy. Teddy Evans was responsible for her transformation into a floating laboratory and fell in love with her: 'I loved her from the day I saw her because she was my first command. Poor little ship, she looked so dirty and uncared for . . .' Her noisome blubber tanks had to be removed and the whole ship scrubbed down and disinfected. Living quarters had to be constructed for officers and men as well as laboratories, instrument and chronometer rooms and store rooms. As the work progressed down in the West India Docks she attracted plenty of visitors but poor Teddy Evans 'often blushed when admirals came down to see our ship, she was so very dirty'. He was operating on a very limited budget but there was much to be bought or scrounged: 'There were boatswain's stores to be purchased, wire hawsers, canvas for sail-making, fireworks for signalling, whale boats and whaling gear, flags, logs, paint, tar, carpenter's stores, and a multitude of necessities to be thought of, selected, and not paid for if we could help it.' He observed wryly that the verb 'to wangle' had not then appeared in the English language, so they just 'obtained'. Much of the work was done by petty officers and men from the RNVR in their spare time. Ironically, moored immediately opposite the *Terra Nova* was the *Discovery*, which was being loaded for a voyage to North America – the *Birmingham Post* noted that Scott's former pride and joy looked 'very unkempt and forlorn'. There was little time to get the *Terra Nova* into shape. Scott had decided to bring the date of sailing forward by two months to 1 June. By arriving earlier in Antarctica he hoped to gain extra time for the depot-laying journey he planned before the onset of the Antarctic winter.

Of course Scott was once again caught in the toils of fundraising, this time with no official sponsors. He estimated the costs at some £40,000, compared to the cost of the *Discovery* expedition, which at over £90,000 had included the construction of the *Discovery* herself, and the press argued that he should have it without quibbling. The *Pall Mall Gazette* announced in a lordly way that the sum required was 'a mere bagatelle' and 'that it should not be forthcoming is unthinkable'. *The Times* threw in its penn'orth suggesting that it would be 'deeply regrettable if, for want either of men or of money, the brilliant recent record of British exploration were at this point to be checked' and, somewhat prophetically, that it would be a shocking thing if the door were left open for a foreigner. The most obvious danger seemed to be from the Americans. In November 1909 Commander Robert Peary, who in April had hobbled toeless towards the North Pole to claim it for his country (it was his sixth attempt and he had lost his toes through frostbite after his fourth attempt), had announced that the Americans would try for the South Pole within the next five years.

However, Scott put such thoughts out of his mind as, helped by Teddy Evans, he fought against time to find the necessary money. It was not until the spring of 1910 that the first £10,000 was raised. Evans described the distasteful business of hustling from one end of the country to the other. While he had gone to South Wales and the west country 'beating up funds' as he called it, 'Scott, himself, when he could be spared from the Admiralty, worked Newcastle, Liverpool, and the North, whilst both of us did what we could in London . . . It was an anxious time for Scott . . .' Evans had a hearty easy way of prodding a prospective donor and saying: 'I want a nice cheque from you!' Scott conversely found it hard, uncongenial, depressing work and his letters to Kathleen are full of gloom but also of his love for her: 'My dear, my heart is very full of you in spite of the hard crust which you find it so difficult to get through.' There are also occasional insights into the practical difficulties of travelling around the country. In February 1910 he sent her an urgent request for socks.[37]

In some quarters there was actual hostility to the idea of funding an expedition. The *Sussex News* of 19 February 1910 carried an angry letter: 'I call it scientific cheek to come along when there are so many thousands of unemployed and ask £50,000 for such a purpose.' There was something of Captain Cook's view in all this that exploration to the south was a futile activity from which the world would derive no benefit. It was also the result of economic pressures – wages were failing to rise with the cost of living and the years between the death of Edward VII and the Great War would see a series of crippling strikes. In November 1910, 30,000

Welsh miners would down tools. In 1911 dockers would strike for eight pence an hour for a ten-hour shift. The rich were also feeling the squeeze with Lloyd George's 'People's Budget' of 1909 which aimed to raise £15 million by new taxation. Unearned or investment income was taxed at 1s 2d in the pound and land was to be valued so tax could be levied from the rising value of real estate. It seems tame stuff today, but it was described by a critic as 'the beginning of the end of all rights of property' and it made rich men less likely to dip into their pockets.[38]

The expedition's prospects became suddenly much rosier with a government grant of £20,000. Its previous parsimony can perhaps be explained by having to stump up £20,000 for Shackleton, who was in financial trouble. In contrast to the cautious Scott he had raised much of the money he needed in the form of loans to be repaid out of fees and royalties from writing books and lecturing. Always the optimist, he had found himself with an embarrassing shortfall. By this time Scott had managed to secure some £12,000 either in donations or promises so that he now only had some £8,000 to find. However, as the expedition was due to sail in June time was short and he set off on a lecture tour of the north.

Scott had a difficult path to tread in explaining the objectives of the expedition. Was it about science or was it about being first at the Pole? It was certainly more than a Pole hunt as far as Scott himself was concerned. He had too much intellectual curiosity to be unmoved by the potential for serious scientific achievement. Yet at the same time he could not be immune to the fame and prestige that would fall to the man who conquered the Pole for Britain. He was seduced by both objectives but astute enough to know that he must tailor his messages to his audience. In an address to the Royal Geographical Society he confirmed that, while the idea of reaching a spot on the globe as yet untrodden by human feet was a matter of national pride 'and an outward visible sign that we are still a nation able and willing to undertake difficult enterprises . . .', the true aim was 'to achieve the greatest possible scientific harvest which the circumstances permit'. However, he divined correctly that whatever he might say in elegant addresses to the Royal Geographical Society, it was the idea of planting the Union Jack on the Pole which would grip the public's imagination and attract the funds and so the published objective of the expedition was to reach the South Pole.

Scott wrote to everyone he could think of for money – from the great and the good to learned institutions and companies. He won some powerful friends. The financier Sir Edgar Speyer, who had been wooed by Kathleen, subscribed £1,000 and agreed to become the expedition's treasurer. Sir Arthur Conan Doyle made a rousing speech at the Mansion House to the effect that that there was one Pole left, it should be a British Pole and that Captain Scott was the man to conquer it.

Scott again had to rely to a large extent on sponsorship and described with satisfaction how 'the advertisement to be derived from the supply of stores to an Expedition such as this is thought of very highly in this country, and thanks to this and to a patriotic wish for our success, we are getting goods on extraordinarily favourable terms.'[39] Some companies donated their products free while, as Scott noted with something approaching glee, they were even handsomely paid to take a wide range of branded products. Colman's supplied 'new ready mixed mustard', flour and semolina. Scott wrote from his winter quarters in Antarctica to thank the company. He also took Bovril, pemmican and Oxo. The makers of Oxo devised an advertisement showing Polar bears advancing on a jar of Oxo but substituted penguins when they belatedly realized that there were no Polar bears in Antarctica. Other products included goods from Imperial Tobacco, Abram Lyle's golden syrup, Henry Tate's sugar and Frank Cooper's Oxford marmalade. Jaeger provided the expedition with special boots, while the brewers Bass donated some cases of the celebrated 'King's Ale', the brewing of which had been inaugurated by King Edward VII during a visit to the brewery in 1902. The directors expressed the hope that Captain Scott would use it to drink to the King's health at the South Pole.

Scott was also delighted with the generous response from schools across the country which he had invited to raise money to buy dogs, ponies, sledges, sleeping bags and tents. More than one hundred public, secondary and private schools took part. Dogs cost £3.3s each, sledges £5 12s 6d, sleeping bags £2 and ponies £5. Each contribution was carefully recorded in the appendix to Scott's journals of the final expedition and Scott made a point of writing to every school himself to thank the girls and boys – he wrote to South Hampstead High School for Girls to acknowledge the donation of a pony nicknamed 'Bones' and a dog nicknamed 'Jackass'.

Throughout this period of frantic hard work – Nansen had been right to warn that the hardest part of an expedition was the preparation – Scott had to be careful to cultivate the right public image. There must be no sign of the inner worry and bouts of depression, 'the black thundercloud' as Kathleen called his darker moods. There was a revealing report in the *Daily Mail* of January 1910 for which Scott must have projected absolutely the right image of a man of action and determination.

> Captain Scott has a personal force which is plain for all men to see. Thick-set, deep-chested, with a thoughtful geniality in his clean-shaven 'naval-officer'

face, he is much of the bull-dog type, with blue eyes that look out sparklingly from a face hard-bitten with adventure. 'Suppose you don't succeed at first?' he was asked. . . . Captain Scott took his cigarette from his lips and brought his finger down on to the table with slow emphasis. '. . . we shall jolly well stop there till the thing is done'.

This display of confidence was at odds with his inner doubts. He later wrote to Kathleen from Antarctica of his worries during the early stages:

And now that I can say these things and feel myself as I do, a competent leader over the team, I must be honest enough to confess a certain amount of surprise at finding everything so satisfactory. I am quite on my feet now, I feel both mentally and physically fit for the work, and I realize that the others know it and have full confidence in me. But it is a certain fact that it was not so in London or indeed until after we reached this spot. The root of the trouble was that I had lost confidence in myself . . .[40]

The tension was heightened when Shackleton wrote to him announcing that he was preparing an expedition in 1911 to map the western coastline between Cape Adare and Kaiser Wilhelm II land. He explained that he had no plans to go to the Pole, promised that his expedition was purely scientific and offered, should Scott still be in Antarctica, to cooperate with him in exploring this western region. Scott's response was lukewarm. While he would welcome cooperation to explore this little known area 'it should be clearly understood that my own programme for a second season will not be modified by the publication of your plans'.[41]

On 3 February came another development which excited public interest. The US National Geographical Society announced that it would launch an American expedition to the Pole from the Weddell Sea coast to begin in December 1911 and with the goal of reaching the Pole a year later. Peary had written to Scott to ask whether he had any objections to these plans. He had replied that he welcomed the plan and would be happy to cooperate in scientific work. However, the press now took up the story, presenting it as a challenge to British ambitions. Scott allowed the correspondence between himself and Peary to be published, adding the rider that the rivalry would be of an entirely friendly character, but that each would naturally be keen that his own nationality should be first. At the end of February Peary gave the public what they wanted, promising 'the most exciting and nerve-wracking race the world has seen'.

The following month Scott was in Norway to consult Fridtjof Nansen, who seems to have been very taken with Kathleen, and to test out a prototype motor sledge at Fefor at the foot of the Jotunheim mountains, north of Oslo. This was built on lines devised by Scott and Reginald Skelton by the Wolsey Tool and Motor Company and its design was a forerunner both of the tank and of the Sno-cats later used by Fuchs and Hillary on the Trans-Antarctic Expedition of 1955–8. He was also able to visit the company that was making his conventional sledges and other equipment, including fifty pairs of skis.

Nansen listened carefully to Scott's plans and did his best to advise him. He personally had little confidence in motorized sledges but approved Scott's decision to take dogs as well as ponies. He also advised him to take an expert skier and introduced him to a good-looking, lively, confident young man, Tryggve Gran. Gran was wealthy (or at least wealthy for a Norwegian as Wilson observed) and had serious plans of his own to go to the Pole.[42] He had had a vessel especially built and his idea, based on advice from Nansen, Shackleton and Borchgrevink, was to ski to the Pole taking dogs. He planned to start out from Norway the following summer and wanted Scott to be aware of his plans. It must have seemed to Scott as if Antarctica was developing into a kind of Piccadilly Circus for explorers with everyone explaining their plans to everyone else to ensure they did not trip over one another or breach understood spheres of interest.

However, one explorer, also Norwegian, was at this time keeping exceptionally quiet about his plans – the thirty-seven-year-old Roald Amundsen. Since serving as second mate on the *Belgica* he had matured as a Polar explorer. He had traversed the North West Passage and been the first to confirm that the North Magnetic Pole was not fixed but migrated. His publicly avowed intent was now to reach the North Pole and explore the Polar basin despite Peary's successful expedition. Significantly, however, although Scott made several attempts to make contact, Amundsen avoided him. Scott even sent a matched set of instruments so that comparative measurements could be taken of north and south. Amundsen accepted these quietly and, although he felt awkward, had no intention of revealing that for the past six months he had secretly been planning to head for the South Pole. Gran, who had tried to engineer a meeting, was deeply embarrassed. Amundsen wouldn't take his telephone calls and when Gran took Scott to Amundsen's house they were told by his brother that, even though he knew Scott might be coming, Amundsen was out. Although they waited an hour, Amundsen didn't return.

Scott decided that the best way to deal with the ardent Tryggve

Gran was to invite him to join his own expedition. He was impressed with the speed with which Gran had been able to ski to the nearest blacksmith to have a motor sledge axle repaired, and by his skiing technique – using two sticks, rather than one – which was new to Scott. The offer was accepted, Gran interpreting it as a mission 'to root out that opposition and ill-will towards skiing which had characterized previous English South Polar Expeditions'.[43] He had a high opinion of his abilities – an expedition colleague later described how he delighted in 'speechmaking and in telling tales of his exploits on ski – our strong man – at any rate by his own accounts'.[44] The trials themselves went quite well. The motorized sledge performed promisingly, although there were problems with the fuel. The sledge was tried out across level surfaces and up hills. It was found that it could haul 10 hundredweight over deep snow and several times that weight at least over firm ice.

Scott flirted with some other novel ideas. The reign of Edward VII had been a revolutionary period in transport. Electrical propulsion was taking over from steam: man was taking to the air in planes and venturing into the deep in submarines. The British and Colonial Aeroplane Company of Bristol offered him the use of a Zodiac monoplane, but he turned it down because he felt it was too experimental. By 1910 there had in fact been considerable advances in aviation. More powerful and reliable engines had been developed and aircraft design improved so that pilots were undertaking more daring feats. The most outstanding achievement of the year was the crossing of the Alps by Georges Charez. By 1911 aviation had developed from a sport for the adventurous to a serious commercial proposition. While Scott was probably correct not to take a plane in 1910, had he been departing just a couple of years later he might have benefited from doing so.

While he was away Kathleen Scott had great fun visiting airshows and becoming only the second British woman to be airborne. Scott was also interested in being the first explorer to use wireless telegraphy in Antarctica but had to reject it because the equipment was too cumbersome to transport and erect. However, the National Telephone Company supplied equipment that would enable Scott to lay a telephone link between his two huts on McMurdo Sound.

Leaving the sledge to undergo final tests and modifications Scott returned to London to be greeted by news of yet further rivals for the Pole. The Germans had announced an expedition commencing, like the Americans, from the Weddell Sea. Not only that, but having reached the Pole they intended to march on across the plateau to McMurdo Sound and thereby complete the first crossing of Antarctica. This roused the Royal Geographical Society to more than its usual acerbity and it sent a sharp rebuke to Berlin, prompting a promise from the Germans to leave the way clear for the British and the Americans. However, Scott was probably more concerned with Shackleton who now published his plans for exploring the western coastline. There was no intention to compete with Scott, but Scott insisted that his own freedom of action be clearly understood and wrote to the President of the Royal Geographical Society that 'I want it settled before I leave that I am free to go where I please without the reproach that I am trespassing on his ground'.[45] In the event, though, Scott need not have worried. Shackleton abandoned his plans and left the work to the young Australian Mawson whom he had intended to accompany.

The final weeks before departure were spent trying to wring some final donations out of an increasingly reluctant public. Scott now put the expedition's costs at £50,000 but hoped to raise

£10,000 from Australia and New Zealand. Nevertheless money continued to trickle in and then in April came the news that Peary was postponing his bid for the Pole because of lack of money. The scene looked set for Scott, but in the first week of May the death of King Edward VII cast a blight over everything including making subscriptions. Scott decided that when the *Terra Nova* sailed he must stay behind to raise the final funds and follow on by steamer.

On the eve of the *Terra Nova's* departure Scott made a revealing visit to Thomas Marlowe, editor of the *Daily Mail*, whom he had known since the *Discovery* expedition. He was already looking ahead to what he could do on his return and asked Marlowe when he believed war with Germany would break out. Marlowe replied with extraordinary prescience, 'I can only tell you that there is a well-informed belief that Germany will be ready to strike in the summer of 1914 and it is thought that she may do so.' Scott mulled this over then replied, 'By that time I shall be entitled to command a battle cruiser of the Invincible class. The summer of 1914 will suit me very well.'[46] The irony is that if Scott had not died in the Antarctic, he could well have perished at the Battle of Jutland in 1915.

10

'Am Going South, Amundsen'

The *Terra Nova* slid out of the London Docks as planned on 1 June 1910. Just before arriving at Cardiff to take on the Welsh coal so generously donated to her, Scott called all hands aft and made an earnest appeal that every man should make a will. He even offered to give advice. However, the warm reception they received banished sombre thoughts for a while.

Cardiff held a special place in the expedition's heart as the city that had given them the most fervent support. The Lord Mayor now produced a further £1,000 for the fund. In recognition, Scott promised to make Cardiff the *Terra Nova*'s first port of call on his return. The Cardiff Chamber of Commerce gave a farewell banquet for the officers in the wood-panelled rooms of the Royal Hotel. The crew were feted in the nearby Barry's hotel, but Scott invited them to join him for a smoking concert. Edgar Evans, as a native of south Wales, was given pride of place between Scott and the Mayor of Cardiff. Described by the *Cambrian* as 'one of the biggest and burliest members of the crew', he made a memorable impromptu speech in which he paid an emotional tribute to Scott declaring that: 'No one else would have induced me to go there again, but if there is a man in the world who will bring this to a successful issue, Captain Scott is the man.' Despite putting up such a magnificent performance Evans had had so much to drink that it took six men to help him re-embark that night. He appears to have fallen out with Teddy Evans at around this time by drawing Scott's attention to the loading of the wrong sort of skis – Teddy Evans's fault. New skis were ordered and Chief Petty Officer Edgar Evans put in charge of them – a slight which rankled with Lieutenant Evans.

On 15 June Edgar Evans's family gathered on the Gower cliffs at Rhosili to watch the *Terra Nova*'s departure for Cape Town after a tremendous send-off from the crowds amid the din of steam sirens and hooters. Her escort of little flag-draped vessels turned back and she was alone. Scott also watched her, proud that she was flying the White Ensign rather than the flag of the Merchant Navy. He had been elected a member of the Royal Yacht Squadron, entitling him to the Ensign – an honour that had cost him £100. However, he would not see her again until South Africa. His time must now be spent arranging newspaper contracts and squeezing out any last subscriptions because the expedition was still underfunded even at this late stage. There was no guarantee that he could even pay his men their modest salaries beyond the outward voyage.

If Scott regretted that he could not be with his men, Kathleen also had regrets. She was determined to accompany her husband as far as she was able but it meant leaving behind her beloved Peter. She described the pain of it: 'I can think of nothing that hurt more hideously than unlocking the sturdy fingers that clung round mine as I left the laughing, tawny-haired baby Hercules for four months . . .' Gritting her teeth she set sail with Scott on the tramp steamer *Saxon*. Shackleton was among those who came to see them off from Waterloo, and they had as travelling companions Oriana Wilson and Teddy Evans's wife Hilda.

Meanwhile the deeply laden *Terra Nova* lumbered on her way. Oates said gloomily that she appeared to have only two speeds – slow and slower. Dropping anchor at South Trinidad, a small volcanic island in the South Atlantic, some of the men found themselves cut off from the ship by the thunderous surf and were forced to spend the night on the shore observed by leery giant land crabs. The arachnophobic Birdie Bowers wrote home, 'it must have been horrible'.[1] Such experiences helped the men to bond and Cherry-Garrard gave much of the credit for this to Teddy Evans who managed to beat down the natural suspicion between the scientist and sailor, 'doing much to cement together the rough material into a nucleus which was capable of standing without any friction the strains of nearly three years'.[2] However, credit was also due to Scott who, according to Griffith Taylor made a point of selecting men who liked one another. Deep friendships began to form – Bowers decided Wilson was the finest man he had ever met; Wilson in turn thought Bowers tremendously hard-working and unselfish.

High spirits sometimes spilled over. Teddy Evans's 'taste for rowdyism and skylarking' set the tone.[3] Wilfred Bruce viewed him as a kind of Peter Pan and Simpson described how:

> Sometimes, especially at dinner, our spirits run so high that we should be taken for a party of school boys rather than a party of men engaged on work which has the attention of the whole of England. The usual form of our madness is the singing of songs & choruses at the top of our voices followed by cheering and other meaningless noises.[4]

Sometimes there would be mock fights and even Oates, fast acquiring a reputation for 'amused taciturnity',[5] would join in, writing:

> We shout and yell at meals just as we like and we have a game which consists in tearing off each others shirts. I wonder what some of the people at home would think if they saw the whole of the afterguard with the exception of the officer of the watch struggling yelling and tearing off each others' clothes, the ship rolling and the whole place a regular pandemonium.[6]

He doesn't say what he thought about the verse composed by Teddy Evans to the tune of Cock Robin:

> Who doesn't like women?
> I, said Captain Oates,
> I prefer goats.

However, Evans was actually deeply impressed with Oates, particularly his appetite for hard work and his ability to get on with the seamen, and wrote that he was more popular with them than any other officer.

A close camaraderie developed between this somewhat odd assortment of individuals. It was not long before most had nicknames. Scott was the 'Owner' and Teddy Evans the 'Skipper' – properly respectful names. Campbell, an eccentric but gifted Etonian who frightened the living daylights out of Cherry-Garrard, was nicknamed 'the wicked mate'. Then imagination ran riot. Pennell was 'Penelope' or 'Pennylope', Bowers was of course 'Birdie', Oates and Atkinson, by now inseparable, were called 'Max and Climax', Wilson was again 'Uncle Bill', Wright was 'Jules Verne' and the quiet George Simpson 'Sunny Jim'.

The *Terra Nova* arrived at Simonstown, the Cape Town naval base, on 15 August 1910. Oates recorded their reception with his usual sardonic humour – 'Hurrah parties, nibs, nobs, and snobs off to welcome us, but they forgot to bring our letters or any bottled beer.'[7] Cherry-Garrard and Bowers took the opportunity to whisk two pretty girls for a spin in a hired car but it broke down 'in the middle of the wild'.[8] Scott had already arrived and was in Pretoria wooing the likes of Botha and Smuts. He had to raise £8,000 from South Africa, Australia and New Zealand to make good his deficit. He managed to secure an official South African grant of £500 and an equivalent sum from private donors, but it was hard work and the necessary socializing was not always congenial as Wilson described:

> . . . for our sins we were entertained by the Cape Town 'Owl Club', a sort of colonial Savage Club and one of the worst we have ever had the ill fortune to attend. We were all seated at small tables and apparently two members were told off to look after two guests. My two hosts first of all made offensive remarks about tee-totallers when I said I didn't drink, and then quarrelled about the payment for a bottle of soda water which I was given and half a glass of sherry which had accidentally been poured into my glass by the waiter while I wasn't looking. The quarrel was not who should pay for it, but who should *not* pay for it, and eventually as both refused to pay for the sherry, and as the old waiter said if *they* didn't he would have to, they said he might! . . . The evening was truly one of the most

awful penalties of being a member of such a public expedition. There was no redeeming feature about the whole thing.

Wilson was equally intolerant of 'white derelicts wallowing in the idleness and dirt of . . . degenerate Kaffirs on equal terms'. Though gifted with great humanity Wilson was also a man of his time.

Wilson longed for the simplicity of life aboard the *Terra Nova*, the mugs of cocoa shared with a companion as the sun rose, the closeness to nature as he sat sketching on the deck and the 'happy family'. He was therefore disappointed when Scott dispatched him ahead to Melbourne by mail steamer to recruit the expedition's geologist, Raymond Priestley, and to persuade the Federal Government to stump up funds. As Scott was going to sail with the *Terra Nova*, Wilson was also given the job of looking after Kathleen Scott – a preposterously difficult task given their diametrically opposed outlooks on life, but luckily she was a bad sailor (or said she was) and they saw little of each other. Hilda Evans and Oriana also sailed with him. Kathleen found the other women trying. Why, she wondered, could the world not be peopled by men and babies? But she recognized that 'my hatred of women is becoming a monomania and must be curbed'. Kathleen was a woman of strong opinions. (She once wrote of Winston Churchill that he might be a genius but, if so, he disguised it well.) Now she seems to have found the saintly Wilson just a little dull and a bit of a prig. She certainly bullied him to take her out to the *Terra Nova* in heavy seas by mail launch as the vessel approached Melbourne so she could be reunited with Scott. She wrote that although Wilson had been furious with her, 'The relief at getting back to sane folk who understood me was more than can be written about.' Wilson's verdict was that '. . . in future I hope it will never fall to my lot to have more than one wife at a time to look after, at any rate in a motor launch, in a running sea at night-time.'

Teddy Evans was very disappointed at having to yield command of the *Terra Nova* to Scott on the voyage to Melbourne, interpreting this as a criticism of himself. However, Scott wanted the opportunity for him and his men to get to know one another. He was also planning to choose the Antarctic shore parties during the voyage. While there was a less exuberant atmosphere than under Teddy Evans, Scott regarded the high spirits of his young team benignly. The physicist Charles Wright described how: 'The Owner has a thirst for scientific knowledge that cannot be quenched. He takes no part in the skylarking – but always looks on with a grin.'[9] Gran also left an interesting pen portrait: 'In Norway I had learned to know Scott as a cheerful and easy man, and this first impression was strengthened when I again came close to him. He was short-tempered and not to be trifled with when angry, but if he had judged someone unfairly and discovered his mistake, he was quick to make amends.' He was to feel something of Scott's impatience himself – Scott was beginning to consider the confident Norwegian a lazy, posing fellow and a shirker.

Scott soon had something else to think about, however. On berthing at Melbourne on 12 October he received Amundsen's famously laconic telegram from Madeira: 'Am going South, Amundsen.' This volte-face was a complete surprise to Scott, Norway and the wider world. Amundsen had been loaned Nansen's *Fram* (by now Norwegian State property), and had put together an expedition on the understanding that his goal was the exploration of the North Polar Basin. However, as Amundsen admitted subsequently, Peary's conquest of the North Pole changed everything. 'Just as rapidly as the message had travelled over the cables I decided on my change of front – to turn to the right-about, and face to the South.'[10] Amundsen told neither his backers, including Nansen, nor most of his fellow explorers until they were already at sea and it was rather too late for a change of mind. In fact, he had only made six people, on board or ashore, aware of his true intentions before sailing. He later tried to justify his secrecy, arguing, perhaps correctly, that if he had made his plans public they would have been stifled at birth.

He wrote in self-defence that: 'I knew I should be able to inform Captain Scott of the extension of my plans before he left civilization, and therefore a few months sooner or later could be of no great importance.' He also maintained that the main object of Scott's journey was scientific research and that the Pole was 'only a side-issue'. Furthermore, he argued, a man with Scott's 'great knowledge of Antarctic exploration' would hardly have been likely to alter his plans.[11] Yet the truth was that Amundsen was a ruthlessly ambitious man. He was also a 'professional' explorer in a way which Scott, with his troupe of gifted amateurs, so thoroughly in the British tradition, was not. Amundsen had chosen exploration as a career, beginning with the Gerlache expedition and studying such scientific subjects as magnetism because he thought they might be useful in attracting sponsors, rather than through any academic interest. However distasteful such an attitude may have appeared to Scott and his men, Amundsen's focused professionalism would show to his advantage later.

It was difficult for Scott to know how to react to the news. Amundsen could hardly have been less informative about his intentions. It was not clear where he would land or what his ultimate goal would be, whereas Scott's own plans had been openly published, including his intention of reaching the Pole around 22 December 1911. What use would the secretive, not to say duplicitous Norwegian, as Scott must have regarded him, make of this piece of information? It was a worrying thought.

Preoccupied as he must have been with the Norwegian threat, Scott was forced to set off on 'yet another begging campaign'. The Australian government had coughed up a mere £2,500, half the sum given to Shackleton and this only after they heard that a Japanese expedition was in the offing. Before departing from Australia Scott talked frankly to the press about the expedition's chances: 'We may get through, we may not. We may have accidents to some of our transports, to the sledges or to the animals. We may lose our lives. We may be wiped out. It is all a question that lies with providence and luck.'[12] This fatalism was both part of his nature and born of his experiences on the *Discovery*. Knowing the uncertainties of Polar travel he must have comforted himself that luck would apply equally to Amundsen.

After lecturing to enthusiastic audiences, Scott and Kathleen embarked by passenger boat for Wellington, where he received the welcome news that a wealthy citizen from Sydney had agreed to make up the £2,500 shortfall in the Australian government's contribution. Reporters also pressed him for a response to Amundsen's challenge. Scott replied with dignity that his plans remained unchanged. He would attempt to reach the Pole but not at the expense of the expedition's scientific goals. The down-to-earth Oates's reaction in a letter to a friend was typical of him: 'Bloody Norskies coming down south is a bit of a shock. I only hope they don't get there first. It will make us look pretty foolish. They say that Amundsen has been underhand in the way he has gone about it, but I personally don't see it as underhand to keep your mouth shut.'

Evans, meanwhile, had sailed the *Terra Nova* to Lyttelton, the tiny New Zealand port that had also hosted the *Discovery*, the *Morning*, and Shackleton's *Nimrod*. Here she was to be joined by those officers and scientists who had not sailed out in her and to spend a month being unloaded and repacked. Ponting described how: 'It was as interesting as it was delightful to note that our leader's wife spent many days checking packages as they were unloaded and then re-stowed'. What others thought, notably Bowers who was the *Terra Nova*'s expert on stowing, is not recorded. There were the three motor sledges to come aboard in their crates and Meares was waiting with his nineteen white Manchurian ponies and thirty-three Siberian sledge dogs.

Oates gloomily assessed the ponies, noting that 'they are very old for a job of this sort and four of them are unsound however we shall have to make the best of them'. He consoled himself by drinking 'a skinful of beer'.[13] Stables now had to be constructed on the *Terra Nova*'s upper deck and under the forecastle, and the seamen volunteered some of their living space for the stowing of extra supplies with Edgar Evans acting as spokesman. Urine dripped from the pony stables on the deck above through leaky planking into their remaining accommodation, making their lives even more uncomfortable. Meanwhile, Oates and Scott argued about the amount of pony fodder to be taken on board. Scott was reluctant to heed Oates's warnings about the dangers of under-feeding the ponies, dismissing the man who knew more about horses than anyone else on the trip as 'a cheery old pessimist'. However, Oates stuck to his guns and they compromised. Oates also smuggled a couple of tons of extra feed on board, bought at his own expense, without Scott's knowledge.

If Cardiff was the expedition's greatest friend in the northern hemisphere, Lyttelton held that place in the south, reacting with true generosity and enthusiasm to her guests. There were

First aerial ascent in Antarctica. The *Discovery's* balloon *Eva*, in which Scott nearly shot into the heavens, is being deflated.

The *Discovery* caught in ice sixteen-feet thick at McMurdo Sound.

The *Discovery* home again in Dundee where she is open to visitors as part of an intriguing exhibition about Scott and Antarctica.

Announcement of Scott's marriage, *The Tatler*, 1908. A conventional end to an unconventional courtship.

Cherry-Garrard, Bowers, Oates, Meares and Atkinson in their quarters in the Cape Evans hut, nicknamed 'the renements' for their austerity. Oates's only luxury was a bust of his hero Napoleon.

Edgar Evans in outdoor clothes at Cape Evans. He had a remarkable physique and was one of the strongest men on the expedition. He was also noted for his extensive fund of oaths.

Captain Oates, the only army man on the expedition and a wry observer of his comrades.

they sleep in the winter, and for how
many hours a day, is a problem full
of interest. Now and again as we
walk among the Weddell's Seals
we find a Crab-eater, seldom
more than one or two, asleep
with the rest.

When we were in the pack
ice these were our daily
food, for we saw
some every day, and
often ate them. Here they are a
rarity, and an interesting
one, as they have hitherto
been considered the peculiar
property of the pack ice.
The "Southern Cross" expedition
found one on the Great Ice
Barrier, and we saw several
as we sailed along it, but
here we have them still
farther South, and
prospect of our
from time to

there seems every
seeing them
time during the winter
and perhaps even some-
-thing of their family
arrangements in the Spring.
I think the
general admiration of our
party is divided somewhat
between the Crab-eater and Ross'
Seal. We have had but few opportunities
of getting to know the latter, though
both are very interesting. No one has
ever met with Ross' Seal except in the
pack ice, and possibly his coat would
be found to vary much if seen at
other seasons of the year,
but he has only been seen
in summer when all have
had a roughish hair

Sea Leopard
chasing Emperor Penguins

E.a.W.

A page from the *South Polar Times* showing Wilson's
lovely fluid drawings of the wild life. Here a leopard
seal swoops after penguins.

Captain Scott's last birthday dinner. Teddy Evans and Edward Wilson are seated on either side of him. An amused Captain Oates, standing to the left, looks on.

Wilson at work at Cape Evans. He worried needlessly that, working by artificial light in the hut, he would be unable to capture Antarctica's subtle colours in his drawings. However, his eye and memory for colour were faultless.

Captain Scott at work in the hut at Cape Evans.
His men called his cubicle 'the holy of holies'.

Captain Scott's 'den' in the hut at Cape Evans today.

Captain Oates tending the ponies on the *Terra Nova*.
He called them 'crocks' but his devotion to them never wavered.

Captain Scott and Kathleen Scott aboard the *Terra Nova*. Kathleen took a close interest in the loading of the ship which was not always appreciated by Scott's men.

The wood-panelled room in the Royal Hotel, Cardiff, where a farewell banquet was given to Captain Scott and Petty Officer Edgar Evans made his memorable impromptu speech.

The end of the Winter Journey. The physical cost of the extraordinary journey to Cape Crozier to collect emperor penguin eggs by Wilson, Bowers and Cherry-Garrard can be seen in their faces.

Kathleen Scott and Peter. Peter was less than a year old when Captain Scott sailed from England but he more than fulfilled his father's ambition that he should grow up loving nature.

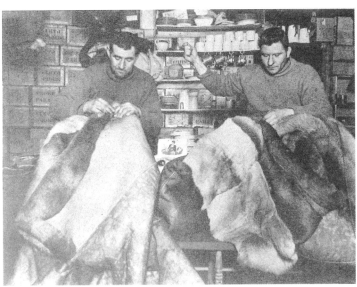

Petty Officers Crean and Evans mending sleeping bags. Crean would one day join Shackleton on his fateful *Endurance* expedition and would again prove his mettle.

Camping near the Polar Plateau, December 1911.
Shortly afterwards Scott selected the four men who
would accompany him to the Pole.

Amundsen's tent at the South Pole. The shock of finding that
Amundsen had beaten them had a profound psychological effect
on Scott and his men.

Roald Amundsen, the victor of the race to the Pole,
called by some 'a Viking raid'.

The famous painting by Dollman of Captain Oates walking to his death in the blizzard. Oates's gesture caught the popular imagination as the epitome of English gallantry and self-sacrifice.

Monument to Captain Scott, Cape Town, South Africa. This was one of several monuments to Scott and his men erected around the world.

Monument to Captain Scott, Christchurch, New Zealand. This was one of a number of monuments sculpted by Kathleen. Another stands in Waterloo Place near St. James's Park in London.

donations of coal, frozen sheep and bullocks, tinned meat, boxes of butter, bacon, beer and biscuits, jerseys and bibles. Lyttelton harbour waived all fees and everyone was given free rail passes. There was also a busy round of parties, dances and race meetings. Oates wrote acidly that: 'Some of the visitors who come in [sic] board write their names on the paintwork which is rather sickening.'[14] Bowers, who in each port the *Terra Nova* had visited had displayed a lively eye for the local girls, wrote 'the charms of the fair sex have not been exaggerated. The girls here are as a whole good-looking and the average would pass as pretty . . . but the little we see of leisure at present precludes the possibility of my falling this time.' Scott complained in an unpublished entry in his diary that in New Zealand he had 'had to hear much talk of Shackleton'. He and Kathleen spent some of their last days together in the beautiful house of Joseph Kinsey, the expedition's agent. It was high on a cliff with wonderful views and a garden ablaze with red and golden flowers. At night they slept outside under clear skies.

On 26 November, the day the *Terra Nova* was due to leave Lyttelton for her final stop at Port Chalmers to take on coal, Edgar Evans fell in the water as he rushed to get aboard after a night out drinking with the locals. Teddy Evans wanted the petty officer dismissed. However, it would have been well nigh impossible for Scott to do this after all they had shared. The fact that in the months to come Kathleen Scott would dream about Petty Officer Evans shows how often Scott must have talked of him and the bonds between them. He therefore decided to overlook this plunge from grace and ordered the Welshman to travel by train to Port Chalmers. In fact they travelled together and the cheerful seaman apparently behaved as if nothing had happened. However, Scott's decision seriously annoyed Teddy Evans who was angry to see the petty officer trotting briskly on board again and the diaries hint more generally at arguments behind the scenes between Scott and Evans. Scott referred to Teddy Evans's 'vague and wild grievances'.

There was also tension between their wives. Bowers attributed it to jealousy between the two. He regarded Hilda Evans as a womanly woman of remarkable beauty and general charm 'who was everything a wife should be'.[15] He was much less in sympathy with the more emancipated and forthright Kathleen and had already reported home that 'he hated to see a woman like her getting out of their proper place in the world'. Now he wrote, 'I don't like Mrs. Scott . . . Nobody likes her on the expedition and the painful silence when she arrives is the only jarring note . . . There is no secret that she runs us all just now and what she says is done through the Owner [Scott]. Now nobody likes a schemer and she is one undoubtedly.'[16]

Oates described a splendid fight between Kathleen and Hilda. 'Mrs Scott and Mrs Evans had a magnificent battle, they tell me it was a draw after 15 rounds. Mrs Wilson flung herself into the fight after the 10th round and there was more blood and hair flying about the hotel than you see in a Chicago [sic] slaughter-house in a month.'[17] He hoped it would not cause coolness among the men when they got down south but added characteristically that it would not bother him if it did. Kathleen decided that if her husband ever mounted another expedition, the wives must be chosen more carefully than the men or, better still, have none. As Bowers remarked, the sooner they were all away the better.

The final farewells in fact came on 29 November. Kathleen, together with Oriana Wilson and Hilda Evans, remained on board until the ship cleared the flag-decked harbour, when they were taken off by tug. Kathleen had left a bundle of letters with Teddy

Evans to be given to Scott on special days. She described in her autobiography 'his face radiating tenderness as the space between us widened, until I held only my memory of that upturned face, but held it for a lifetime'. To cheer herself up she visited a babies' home but found them very plain. Hilda Evans was 'ghastly white' and Oriana Wilson 'sphinx-like' as the tug turned back. Wilson wrote in his diary of his Ory's 'temporary widowhood', little guessing that it was to be permanent, saying that he was taking with him the memory of the most perfect companionship he had ever known.

Back in Britain the news of the *Terra Nova's* departure south received only muted attention. Perhaps the most frequent reminder of the great adventure was the advertisements for a brand of underwear which the expedition had taken with them, under the bold headline 'GONE WITH SCOTT'.

11

Stewed Penguin Breast and Plum Pudding

'All links with civilization are cut, and as night falls New Zealand sinks from sight. It is almost sad to think that years will pass before we shall once more see land with forests and green fields,' wrote an unusually sombre Tryggve Gran as the *Terra Nova* creaked on her way. She was heavily overladen. The crated motor sledges covered in tarpaulins took up most of the deck, together with sixty wooden components for the hut, sacks of coal and drums of fuel. Birdie Bowers described how the decks were crowded with 'garbage fore and aft' but added 'risk nothing and do nothing; if funds could not supply another ship, we simply had to overload the one we had or suffer worse things down south'.[1] She was also a floating menagerie. The thirty-three dogs were billeted on the open deck, chained up around the other cargo and exposed to the wind and the spray, the picture of canine misery. 'The dogs sit with their tails to this invading water, their coats wet and dripping. It is a pathetic attitude, deeply significant of cold and misery; occasionally some poor beast emits a long pathetic whine. The

178

group forms a picture of wretched dejection; such a life is truly hard for these poor creatures,' wrote Scott. He also worried about the fifteen ponies accommodated under the forecastle: 'One takes a look through a hole in the bulkhead and sees a row of heads with sad, patient eyes come swinging up together from the starboard side, whilst those on the port swing back; then up come the port heads, whilst the starboard recede. It seems a terrible ordeal for these poor beasts . . .' The ponies also posed an ordeal for the seamen since some were housed directly above the seamen's mess-table and what they euphemistically described as 'mustard' dripped down.

What fate awaited this ungainly cargo of humans and animals? Scott set great store by luck but the coming weeks would bring a series of misfortunes. On 2 December, just two days out from New Zealand, the *Terra Nova* ran straight into the teeth of a Force 10 gale. Shrieking winds dislodged the deck cargo, sending sacks of coal and cans of fuel cannoning hither and thither. The wretched dogs, chained by the neck, were washed backwards and forwards across the deck. One was actually hurled overboard with such force that his chain broke, but by a miracle a great wave deposited him back again. The ponies were in danger of breaking their legs as the ship pitched and tossed.

The storm was a defining event which showed Scott the calibre of his companions. Oates and Atkinson worked 'like Trojans' among the ponies. Teddy Evans described Oates's 'strong brown face illuminated by a swinging lamp as he stood amongst those suffering little beasts. He was a fine, powerful man and on occasions he seemed to be actually lifting the poor little ponies to their feet as the ship lurched . . .'[2] Scott himself remained calm and stoical – a storm at sea was well within his range of experience. Bowers later described Scott's coolness with awe: 'Captain Scott was simply splendid, he might have been at Cowes . . .'[3] However the reality, as Scott later told Griffith Taylor, was that it was touch and go. The ship's pumps had become clogged with balls of coal dust and engine oil and the ship was taking in water and slowly sinking. Scott and Teddy Evans set the afterguard to baling out by hand and Wilson, one of the lucky ones not to suffer from seasickness, described the desperate scenes:

> It was a weird night's work with the howling gale and the darkness and the immense sea running over the ship every few minutes, and no engine and no sail, and we all in the engine-room black as ink with engine-room oil and bilgewater, singing chanties as we passed up slopping buckets full of bilge, each man above slopping a little over the heads of all of us below him, wet through to the skin, so much so that some of the party worked altogether naked . . .

The storm began to abate and after a twelve-hour struggle a hole was eventually cut through the engine-room bulkhead to reach the suction well of the hand pump which was flooded. Teddy Evans squeezed through and worked neck-high to clear the valves when 'to the joy of all a good stream of water came from the pump for the first time,' wrote a grateful Scott. The danger was past – fires could be re-lit, bilges dried out and the cost counted. Everything was sopping, including Gran's wellington boots which were 'like eel-pots'. More importantly, two ponies had died and their bodies had to be pushed out of the forecastle skylight. Teddy Evans described it as 'a dirty job, because the square of the hatch was so small that a powerful purchase had to be used which stretched out the ponies like dead rabbits'. In addition, one dog had drowned and 10 tons of coal and 65 gallons of petrol had been lost, together with a case of biologist's spirit.

The phlegmatic Edgar Evans took it in his stride, writing to his mother simply that 'Since leaving New Zealand we have had some pretty bad weather . . .'[4] To Wilson, the *Terra Nova's* salvation had been God's work signalled by 'a most perfect and brilliant rainbow' which had appeared at the storm's height, though it apparently went unnoticed by his less spiritual colleagues. Wilson took it as a sign that 'seemed to remove every shadow of doubt, not only as to the present issue, but as to the final issue of the whole Expedition . . .' Bowers was similarly sustained by a deep faith that: 'Under its worst conditions this earth is a good place to live in'.[5] Cherry-Garrard after forty-eight hours without sleep was more down to earth. 'For sheer downright misery,' he wrote, 'give me a hurricane, not too warm, the yard of a sailing ship, a wet sail and a bout of seasickness.'

However, a second blow followed swiftly on the first. Just ten days after leaving New Zealand the first iceberg was sighted, heralding the approach of the pack. A delighted Ponting described this great white floating island: 'flat as a table; about eighty feet in height, and a mile or more long. Its vertical cliffs were seamed with fissures, and near the water line the great mass was pitted with caverns into which the waves rushed and foamed, or, dashing against the cliffs, rose with a roar, far up the perpendicular precipices.' On 9 December the *Terra Nova* collided with her first big ice floe. To eager young men like Cherry-Garrard the pack was a fantasy world: 'The floes were pink, floating in a deep blue sea, and all the shadows were mauve. We passed right under a monster berg, and all day have been threading lake after lake and lead after lead. "There is Regent Street," said somebody, and for some time we drove through great streets of perpendicular walls of ice.' However, they did not grasp the significance. They had sailed into the pack much farther north than Scott had anticipated. He worried that it would delay their arrival at Cape Crozier, his intended base.

The *Terra Nova* made slow progress, using up her coal at an alarming rate. Scott, always an impatient man, fretted. 'Oh, but it's mighty trying to be delayed and delayed like this . . .' he raged inwardly, but he took care to conceal his frustration from his men. Wilson's feelings were rather different: 'the soft seething noise of moving ice and an occasional bump and grating noise along the ship's side gave one a feeling of old times.' Soon he was again sketching the prolific wildlife. There were emperor penguins and less stately but more acrobatic Adélies. Flocks of Antarctic petrels roosted on the ice floes, snowy petrels circled and schools of blue whales passed by – 'their blows were very high and looked almost like factory chimney smoke as they rose dark grey against the white ice blink of the pack ice sky . . . a grey column of foggy, frosty breath.'

Wilson's diary captures the magical beauty:

> The sunlight at midnight in the pack is perfectly won-
> derful. One looks out upon endless fields of broken ice,
> all violet and purple in the low shadows, and all gold
> and orange and rose-red on the broken edges which
> catch the light, while the sky is emerald green and
> salmon pink, and these two beautiful tints are reflected
> in the pools of absolutely still water which here and
> there lie between the ice-floes. Now and again one
> hears a penguin cry out in the stillness . . . and then,
> perhaps, he appears in his dress tail coat and white

waistcoat suddenly upon an ice-floe from the water –
and catching sight of the ship runs curiously towards
her, crying out in his amazement as he comes . . . but
only intensifying the wonderful stillness and beauty of
the whole fairy-like scene as the golden glaring sun in
the south just touches the horizon . . .

Ponting wanted to obtain 'a moving-picture film showing the
bow of the *Terra Nova* cleaving the ice-floes'. He clambered onto
some overhanging planks rigged up by the crew and filmed one of
his most dramatic sequences. Nine months later Kathleen Scott
would watch it at the Gaumont cinema in London.

Despite the delay and uncertainty, the ice floes did at least
provide an opportunity for ski practice 'or in current parlance
(à la Gran) to go "mit dee shee op",' as Griffith Taylor described
with some mirth. Tryggve Gran marshalled his slithering, tot-
tering companions and demonstrated how to use two ski sticks,
rather than the one which until recently had been customary. Not
everyone was enthusiastic. Petty Officer Evans referred darkly to
the skis as 'planks'. However, officers, scientists and seamen were
soon hurtling about. Griffith Taylor recorded: 'We learned from
Gran that a knock-kneed man has the advantage in ski-ing; at any
rate we had to keep our knees together to counteract a tendency
of the ski to spread.'

Christmas Eve brought about the usual high jinks which
Cherry-Garrard recorded:

> Jane [Atkinson] and Soldier [Oates] entered the mate's
> cabin and said that they did not want to use force, but
> they wanted the return of twenty matches which he
> had taken from the Eastern Party. There was such a

fight that afterwards Campbell was hanging over the side feeling very sick! Titus dragged all Bill's clothes off and Bill burst naked into the wardroom dragging Titus along on his back.[6]

Christmas dinner included an entrée of stewed penguin breasts with redcurrant jelly and concluded with a flaming plum pudding, mince pies and chocolates washed down with heroic quantities of champagne, port and liqueurs. The whole company then gathered around the pianola and the usually taciturn Oates amazed everyone by bursting into song. The next morning Bowers, who took pride in washing in cold water, emptied a bucket of icy water over his naked body to sober himself up and offered to do likewise for his colleagues.

Kathleen Scott's Christmas was rather more muted. She took Peter to stay with his grandmother at Henley who 'said how sad it was that Peter didn't know the divine meaning of Christmas Day. I had to be a little stern, and told her that Peter knew that there was a little baby in history born in a stable who grew up to be a very wonderful man, and that was more than most babies of two knew.'

Scott was glad to see his men in such spirits, though, as he could not join in, it heightened his sense of isolation from them. The responsibility for a successful outcome weighed on him. His anxiety about the delays and about the condition of the animals overshadowed everything. Nevertheless, while impressed with Oates's ceaseless efforts with the ponies, he felt inhibited from making suggestions to him. His diary expressed surprise that Oates did not take advantage of the relative stability of the ship in the pack to exercise the ponies on deck, but he did not suggest it. Perhaps the reason was a sense of social and/or professional inferiority. Oates had quickly divined that neither Scott nor Evans understood animals, writing to his mother that 'their ignorance is colossal'.[7] A lack of communication betweem Scott and Oates would remain a feature of the expedition.

On 30 December the *Terra Nova* at last broke free. She had been in the pack ice for twenty days compared with the *Discovery's* four and had used up 61 tons of coal. According to Debenham, Scott attributed the delay to a combination of starting so early in the season and to 'rank bad luck'. On New Year's Eve came the first glimpse of Antarctic land – the peaks of the Admiralty range appeared in the distance, lit up by the sun 'like satin, above the clouds'. Two days later the towering mass of Erebus was sighted and Ponting photographed it in the brilliant light of the midnight sun. This familiar landmark brought a lump to the throats of the *Discovery* veterans. However, the swell at Cape Crozier was too fierce to allow them to land and set up their winter base as they had intended. They would have to seek another haven with easy access to the Barrier, but it would not be so close to the Pole.

The *Terra Nova* now made for the familiar territory of McMurdo Sound and a landing place was found on the northern side of a tongue of land formed by an old lava flow from Mount Erebus. This site had been known in the *Discovery* days as 'the Skuary' because of the skua gulls nesting there. It lay some fifteen miles north of the *Discovery's* old winter quarters at Hut Point and was separated from it by two deep bays which, when frozen, could be marched over in a day. The bays themselves were divided by a jutting spur of ice, Glacier Tongue. With characteristic generosity, Scott named their new home Cape Evans in honour of his number two.

The *Terra Nova* was secured with ice-anchors and unloading began as fast as possible. Scott was relieved to be able to get his ponies on land again, a reaction they shared – Ponting's film shows them rolling joyfully in the snow. Scott's account of their antics was coloured by his tendency to anthropomorphise. He described how they obligingly nuzzled away at each other to relieve the itch which had tormented them on board. Some of the ponies were strong enough to begin work almost straight away, though they did not always take to sledge-pulling, showing a tendency to bolt. The dogs were also brought ashore and were in quite a sorry state, though not too weak to massacre any curious Adelies who waddled up to take a look.

Ponting was nearly devoured by a school of killer whales he had run onto an ice floe to photograph. Before he realized what was happening, the whales spotted him and launched a concerted attack, swimming under the ice and rising in unison to dislodge him into the water. His horrified colleagues watched Ponting leap across the ice pursued by these demonic creatures with their 'tawny head markings, their small glistening eyes, and their terrible array of teeth . . .'[8] He described his escape graphically:

> The ship was within sixty yards, and I heard wild shouts of 'Look out!' 'Run!' 'Jump, man jump!' 'Run, quick!' But I could not run; it was all I could do to keep my feet as I leapt from piece to piece of the rocking ice, with the whales a few yards behind me, snorting and blowing among the ice-blocks. I wondered whether I should be able to reach safety before the whales reached me; and I recollect distinctly thinking, if they did get

me, how very unpleasant the first bite would feel, but that it would not matter much about the second.

Ponting scrambled to safety to be greeted by an ashen Scott with the words, 'My God! That was about the nearest squeak I ever saw!'

The operation of unloading was a good opportunity to test out the motor sledges but further disaster struck when one of them fell through a patch of rotting ice. Priestley, one of the unloading party, described what happened:

> We realised that the ice was getting very rotten but when a message came back from an anxious Scott to hurry with the unloading, no one had the courage or the sense to ignore it. The Ship Party had got the sledge down on to the ice when without warning Williamson went through to his thighs. The motor sledge suddenly dipped, the ice gave way beneath her afterend and she fell with all her weight vertically on the rope. The rope began cutting through the thin ice . . . Man after man was forced to [let the rope go] and when only five of us were left, [the sledge] took charge at a gallop and is now resting on the bottom at a depth of 120 fathoms.

Scott took the loss calmly, even though the £1,000 the sledge cost represented a sizeable slice of the money so painstakingly raised, blaming himself for his own impatience. Wilfred Bruce attributed his generally relaxed attitude to the fact that he had reached Antarctica safely: 'Having landed, and feeling a bit more settled he bucked up a lot and said many pretty things to all of us.'[9] Scott's growing confidence can be seen in his reassuring letter to his mother: 'My companions are a far abler lot of men than I had in the *Discovery* and all are devoted to the work and loyal to me.'[10] Scott was also quite pleased with Cape Evans, writing to Kathleen that: 'Fortune has been kind after all, and every day shows the advantages of the spot we have chosen for our winter station.'[11]

Scott was anxious to establish his base quickly so that the various expeditions could start before the weather grew too cold. The most crucial thing was to erect the hut – a fine structure 50 feet long by 25 feet wide and 9 feet to the eaves. The double walls were insulated with quilted seaweed and lined with felt. The roof was covered with 'three-ply ruberoid' and the floor with linoleum. In line with strict rules of naval discipline the hut was subdivided into the wardroom, for use by the officers and scientists, and the mess-deck for the others. Although each side could hear everything which went on, the protocol was that they could not, thus giving a sense of comfort and privacy to both groups, important in the stressful isolated conditions of Antarctica. By 18 January the hut was ready for occupation – stove, cooking range, gramophone and pianola were all installed. A cave, hewn from the ice, housed the magnetic instruments while an ice grotto was crammed with supplies of mutton, penguin and seal. Stables for the ponies were built on the leeward side of the hut. In his diary Scott wrote that he had been wondering how the ponies would be accommodated. It seems at the least curious that he had not thought about this earlier, given the ponies' supposedly crucial role, but perhaps he was trusting to Oates. Whatever the case, he was delighted with progress, though he continued to fret that there must be 'some drawback hidden by the summer weather' which they had overlooked.

On 15 January Scott set out with Meares and a dog team to

visit Hut Point. He was shocked to find that Shackleton and his men had left a window open so that the hut had filled with snow and ice. It had also been left in a squalid state in Shackleton's rush to depart. He had re-embarked on the *Nimrod* just three days after returning to the hut, having spent two of them rescuing comrades left out on the ice. Scott's resentment of his rival's behaviour caused him to write an angry passage in his journal, later deleted for publication, describing how: 'Boxes full of excrement were found near the provisions and filth of a similar description was thick under the verander [sic] . . . It is extraordinary to think that people could have lived in such a horrible manner and with such absence of regard for those to follow.'

However, Scott had little time to brood as sledging was about to begin. His diary again shows a surprising uncertainty. He wrote: 'my head doesn't seem half as clear on the subject as it ought to be.' In the event, he decided to lead a party of thirteen men with eight pony sledges and two dog sledges in the limited time before winter set in to lay the series of supply depots crucial for next season's Polar attempt. The depots would provide substantial amounts of food and fuel to supplement the supplies which the Polar team and their supporting parties would be able to transport, thus increasing the effective range of operation to allow the Pole to be reached with an adequate safety margin. Lieutenant Campbell, the so-called 'wicked mate', was to lead a team to explore the coast of King Edward VII Land, while the Australian Griffith Taylor and three others were to carry out a geological survey of Victoria Land's mountains and glaciers. The *Terra Nova* would drop Campbell's and Griffith Taylor's parties and then sail on to New Zealand since, unlike the *Discovery*, she would not winter in McMurdo Sound. As Scott had rejected the idea of bringing a wireless, from the time of the *Terra Nova*'s departure until her return Scott and his men would be entirely cut off from the outside world.

Scott's depot-laying party of thirteen men marched out on 24 January, just three weeks after landing. There was a sense of occasion with, in Wilson's words, '. . . a great deal of photographing and a good deal of trouble and excitement' as the dogs and ponies slithered about on the ice. The men were amused by the figures they cut in their sledging garments. Debenham decided that their windclothes, cut very full to go over other clothing, were 'not at all elegant and make a man look very corpulent even dropsical!'

The plan was to march across the Barrier along the Polar route for a hundred miles or so, depoting such essential supplies as pony fodder, sledging rations, dog biscuits and paraffin at strategic points. The need for haste became immediately apparent – the sea ice which provided the only direct route to the Barrier was already breaking up. According to Cherry-Garrard the party crossed it in the nick of time 'in a state of hurry bordering on panic'.

Wilson and Meares were responsible for the two dog teams with Dimitri Gerov, while Scott, Oates, Atkinson, Cherry-Garrard, Birdie Bowers, Gran, Crean, Forde, Keohane and Teddy Evans led or marched alongside the ponies. Wilson thoroughly enjoyed his dog driving, finding it 'a very different thing to the beastly dog driving we perpetrated in the *Discovery* days'. He developed a deep affection for the leader of his team, 'Stareek', Russian for old man, 'quite the nicest, quietest cleverest old dog gentleman I have ever come across. He looks . . . as though he knew all the wickedness of all the world and all its cares and as though he was bored to death by both of them.' He had discussed dog driving with Meares on the voyage south from New Zealand and had concluded that 'if any traction except ourselves can reach the top of Beardmore Glacier it will be the dogs.' Scott's attempt at driving dogs was less successful, causing him to write in his journal that, 'I withhold my opinion of the dogs, in much doubt as to whether they are going to be a real success – but the ponies are going to be real good.'

The party soon encountered problems. Atkinson's foot became so badly chafed that he had to return to Cape Evans. Scott was not particularly sympathetic on the grounds that Atkinson 'ought to have reported his trouble long before'. Also, the surface of the Barrier proved softer and more yielding than the mirror-hard surface they had expected. The ponies found it hard going and floundered badly. Scott had to acknowledge that the conditions did not suit them: 'The great drawback is the ease with which they sink in soft snow . . . they struggle pluckily when they sink, but it is trying to watch them.' Oates saw what was happening and grew despondent, but Scott dismissed his concern on the grounds that 'he is not an optimist'. Pony snow shoes – circles of wire hooped with bamboo – were tried out on one pony, Weary Willie. Much to everyone's surprise, including Oates who had so little confidence in the shoes that he had brought only a single set, they had a magical effect. Meares and Wilson were sent back to get some more but found that the ice had broken up, making a return to Cape Evans impossible. Scott understandably fretted that 'so great a help to our work has been left behind at the station'.

The party struggled on south and east to reach a position due south of Cape Crozier, which they nicknamed Corner Camp. It gave a straight course for the Beardmore Glacier, the path taken by Shackleton, which was to be Scott's gateway to the Pole. However, before they could move on, the first blizzard struck – it was an awesome encounter with what Cherry-Garrard called 'raging chaos' and it delayed them for three days. When it cleared they pushed south again past Minna Bluff (named for Sir Clements Markham's wife Minna), and set up Bluff Depot near the 79th parallel. Cherry-Garrard described what it was like sharing a tent with Scott:

> Scott's tent was a comfortable one to live in, and I was always glad when I was told to join it . . . He was himself extraordinarily quick, and no time was ever lost by his party in camping or breaking camp. He was most careful, some said over-careful but I do not think so, that everything should be neat and shipshape . . . And if you were 'sledging with the Owner' you had to keep your eyes wide open for the little things which cropped up, and do them quickly, and say nothing about them.

Life with Scott sounds wholly admirable, if a bit of a strain. Disciplined himself, he expected others to be similarly meticulous. Wright later recalled how some of the men were so in awe of Scott that they went outside into the cold to urinate, rather than doing so in the corner of the tent as was usual.

Although they had only been sledging for eighteen days, the ponies were weakening. Scott's journal shows his distress and anxiety – not only was he depending on the ponies for the Polar journey, but he was haunted by their suffering. Oates, who loved horses too but was less sentimental, took a more pragmatic view, arguing that it would be better to drive the ponies as far south as possible and then kill them and depot the meat for the men and dogs of the Polar party. He thought it unlikely that many of the ponies would survive the journey back to Cape Evans. Nevertheless, Scott decided to send the three weakest – Blossom, Blucher and James Pigg – back with Teddy Evans, Keohane and

Forde. Blossom died almost immediately and Blucher after just thirty miles, vindicating Oates's view.

Oates continued to argue for pushing on and killing the ponies, particularly Weary Willie, who was now very weak, having been set on by some of the dogs, but Scott refused, according to Gran, and there was a telling exchange: 'I have had enough of this cruelty to animals,' was Scott's reply, 'and I'm not going to defy my feelings for the sake of a few days' march.' 'I'm afraid you'll regret it, sir,' said Oates in the end. 'Regret it or not, my dear Oates,' Scott answered, 'I've made up my mind, like a Christian.'[12] In the event the farthest south they reached was only 79° 29'S, 130 geographical miles from Cape Evans and thirty miles farther north than Scott had intended. They laid a depot, called it 'One Ton' because of the enormous amount of stores left there, and marked it with a black flag. Scott now wrote in his diary that 'we shall have a good leg up for next year and can at least feed the ponies full up to this point'. But as events would prove, if Scott had listened to Oates and laid the depot further south, nearer the Pole, the returning Polar party, frozen, starving and exhausted, might have gained at least temporary relief.

By now the temperature had dropped to around -21°F and many of the party were feeling the cold – Oates in particular was suffering with a frostbitten nose. Reflecting that this did not bode well for the next season's journeys, Scott now divided the party for the return journey. Scott, Wilson, Cherry-Garrard and Meares went ahead with the two dog teams. Bowers, Oates and Gran followed at their own pace with the five exhausted ponies. An interesting exchange took place between Oates and Gran as they tramped northwards again. According to Gran: 'Oates was a completely closed book to me until I shared camp life with him . . . I (had) gained the impression that I did not find grace in his eyes . . .' Gran was correct. On 31 January Oates had written to his mother: 'I can't stand this Norwegian chap, he is both dirty and lazy. I have had one row with him and I should think it won't be very long before I have another.' However, as Gran described, on the return journey from One Ton Depot:

> Oates told me straight out that what he had against me was not personal; it was just that I was a foreigner. With all his heart he hated all foreigners, because all foreigners hated England. The rest of the world led by Germany were just waiting to attack his Motherland, and destroy it if they could. I was about to reply when Bowers quickly intervened: 'Could be something in what you say, Oates, but all the same I wager what you will that Gran would be with us if England is forced into war through no fault of her own.' 'Would you?', asked Oates. 'Of course,' I replied, and the next instant he grasped my hand. From this moment the closed book opened, and Oates and I became the best of friends.

Scott meanwhile was increasingly impressed by the dogs' perform-ance. They made excellent time on the return journey and he had begun to consult Meares about how dog teams might perform on the Polar plateau. However, his confidence was soon shaken again. He and Meares narrowly escaped death when a snow bridge collapsed as they were crossing a crevasse. All but the leader of their team, the magnificently strong Osman, who had survived being washed overboard during the storm, tumbled in. Looking down, an appalled Wilson saw 'a great blue chasm in which hung the team of dogs in a festoon'. They managed to haul up eleven dogs, but two had slipped from their harness, fallen onto a snow shelf 65 feet below and promptly gone to sleep. Forgetting his responsibilities as leader and ignoring the strenuous objections of the others – Wilson thought it was an insane risk – the sentimental, animal-loving Scott insisted on being lowered on a rope to rescue them. This he managed, and the weary party reached Safety Camp on 22 February without further incident to find Teddy Evans with his solitary pony, James Pigg.

However, worse was to come. Atkinson, whose foot had recovered, delivered a bag of mail left at Cape Evans by the *Terra Nova* before she sailed on to New Zealand. The post included a letter from Campbell containing the dire tidings that he had discovered Amundsen camped on the ice at the Bay of Whales, a bight in the Great Ice Barrier near Edward VII Land. This was where Scott had made his precarious ascent in a balloon in 1902 and the most southerly point that a ship could reach. It was also a mere 400 miles from Scott's own winter quarters. The challenge could not have been clearer. A bitterly angry Scott pored over Campbell's account of the tense encounter between the Norwegians and the British.

Campbell described how his party had been unable to land as planned on King Edward VII Land because ice barred the *Terra Nova*'s way. Turning back, Campbell had decided to seek a wintering place on the Barrier itself and, rounding a point, the men of the *Terra Nova* had been astounded to see the *Fram*, as welcome as a Viking raiding ship, moored snugly at the Barrier's edge. As Wilfred Bruce wrote to Kathleen, 'Curses loud and deep were heard everywhere.'[13]

The crews visited each other in an atmosphere of excruciating politeness. The Norwegian shore party consisted of nine men and 110 dogs, compared to Scott's two shore parties totalling thirty-three men and their assorted transport. The Norwegians were quite open about their plans. Amundsen intended to make a dash for the Pole with their dogs and on skis and to start as early as the weather allowed. He invited Campbell to stay at the Bay of Whales and make use of some of his dogs but Campbell declined. After meticulous civilities on both sides he took his leave, preferring to sail on with the *Terra Nova* on her passage to New Zealand and attempt a landing beyond Cape Adare.

Scott's first reaction, as Cherry-Garrard described many years later to George Bernard Shaw, was fury. He had to master the temptation to rush to the Bay of Whales and have it out with Amundsen. Cherry-Garrard had never seen his captain so distressed. There are overtones here of Scott the child who hated losing. The thought of having the prize plucked from his grasp, plus the fact that Amundsen had not 'played the game' were unbearable. It was not fair! However, more sober reflection convinced him that, 'The proper, as well as the wiser, course for us is to proceed exactly as though this had not happened. To go forward and do our best for the honour of the country without fear or panic.'

However, whether Scott liked it or not, the Polar journey would now be a race. He began to weigh up their respective chances, reflecting gloomily that at the Bay of Whales Amundsen was some sixty miles closer to the Pole. He pondered Amundsen's reliance on dogs, admitting that his plans for running them seemed excellent and that he would be able to start earlier with dogs than he could with ponies. It would have depressed him further to know that on his final depot-laying journey Amundsen had achieved nearly sixty miles on his best day, his dogs whisking effortlessly over the frozen surface of the Barrier, and that he had laid his final depot 150 miles farther south than Scott's. On average Scott had only managed between a third and a half of Amundsen's speed.

Scott anyway found it difficult to accept that intelligent animals like dogs could be driven for hundreds of miles over featureless terrain all the way to the Pole. He believed that 'A dog must be either eating, asleep or *interested*. His eagerness to snatch at interest, to chain his attention to something, is almost pathetic. The monotony of marching kills him.' Yet, even if Scott had now wanted to alter his plans and abandon his reliance on ponies, there was the danger of being accused of copying Amundsen.

While Scott was still reflecting on this strange twist of fate, Bowers, Oates and Gran arrived at Safety Camp with all five ponies, but Weary Willie was in a bad way. Scott stayed with Oates and Gran, trying unsuccessfully to nurse him but he died in the night. It emphasized even more clearly to Scott that 'these blizzards are terrible for the poor animals . . . It makes a late start *necessary for next year.*'

Meanwhile Scott had sent the others ahead to the safety of Hut Point, which Wilson and Meares reached with the dog teams. However, a nightmarish sequence of events awaited Bowers, Cherry-Garrard and Crean. Unlike Wilson they decided to cross the sea-ice with their four emaciated ponies. As Bowers described, 'it was a beastly march back: dark, gloomy and depressing.' Progress was slow and they made camp on ice which seemed solid enough but extreme weariness probably affected their judgement – Bowers made the customary cocoa with curry powder and Crean did not even notice. They awoke to the unpleasant discovery that, as Bowers described, 'We were in the middle of a floating pack of broken-up ice.' One pony, Guts, had vanished and a desperate race now ensued to drag their sledges and the remaining three ponies from floe to floe to reach the safety of the

Barrier. As if this were not enough, Bowers described the 'further unpleasantness' caused by the sight of squadrons of killer whales cruising with 'fiendish activity' in the thirty to forty feet or so of open water which lay between them and the Barrier.

Thomas Crean, the huge Irish petty officer with a profile like the Duke of Wellington's, leapt across the floes. Gaining the Barrier, he raised the alarm and Scott hurried to the Barrier's edge. Meanwhile Bowers and Cherry-Garrard had their work cut out to calm the ponies terrorized by the sight of 'Huge black and yellow heads, with sickening pig eyes only a few yards from us'.[14] Luckily their floe came to rest against the edge of the Barrier and a mightily relieved Scott shouted down, 'My dear chaps, you can't think how glad I am to see you safe!'[15] Bowers wrote how he 'realised the feeling Scott must have had all day. He had been blaming himself for our deaths and here we were very much alive.'

However, Scott saw continuing danger. At any moment the current might shift and the floe with its bedraggled and exhausted cargo would float out to sea. He therefore ordered Bowers and Cherry-Garrard to abandon the animals. They did so but while they persisted in trying to cut steps to lead the ponies up on to the Barrier after them, the ice floe broke loose again. They had to endure the sight of the three disconsolate beasts floating away. The next morning Bowers spotted the ponies about a mile to the north west where their floe had again come to rest. However, in the frantic efforts to hustle them once more across a moving bridge of ice floes to the safety of the Barrier two fell in and Oates and Bowers had the sickening task of killing them with pickaxes to save them from the whales. Only one survivor, Nobby, made it to safety. It was a great blow to Scott's plans for the Pole. 'If ever a man's footsteps were dogged by misfortune, they were surely our leader's,' wrote an unusually sombre Teddy Evans. The fatalistic

Wilson put the sequence of calamities down to God's will, just as he had their survival from the storm at sea.

The break-up of the sea-ice also meant that the party was now trapped at Hut Point. They were forced to exist in the smoky, reeking atmosphere of the old *Discovery* hut whose stove was fuelled with lumps of seal blubber. Their plight was made even more frustrating by the knowledge that 'Cape Evans, though dimly in sight, was as far off as New Zealand till the sea froze over,' as Bowers wistfully described. Living conditions became even more cramped when on 14 March Griffith Taylor and his band of geological surveyors, including Edgar Evans, arrived. Petty Officer Evans had won the admiration of Griffith Taylor and his fellow academics for his strength and courage, his inexhaustible supply of anecdotes and unusual swearwords and his choice of reading matter. They had abandoned their more erudite tomes in favour of his William le Queux novel and copy of the *Red Magazine*.

The men rubbed along well enough in a spirit of camaraderie. They dined on fried seal liver and penguin breast and Wilson invented a penguin lard which tasted like very bad sardine oil. Oates put in a plea for plain cooking, remarking in a loud voice: 'Some of our party, who rather fancy themselves as cooks, quite spoil the meals by messing up the food in their attempts to produce original dishes.'[16] However, he appears to have enjoyed Wilson's chapattis. He tried unsuccessfully to get Wilson to give him some brandy 'for medicinal purposes' by pretending to throw a fit but Wilson saw through it: 'Yes, he's got a fit all right; rub some snow down his neck, and he'll soon get over it.'[17]

Scott was pleased to see such high spirits but his own confidence had been severely jolted by the events of the depot journey, compounded by the news about Amundsen. He wrote: 'It is ill to sit still and contemplate the ruin which has assailed our transport . . . The Pole is a very long way off, alas!' As soon as the sea-ice began to re-form Scott leapt at the chance to be off, though some of the group had misgivings. Soon men and sledges were descending onto the sea-ice by alpine ropes. Teddy Evans admired Scott's resolution, writing that 'a more nervous man would have fought shy because once down on the sea ice, there was little chance of our getting back'. It is a measure of Scott's frustration that he was prepared to take such a risk, but he was worried about what he might find at Cape Evans, fearing that 'misfortune was in the air' and that 'some abnormal swell' might have wrought havoc.

The gamble paid off and on 13 April they regained the relative luxury of Cape Evans, where a relieved Scott found 'all safe'. They looked so changed with their beards, weatherbeaten skins and clothes soaked in seal blubber and soot, that Ponting took them for Norwegians. When he realized who it was he rushed for his camera but, as he later wrote:

> To my intense disgust . . . Petty Officers Evans and Crean had clipped off their bushy, black beards before their turn came round, leaving only a lot of bristles that were sufficient to dismay any self-respecting camera . . . But Griffith Taylor, with a lofty scorn for gibes, which added greatly to my respect for him, declined to sacrifice his 'Keir-Hardie' whiskers for anyone.

Ten days later the sun rose for the final time for four months, heralding the arrival of winter. In the dark days to come Scott would have much on which to reflect. On the voyage south he had written: 'Fortune would be in a hard mood indeed if it allowed such a combination of knowledge, experience, ability and enthusiasm to achieve nothing.'[18] But Fortune had not smiled. Instead she had allowed in an interloper.

12

Winter

As the darkness fell, life settled into an orderly routine. The hut was comfortable, even cosy, with acetylene gas jets, stoves, clothes lines, clocks and the all-important gramophone on which the men played such sentimental favourites of the age as 'A Night Hymn at Sea' by Clara Butt and K. Rumford and 'Tis Folly to Run Away From Love' by Margaret Cooper. The nine men of the mess-deck lived their separate existence, separated from the wardroom by a shelved wall and warmed by the galley stove, the hut's main source of heat. Debenham described how: 'In the hut the temperature at floor-level was kept below freezing point so that any snow brought in could be swept out daily, but at table height it would be about 50°F., while at the peak of the hut it could rise to 70°F., where we could thaw a bucket of ice for our weekly wash.'

On the other side of this partition the sixteen officers and scientists eked out the space as economically as they could. Scott had a curtained alcove six foot square where he worked at a linoleum-covered table. When he looked up his eye would fall on photographs of Kathleen, Peter and his mother and sisters. For solace he had his volumes of Hardy, Galsworthy and Browning and his much cherished 23-year-old Royal Navy greatcoat which had become something of a mascot and which he often used for a bedspread. Given that Scott, like most of the men, was a smoker, his section of the tightly sealed hut, like the rest of it, would have had a permanent smoke haze. (Wilson, a non-smoker himself, had written in his medical report on the *Discovery* expedition in the *British Medical Journal* in July 1905 that tobacco was invaluable on sledge journeys as 'a sedative to chronic and insatiable hunger'.)

There was a meticulously clean darkroom which Ponting had designed for himself and where he also slept. Next door was Atkinson's laboratory full of microscopes and test tubes, while adjacent to him was the meteorologist Simpson, whose wonderful collection of state-of-the-art instruments hummed, ticked and whirred. These included Dine's Anemometer which recorded each gust of wind by means of a vane attached to a two-inch pipe projecting above the roof. Ponting described its eerie sound effects: 'When blizzards raged, the sighing and moaning and utterly unearthly sounds emitted by this tube at night were most depressing.' They contrasted with the sound of Clissold the cook's improvised bread-making machine. Clissold made his dough, placed it in a big pot to rise and retired to bed. According to Griffith Taylor: 'When the dough rose sufficiently it pushed up a disc, which overbalanced a gutter. Down this ran a lead ball which made contact and rang a bell! Further, the bell actuated a pulley and wire and made another contact whereby a red light appeared at intervals above his head!'

Wilson's corner was opposite Simpson. Each day would find him hard at work from five in the morning, noting and drawing. Nelson and Day shared one cubicle while the Australians,

Debenham and Griffith Taylor, shared another with Gran. In a letter to his mother Debenham confessed rather mysteriously to misgivings about Gran's 'morals'.[1] Whether this was a reference to his boasting about women or something else, perhaps masturbation, is hard to tell. They curtained off their entrance with some photographic blackout material begged from Ponting, a refinement that was irresistible to Oates, who declared their accommodation no better than an opium den or ladies' boudoir. He himself shared a cubicle with Cherry-Garrard, Bowers, Meares and Atkinson which earned the nickname 'The Tenements' on account of its Spartan austerity. Oates's only luxury was a small bust of Napoleon whom the chauvinistic soldier admired passionately despite his nationality. The philosophy of the tenement dwellers was 'Down with Science, Sentiment and the Fair Sex' and they engaged in a good-natured war of words with their scientific neighbours which sometimes spilled into high-spirited horseplay. Scott described how: 'Tonight Oates, captain in a smart cavalry regiment, has been "scrapping" over chairs and tables with Debenham, a young Australian student'. Oates in fact spent much of his time in the stables, conscientiously tending the ponies with Anton, who worried about his one-legged girlfriend back in Russia. The latter was so perturbed by the darkness and the dancing Aurora Australis that he left cigarettes out on the ice to appease these spirits of winter. Anton became devoted to Oates. When asked about him he would reply in his broken English that Captain Oates was good to horses, good to Anton.

Scott was pleased with 'the universally amicable spirit'. The relatively happy and relaxed atmosphere was due, at least in part, to the fact that everybody was busy. There were scientific experiments to be carried out, instrument readings to be taken, sledging equipment to be checked and mended. Cherry-Garrard revived the *South Polar Times* and painted a comfortable picture of daily life during the Polar winter.

> Probably anyone arriving here from England would be surprised to find how much work there is to be done during a long and dark winter. There are ten ponies to be exercised every day and they seem to get fresher every time they go out, and seals have to be killed and skinned. There is constant work on the sea-ice, collecting fish and other animals for scientific work, taking soundings and measuring the tides. With the care of the dogs and ponies, meteorological observations, night watch for Aurora, working up the results of last season's sledging and preparation for the coming season, there is not much spare time . . . And so we live very comfortable . . . and we are all as fit as we can be.

Ponting caused much amusement when his companions learned that some joker at home had told him that pepper was excellent for warming the feet and that credulously he had brought a case of cayenne with him and was assiduously putting it onto his boots. Sometimes the men played football in the half-light, a game that puzzled the tiny Anton exceedingly, though he joined in. Atkinson was the star, even though Gran had played for the Norwegian national team. Bowers stuck to his daily routine of going outside in his pyjamas to collect snow to rub himself down to keep clean. Wilson sometimes joined him, but the others preferred to let the dirt accumulate.

The *South Polar Times* also gave a lively picture of the evening lecture programme instituted by Scott. Oates was an unexpected success with his wry talk on horse management or 'mismanagement', which reduced his audience to helpless laughter. Invited to give a second performance he concluded with the story of a young lady who, arriving late at an elegant dinner party, blamed the slowness of the cab-horse. 'Ah, perhaps he was a jibber,' suggested her hostess. 'Oh, no,' smiled the damsel, all unknowing, 'he was a bugger. I heard the cabby say so several times.' Ponting's magic lantern shows were also very popular, particularly his exquisite pictures of Japan. In her book on Captain Oates, Sue Limb recounts how Oates would say to Meares, 'Coming to the pictures tonight, dearie?' He often called Meares 'dearie' and Atkinson, his other boon companion, 'Jane'. It is tempting to draw certain conclusions but there is no evidence of homosexual leanings. The badinage and nicknames, like the horse play, were probably no more than the humour of a closed male society.

Another well-attended lecture was by Atkinson on scurvy. He like others before him suggested that tainted tinned food might be a primary cause. Scott himself, however, recognized from the *Discovery* experience the value of fresh meat in avoiding the disease and insisted that his men ate fresh seal and penguin meat despite the reluctance of several, including Edgar Evans.

On 22 June, they celebrated Midwinter Day, the equivalent of Christmas Day and still the high-holiday of Antarctica. After lunch Cherry-Garrard handed Scott the first edition of the *South Polar Times*. As Debenham described with some amusement: 'A silhouette of the Owner by Bill was very good but, as it represents him with his hair awry as it always is here, he didn't like it at all and said, "Well I'm damned, I didn't think I was so ugly."' Later that day, as blizzards rampaged around the hut, they ate a 'gorgeous' dinner of seal soup, roast beef and Yorkshire pudding, plum pudding, mince pies, crystallized fruits, chocolates, custards, jellies and cake, with sherry, Heidsieck 1904 vintage champagne, brandy punch and liqueurs – a degree of luxury and sophistication which would have amused and surprised the plain-living Amundsen, celebrating over at the Bay of Whales more restrainedly by eating 'a little more than usual' and smoking a cigar.[2] Birdie Bowers devised a fine candle-lit Christmas tree out of ski sticks decked with skua feathers and gifts from Oriana Wilson's sister and there were toasts and speeches galore. Oates danced the lancers with Anton and nearly everyone had too much to drink.

However, this jollity marked a watershed. The new sledging season was approaching, with everything that implied. Scott felt the mantle of responsibility settle even more firmly on his shoulders. He was also concerned about a strange quest which three of his men were about to attempt – the famous 'Worst Journey in the World'. Wilson had persuaded Scott to allow him to lead an expedition in the depths of the Antarctic winter to the emperor penguin rookery at Cape Crozier. Previous explorers thought that the male penguins tended the eggs during the winter months but no one had proved it. Neither was it known when the eggs hatched. Wilson hoped to answer some of these questions and by retrieving some eggs and studying their embryology to explore the link between birds and reptiles. The scheme had been in Wilson's mind since the discovery of their breeding ground at Cape Crozier nine years earlier and he had revealed this ambition to Cherry-Garrard in London.

Shackleton had vetoed a similar proposal from his men and the more cautious Scott was initially very reluctant to allow Wilson to take such a risk. He would be battling against gale-force winds, appallingly low temperatures and a circuitous route of some seventy miles of deeply crevassed ice and cliff. Twice during the winter he had taken Wilson for a walk to try to dissuade him, but without success. He could not find it in his heart to disappoint him and reasoned that some useful experience would be gained for the Polar attempt. More would be learned about the conditions on the Barrier, and he asked Wilson to experiment with diet, trying out different proportions of fats, carbohydrates and proteins. He allowed Wilson to take Cherry-Garrard and Bowers, whom Wilson described in a letter to Ory as 'the two best sledgers of the whole Expedition'.[3] Cherry-Garrard thought he might have done better to take Lashly rather than himself, but described how Wilson had a prejudice against seamen for a journey of that type on the grounds that 'They don't take enough care of themselves, and they *will* not look after their clothes'.

And so 'the weirdest bird's-nesting expedition' began.[4] Ponting took a flashlight photograph and Scott saw them off with a mixture of hope and foreboding, writing in his journal: 'This winter travel is a new and bold venture, but the right men have gone to attempt it. All good luck go with them!' Cherry-Garrard's moving and evocative book, *The Worst Journey in the World* captures their excitement and apprehension: '. . . three men, one of whom at any rate is feeling a little frightened, stand panting and sweating out in McMurdo Sound.' Their two nine-foot sledges were lashed one behind the other and carried between them some 750 pounds of food and equipment. The surface they had to cross was considered unsuitable for dogs or ponies and so they were to manhaul. They had given up the idea of going on skis because they felt too inexperienced to use them in the darkness. Wilson warned Ory that the trek would be 'a regular snorter' but this proved something of an understatement.[5]

Existing on a diet of pemmican, biscuit, butter and tea the three men tried to adjust to camping in the dark, finding that everything took much longer. Close to the Barrier the temperature dropped to -47°F. and then -56°F. A badly frostbitten

Cherry-Garrard painted a ghastly picture of the nineteen days it took to reach Cape Crozier. 'I for one had come to that point of suffering at which I did not really care if only I could die without much pain . . . It was the darkness that did it. I don't believe minus seventy temperatures would be bad in daylight, not comparatively bad, when you could see where you were going . . .' Their clothes became so frozen that it took two men to bend them into the required shape. One morning Cherry-Garrard went outside the tent, raised his head to look around 'and found I could not move it back'. He had to walk for four hours with his head stuck at a curious angle. The only solace was the magical lights of the Aurora Australis which sometimes danced overhead, though Cherry-Garrard could not appreciate it with his poor eyesight. It was too cold for him to wear his spectacles.

The temperature continued to fall and the lowest recorded on the journey was an unimaginable -77.5°F. The question inevitably arose of whether to go on. '"I think we are all right as long as our appetites are good," said Bill [Wilson]. Always patient, self-possessed, unruffled, he was the only man on earth, as I believe, who could have led this journey.' He also kept a close eye on the state of their feet, recognizing that: 'We couldn't afford to risk getting anyone crippled in the feet above all else.' Bowers remained unremittingly cheerful and somehow the party struggled onwards. Finding it too hard now to pull both sledges they resorted to relaying, progressing a bare two or three miles a day but walking three times the distance. Sometimes Cherry-Garrard felt like howling. They were now among deep crevasses and only a fleeting sliver of moonlight saved them from tumbling into an abyss.

On 15 July, Wilson's wedding anniversary, after a terrible struggle through crevasses and pressure ridges they reached their destination. Choosing a position high on the cliffs overlooking the rookery they began building themselves an igloo of rock and snow with a canvas roof to be heated with a blubber stove. Wilson named it Oriana Hut. On 19 July they set out to look for the penguins but could find no way of scrambling down on to the sea-ice, though they could hear 'the emperors calling'. Their cries echoed tantalizingly in the silence. There was no alternative but to return to camp and try again. The second attempt was more successful. Working their way over the pressure ridges they at last found a way down through the ice like a foxhole, and there below them were the emperors, huddled under the cliff, incubating their eggs. They were gazing on a sight never before seen by man, but Wilson was disappointed to find a mere hundred or so birds compared with the several thousands he had been expecting. While the startled penguins kicked up a rumpus, Birdie and Wilson lowered themselves down and collected five eggs. They also killed and skinned three birds to provide fuel for the blubber stove.

However, the weather was closing in, there was a bitter wind and in the struggle to regain the hut short-sighted Cherry-Garrard stumbled and broke the two eggs he had been clutching in his fur mitts. The men were frozen, exhausted and near the end of their tether by the time they reached shelter. That night a gob of hot fat from the blubber stove hit Wilson in the eye, leaving this normally stoical man writhing in agony, afraid that he was blinded. He admitted that they had 'reached bed-rock' – strong language for Wilson – but his belief that things would improve was misplaced. A storm blew up which sounded to Cherry-Garrard 'as though the world was having a fit of hysterics'. In the maelstrom, the tent, which had been pitched against the igloo to store equipment, blew away. All they could do was struggle to bring what was left into the igloo: 'to get that gear in we fought against solid walls of black snow which flowed past us and tried to hurl us down the slope.'

Conditions grew yet more desperate when the canvas roof of the hut ripped off, leaving them exposed. Wilson yelled to the others to get deep into their sleeping bags. When Cherry-Garrard tried to help him, 'Wilson leaned over and said, "*Please,* Cherry . . ." and his voice was terribly anxious. I know he felt responsible: feared it was he who had brought us to this ghastly end.' Ironically, it was Wilson's birthday. As Bowers later described, 'I was resolved to keep warm and beneath my debris covering I paddled my feet and sang all the songs and hymns I knew to pass the time. I could occasionally thump Bill, and as he still moved I knew he was alive all right – what a birthday for him!'[6]

However, what happened now was close to a miracle and Wilson and Bowers probably interpreted it as such. Bowers thanked God for his mercy in his diary. The hurricane abated, the three of them were still alive, though barely and, most extraordinary of all, their tent had landed intact just half a mile away. As Cherry-Garrard wrote, 'We were so thankful we said nothing.' A return journey to Cape Evans without a tent would have been well nigh impossible. Wilson was determined to take no more risks, although Birdie actually urged another visit to the penguins. Failing that he suggested that the Polar party should return that way rather than back down the Beardmore Glacier. The frozen men, somewhat surprised at still being alive, packed up and turned their steps homewards. The remnants of their camp would be found by Sir Vivian Fuchs during the Commonwealth Trans-Antarctic Expedition of the mid 1950s. Birdie was in the best physical condition, exactly the 'sturdy, active, undefeatable little man' lauded by Scott,[7] but 'Bill looked very bad' according to Cherry-Garrard, while he himself felt so weak that he had at last agreed to accept Birdie's offer of the loan of his eiderdown, a gesture of such generosity that it almost reduced him to tears.

The return journey was so grim that Cherry-Garrard wrote that its horrors were blurred in his memory. What he did remember was that as they neared Cape Evans Wilson and Birdie had quite an angry argument about its exact location, the only time they had ever squabbled. He attributed it to the sudden release of tension at nearing home. He also remembered their arrival back at Cape Evans, three frostbitten emaciated scarecrows who were greeted by a cry of 'Good God! Here is the Crozier Party'. Debenham described how: 'Three ice-clothed objects came in, sooty, lank-haired and clothed in an armour of ice.' Some wag suggested a can opener be fetched to release them.

And so ended this extraordinary Winter Journey. Each man had lost weight but not as much as expected. Cherry-Garrard's sleeping bag had on the other hand increased in weight from 18 pounds to 45 pounds entirely due to the extra burden of his frozen sweat and breath. Scott was relieved to have his men safely home. Every time the weather had deteriorated around Cape Evans his thoughts had turned anxiously to the Cape Crozier party. He now gave full vent to his feelings in his diary: '. . . to me and to everyone who has remained here the result of this effort is the appeal it makes to our imagination as one of the most gallant stories in Polar History. That men should wander forth in the depth of a Polar night to face the most dismal cold and the fiercest gales in darkness is something new; that they should have persisted in this effort in spite of every adversity . . . is heroic. It makes a tale for our generation which I hope may not be lost in the telling.'

However, this would also have been a fitting tribute to the journey he was about to undertake and which would truly prove to be 'the worst journey in the world'.

13

'Miserable, Utterly Miserable'

Twenty-third August saw the end of the Antarctic night, but a gale blotted out the returning light. It was three more days before the sun once again gilded the floes. 'It was glorious to stand bathed in brilliant sunshine once more. We felt very young, sang and cheered . . .' wrote the forty-three-year-old Scott euphorically. They also drank champagne and even the animals perked up in the sparkling air, going 'half dotty' in Teddy Evans's words. The expedition had come through the winter relatively unscathed. The Cape Crozier party had returned safely, if on their last legs. Atkinson had got lost in a blizzard, blundered about for five hours but survived, albeit with a badly frostbitten hand disfigured with slug-like blisters. 'The other excitement', as Wilson put it, 'was that one of the ponies very nearly died of colic.'

Everyone's thoughts now turned to the Polar journey. However, as Scott began to lay his final plans, the expedition's finances back in England were in a sorry state. The news of Amundsen's arrival in the Bay of Whales had reached England and did not help Scott's appeal. Instead of arousing patriotic generosity, people wondered why they should subscribe to an expedition which now looked likely to fail. Kathleen Scott had received the unwelcome information that there was barely enough money to meet outgoings until the end of October. The London and the New Zealand agents between them needed £1,500. Kathleen sensibly suggested that the expedition's accounts be published to show how desperate things were and set off on a round of energetic fund-raising. Unlike Scott she felt no embarrassment, though she baulked at an offer from the *Daily Mirror*, who wanted to print a photograph of Peter to help launch a new appeal. She could not 'bear my weeny being bandied about in the half-penny press'. Practical as ever, she also doubted whether it would really raise much money. However, her natural resilience was dented by an unusual sense of foreboding. On 20 September she wrote: 'Rather a horrid day today. I woke up having had a bad dream about you, and then Peter came very close to me and said emphatically: "Daddy won't come back," as tho' in answer to my silly thoughts. Happily I am not often silly.'

Scott, meanwhile, was ignorant of the latest financial crisis, but he did know that on the voyage south he had failed to raise the funds for which he had hoped. He confided in Ponting more than once that 'he was troubled by the fact that the cost of the enterprise had greatly exceeded his estimate, and that there would be a considerable deficit to face'. In mid-October he gathered his men together, explained that the expedition was in debt and asked all those who could to forgo their pay for the next twelve months. Those men who could afford to responded with warmth and generosity and Scott signed a formal note of indemnity, relieving the expedition fund of the liability for a number of salaries including his own.

Meanwhile, as the weeks drew on the sledging equipment was readied and dogs and ponies exercised. Scott spent much time at his lino-covered table in his cubicle, the 'holy of holies' as the others called it, going over the details for the assault on the Pole with Bowers, checking and rechecking lists of equipment and calculations. The latter included 'Sunny Jim' Simpson's data on the weather and temperature likely to be encountered on the journey, as well as other information on the most suitable diet and the amount of food and fuel to be carried. In the light of the experience of the winter party, more fat was added to the rations for the Polar team, which they called 'the summit rations'. In fact, Scott regarded Bowers as the only man he could trust to get the figures right.

Gathering his men together on 13 September Scott presented his detailed plans. They followed the principles he had outlined in May when he told them that he intended to rely on ponies and then on manhauling. His experiences during the depot journey had failed to convince him that the dogs could be taken far and he had recorded that: 'With this sentiment the whole company appeared to be in sympathy. Everyone seems to distrust the dogs when it comes to glacier and summit.' Indeed, Bowers had positively welcomed the news of the manhauling 'in these days of the supposed decadence of the British race'.[1] It seemed the correct and manly thing to do, though it meant that the Polar party would have to manhaul for over 1,200 miles.

Scott now explained that his plan assumed a journey of nearly 1,600 miles to the Pole and back in 144 days. The southern party would consist of twelve men, only four of whom would go to the Pole. Others would support them up to the final stages of the journey, turning back successively. The motors would set out in advance of the main party, dragging fuel and forage. The ponies would pull light loads until Corner Camp and then full loads to One Ton Camp and beyond. The dog teams would pull more

215

fodder for the ponies. The intention was to shoot the ponies when they had reached the end of their endurance and to send the dogs back. After that it would be manhauling all the way to the Pole and back. Scott wrote in his diary that 'The scheme seems to have earned full confidence: it remains to play the game out'. He also recorded his gratitude to Bowers and Edgar Evans for the fact that 'there is not a single detail of our equipment which is not arranged with the utmost care and in accordance with the tests of experience'.

Scott was an ardent student of human nature. He had spent much of the winter observing his companions and writing shrewd rather than universally flattering pen-portraits, many of which were edited out or toned down in the published version of his diary. His observations also helped him decide how to deploy his men on the southern journey. The main party was to include Wilson, Bowers, Oates, Cherry-Garrard together with Atkinson, Wright, and Petty Officers Evans, Crean and Keohane. The advance motor party was to be under the command of Teddy Evans, whom Scott described on the eve of his departure in a letter to his agent in New Zealand as 'a thoroughly well-meaning little man' but a bit of a duffer outside naval work and unsuited to be his second-in-command. These comments chime with similar ones Scott made in his diary in May of that year, which were excised before it was published, including that 'he is not a rock to be built on' . . . 'well meaning but slow to learn . . . very desirous to help everyone, but he is mentally incapable of doing so'. They seem to reflect his settled view of his second-in-command.[2]

Of course, the plans fuelled intense speculation about who would be in the Polar party. Wilson wondered whether he would have the chance to go to the Pole but reflected that there were many 'young bloods' more youthful and fitter than he. He was, however, sorry to realize that the returning party would arrive too late to sail home on the *Terra Nova*, or to answer the letters she would have brought, but wrote: 'Obviously I cannot shirk the southern sledge journey on this account, having come down here to take part in it.' Oates tried to reckon up his chances. 'I think I have a fairish chance that is if Scott and I don't fall out. It will be pretty tough having four months [with him], he fusses dreadfully.'[3] Ponting recorded a telling discussion in the privacy of his darkroom:

> The point was raised as to what a man should do if he were to break down on the Polar journey, thereby becoming a burden to others. Oates unhesitatingly and emphatically expressed the opinion that there was only one possible course – self-sacrifice. He thought that a pistol should be carried, and that 'If anyone breaks down he should have the privilege of using it'.

In the month before departure there was a series of mishaps. The dogs were attacked by a mysterious disease and several died, while some of the ponies looked very shaky. Petty Officer Forde's hand was badly frostbitten, making him unfit for sledging; Clissold, the excellent cook who should have gone with the motor party, tumbled off a small iceberg and concussed himself while posing or 'ponting' as it had come to be known – Griffith Taylor, with his usual wit, had defined 'to pont' as 'to spend a deuce of a time posing in an uncomfortable position'. Debenham hurt his knee playing football on the ice, also for the benefit of Ponting's camera. The photographer later described a furious Scott advancing on him with the words: 'So that's another member of the expedition *you've jiggered up!*' Scott apologized later the same evening and was 'so charming I loved him all the more, and as one realized the anxieties with which he was weighted one's whole heart went out to him in pity'.[4] Ponting had in fact spent some time instructing Scott in the rudiments of photography. Scott was 'pleased as a boy' though he made many mistakes and grew impatient.

There is a sense of frustration in Scott's writing as the time for departure approached, as if he felt that he alone understood the seriousness of what lay ahead while the others treated it all as a bit of a lark. Ponting put his finger on it when he described Scott's behaviour over the winter months and in particular the periods of moodiness and reticence:

> It was obvious on such occasions that he was silently weighted with the problems of the future – so infinitely increased by the heavy losses to his transport. When this mood was upon him I felt instinctively that he was oppressed by the sense of obligation to his country to push the venture to success, be the enhanced difficulties what they may.

Scott was in the classic trap of doubting his own capacity to pull the venture off, but being afraid, both because of his buttoned-up character and leadership responsibilities, to reveal his uncertainties to anyone or be seen to be seeking advice. This left him at times in a state of nervous indecision.

After the disaster of the depot journey Scott was particularly worried about the ponies. As Oates fed them up and exercised them Scott noted their characteristics as carefully as he did those of his men. There were ten – Victor, Nobby (who had had the narrow escape from the killer whales), Jehu, Chinaman, Michael,

Snatcher, Bones, James Pigg, Christopher – an animal of truly
fiendish temperament – and Snippets. Oates's view remained that
the ponies were 'without exception the greatest lot of crocks I
have ever seen that were seriously meant for use'.[5] He too was
worried about the weight of responsibility resting on his shoulders – the success of the whole expedition was predicated on the
ponies' performance and his anxiety led to anger with Scott for
expecting so much from such an unpromising bunch. He wrote:

> I am of course very annoyed as it is perfectly wretched
> starting off with a lot of cripples and Scott won't believe
> how bad they are, he thinks I am always making them
> out worse than they are. Scott has put two or three
> people's backs up lately and Meares, who looks after
> the dogs . . . had a regular row with him, myself I dis-
> like Scott intensely and would chuck the whole thing
> if it was not that we are a British Expedition and must
> beat those Norwegians.

He also wrote that though Scott had always been very civil to him
and they had the reputation for getting on, 'the fact of the matter
is he is not straight, it is himself first the rest nowhere'.[6] However,
he wrote those comments when he was hungry and acknowledged
that he might feel more kindly towards his leader when he had
eaten. A letter sent on the very eve of his departure to his mother
told her that if anything happened to him she should remember
that 'when a man is having a hard time he says hard things about
other people which he would regret afterwards'.[7]

Oates's reservations about Scott after a long winter spent with
him were echoed to an extent by Debenham. In a letter to his
mother he set out his views on Scott with complete frankness:

I must tell you what I think of him. I am afraid I am
very disappointed in him, tho' my faith died very hard.
There's no doubt he can be very nice and the interest he
takes in our scientific work is immense, he is also a fine
sledger himself and as an organiser is splendid. But there
I'm afraid one must stop. His temper is very uncertain
and leads him to absurd lengths even in simple arguments. In crises he acts very peculiarly. In one, where
Atkinson was lost for 6 hours in a blizzard, I thought he
acted splendidly but in all the others I have been quite
disgusted with him. What he decides is often enough
the right thing I expect, but he loses all control of his
tongue and makes us all feel wild . . . but it is difficult
to judge one's leader . . . But the marvellous part of it is
that the Owner is the single exception to a general sense
of comradeship and jollity amongst all of us.[8]

However, like Oates's, these remarks must be taken in their context. The winter had been a debilitating time for everyone and
Scott could undoubtedly be a martinet. The stress of planning the
coming journey, his responsibility for everyone's safety, his fear
that Amundsen would rob them of the prize, had not improved
his usually quick temper and sharp tongue. The remarkable thing
is that Scott's relationship with most of his men was still so good.

The two motor sledges set out on their pioneering journey on
24 October with Teddy Evans, Day, Lashly and Hooper, each
pulling three loaded sledges with orders to proceed via Corner
Camp to One Ton Depot and then south to 80°30′S. Scott
watched them depart towards the Barrier with an anxious eye. If
the motors worked they would make the journey to the foot of
the great Beardmore Glacier much easier.

On the eve of his own departure Scott wrote to Kathleen and reassured her about his attitude to Amundsen:

> I don't know what to think of Amundsen's chances. If he gets to the Pole it must be before we do, as he is bound to travel fast with dogs, and pretty certain to start early. On this account I decided at a very early date to act exactly as I should have done had he not existed. Any attempt to race must have wrecked my plan, besides which it doesn't appear the sort of thing one is out for. You can rely on my not doing or saying anything foolish, only I am afraid you must be prepared for the chance of finding our venture much belittled. After all, it is the work that counts not the applause that follows.[9]

In fact Amundsen had set out with four companions on 15 October and was already beyond the 80th parallel. He had had to abort an earlier attempt with seven companions in September, returning after seven days because of the extreme cold. An ugly disagreement had ensued in which one of his most senior men, Johansen, criticized Amundsen in front of the other men for abandoning him and a frostbitten colleague on the ice in the race to regain their hut. Amundsen ruthlessly dropped Johansen and two others from the Polar party when it set out again.

Scott's letter of farewell to his 'dear, dear Mother' was very affectionate, reassuring her that he had never been fitter, that his 'little cavalcade' was ready for the long southern journey and that it would not be long until he returned. He admitted that 'there will be a tough bit at the end' but he wrote of his belief that he and his companions would pull through.[10] Scott also wrote to

Edgar Evans's wife, referring to the petty officer as 'such an old friend of mine' and praising his contribution to the expedition.[11] To Birdie Bowers's mother he wrote a glowing tribute to Birdie's energy, tact and popularity, concluding with the poignant remark, 'He has such a happy knack of coming through difficulties with a smiling face that I haven't any doubt he will be as flourishing in health and spirits when you see him next . . .'[12]

On 1 November 1911 Scott and his party set out at last. In the rush Queen Alexandra's Union Jack flag for the Pole was left behind, but Scott was able to phone Cape Evans from Hut Point. Meares had laid an aluminium-clad telephone line between the two, something which Scott found wonderful in this primitive land. Ironically, it was the Norwegian Gran who carried the flag on the first lap, skiing rapidly after the party. 'The irony of fate, my dear Gran,' was Scott's response.[13] Ponting followed the party out to Safety Camp and his cinematograph captured the scene of small figures plodding off to an unknown destiny. Scott was feeling fatalistic. He had written: 'I am past despondency. Things must take their course . . . All things considered, I shall be glad to get away and put our fortune to the test . . . The future is in the lap of the gods; I can think of nothing left undone to deserve success.'

However, as he had often observed, fortune had as much to do with success as merit. And fortune did not appear to be smiling on him. In the first place 'those dreadful motors' failed.[14] One broke down just fourteen miles from Hut Point, the big end of one of its four cylinders broken. The other managed to crawl nearly fifty miles to just beyond Corner Camp. Lashly described how the 'trouble always staring us in the face' was the overheating of the engines.[15] A recent analysis, in 1982, of some of the fuel left at Cape Evans showed that it was of low octane, which probably accounted for the overheating problems.[16]

Scott was disappointed but wrote to Lord Howard de Walden, who had sponsored the development of the sledges, to say that there was nothing wrong with the principles behind them. He predicted correctly that there was a big future for traction motors of this sort in Canada and other places and urged him to ensure that the patents were properly protected. However, Oates had scant sympathy over the motors' fate, writing grumpily in his diary, 'Three motors at £3000 each, 19 ponies at £5 each, 32 dogs at 30/- each. If Scott fails to get to the Pole he jolly well deserves it.' The motor party, Teddy Evans, Day, Lashly and Hooper, now switched to manhauling, and, once beyond One Ton Depot, began laying smaller depots in advance of the main party.

In the second place the weather was dire. Scott was to face conditions on this journey that he had never foreseen and which he had not thought possible. At first, though, they made good progress and Oates recorded Scott's satisfaction with the ponies' performance while Scott wrote 'even Oates is pleased'. However, within the first week blizzards struck and on 12 November Scott was recording weather that was 'horrid, overcast, gloomy, snowy. Our spirits became very low'. Cherry-Garrard was right when he observed that 'indefinite conditions always tried Scott most'. The ponies were clearly faltering under their burdens of 500 pounds apiece and Scott's diary becomes increasingly preoccupied with them – 'I am very anxious about these beasts – very anxious . . .' – and deeply appreciative of Oates's efforts – 'if they pull through well, all the thanks will be due to Oates'. Oates had even invented a fringed device to save the ponies from snowblindness. As Teddy Evans wrote: 'The Soldier hated to see his animals suffering . . .'[17] However, there was little he could do to protect them from the cold. Bowers described how: 'Huge icicles form under [the ponies'] noses during the march. Victor generally rubs his off on my sleeve.'

Oates was soon warning Scott that he doubted whether the beasts would pull through. He himself was having the devil of a time with the temperamental Christopher. Once harnessed there was no stopping him and Oates was forced to cling grimly to his bridle until the end of each day's march, thus forgoing a midday rest and food, which affected his stamina. He had words with Scott, complaining that he was a very difficult man to get along with. Scott also seems to have argued with Bowers, accusing him of overloading some of the sledges. However, Bowers was more forgiving than Oates and wrote that he could 'quite understand his feelings . . . and after our experience of last year a bad day like this makes him fear our beasts are going to fail us'. Tensions were beginning to tell and understandably so.

On 15 November the party struggled in to One Ton Depot to find a note from Teddy Evans saying he and his companions had gone ahead. Scott called a council of war to discuss how best to proceed and according to Cherry-Garrard it was at this stage that he finally abandoned any thought of trying to get any of the ponies up the glacier. It was decided they would take just enough fodder to reach the foot of the Beardmore Glacier and then kill any surviving ponies. Cherry-Garrard, who had moved into Scott's tent for a while enjoyed the lively conversation: 'we had a jolly lunch meal, discussing authors. Barrie, Galsworthy and others are personal friends of Scott. Someone told Max Beerbohm that he was like Captain Scott, and immediately, so Scott assured us, he grew a beard.'

Six days later the main party caught up with Teddy Evans and his group at the appointed rendezvous. Wilson noted that they were extremely hungry – it was the consequence of manhauling and the significance of this, given what was to come, was not fully appreciated. They had been amusing themselves by reading

The Pickwick Papers and looked, in Teddy Evans's words, as if they had come out of 'a bull-fight in a barn' with hair and beards full of loose reindeer hairs from their sleeping bags. They were instructed to march ahead of the main party, erecting marker cairns at intervals and selecting campsites.

Scott had now decided that it would be easier for the ponies to rest by day when the temperatures were higher and to march by night when the more frozen ground would provide a better surface for them. The dogs, driven by the enigmatic Meares and Dimitri Gerov, followed behind in excellent form, but the ponies continued to struggle and Scott's mood grew sombre. Oates described Scott's face as 'like a tired sea boot'. On 24 November the first pony, Jehu, was shot and fed to the dogs, an event which Scott found traumatic and in which he could take no part. Oates, who did the deed, regarded it as a brutal act while Bowers tried to comfort himself: 'A year's care and good feeding, three weeks' work with good treatment . . . and then a painless end. If anybody can call that cruel I cannot either understand it or agree with them.'

Day and Hooper were now sent back to Cape Evans, taking a sledge and two sick dogs. Atkinson, who had been leading Jehu, joined the manhaulers. Two days later Middle Barrier Depot was laid, but progress was disappointingly slow across the soft surface of the Barrier and the scenery monotonous and depressing. On 28 November Chinaman was shot and his driver Wright began manhauling. There were now just eight ponies left.

The next day the party passed Scott's farthest south of 1902 at 82°17′ and it cheered their spirits. Less then seventy miles now separated them from the Beardmore and ahead lay the dramatic peaks of Mount Markham. What also cheered their spirits was the fact that they were adding pony meat to their hoosh. Hunger had overcome sentiment and the meat gave them vitamins that their diet otherwise lacked. No lime juice had been brought – Atkinson had given a lecture on scurvy during the winter and Debenham wrote in his diary: 'Tho' the incidence of scurvy in the Navy has decreased since lime-juice was made a ration, it is the general opinion that lime-juice by itself is not a preventative.' They pushed on at an average speed of about two miles an hour but with the ponies up to their knees in snow. On 1 December the Southern Barrier Depot was laid and Oates dispatched the troublesome Christopher, who, true to form, was the only pony not to be killed cleanly. He moved as Oates shot him and perhaps his hand had been less than steady for Christopher had been his special charge. The pony careered about the camp before being finally caught and killed.

Bowers wrote revealingly in his diary: 'Meares and Dimitri do all the cutting up as the dogs do the whole march in three hours and they have little else to do for the rest of the day. The dogs are doing splendidly; when one sees how well our two teams have done I must say that Amundsen's chance of having forestalled us with 120 dogs looks good.'

As they continued to inch forward with the remnants of the ponies, Scott observed the difference snowshoes could make, noting that Nobby came along splendidly for some five miles while wearing a pair: 'There is no doubt that these snow-shoes are *the* thing for ponies . . .' However, this begs the question of why, particularly after the experience on the depot journey, the winter months had not been spent trying to design some effective snowshoes. They had been discussed after one of Oates's lectures on horse management but little seems to have been done. Perhaps Oates still at bottom distrusted them and thought them merely a fad of the fussy Scott's.

They were now nearing the Beardmore, but the conditions were still poor and they had to push the ponies onward. Bowers's pony Victor had to be killed because the fodder was running out. Scott broke the news to Bowers and the only trace of bitterness in his whole diary was now: 'Good old Victor! He has always had a biscuit out of my ration, and he ate his last before the bullet sent him to his rest . . . I feel sorry for a beast that has been my constant companion and care for so long.' However, they were all now eating pony meat with increasing relish. Wilson noted that it tasted like boiled beef and cheerfully recorded a supper of 'hoosh with plenty of Victor in it'.

Scott had been trusting that the weather would turn but he was disappointed. On 3 December a violent gale and thick snow made progress almost impossible. Scott felt his luck was 'preposterous'. The next day brought blizzards and Scott brooded on his ill-fortune, knowing that Shackleton had faced quite different conditions at precisely the same time of year. On 4 December Bowers recorded: 'Wild one of Shackleton's quartette [sic] wrote in his diary about December 15th. "This is the first day for a month that I can say we have not had glorious weather." Either he must have had a phenomenally fine season or we have an extraordinary bad one. The sailors are debating who is the Jonah.' Making agonizingly slow progress they reached a point twelve miles from the gateway to the glacier, where another pony was killed. Scott hoped that just one more march would see them camped on the Beardmore, but 5 December brought weather from hell. Another blizzard descended of such ferocity that 'One cannot see the next tent, let alone the land'.

'What on earth does such weather mean at this time of year?' Scott railed. 'It is more than our share of ill-fortune . . .' The blizzard brought the greatest snowfall Scott had ever seen.

Oates and Bowers struggled to keep the ponies from being snowed up though the dogs were snug enough in their snow holes. The warmer temperatures that came with the blizzard meant wet tents and soggy sleeping bags. Their bodies lay in pools of water – 'a snipe marsh' Bowers called it. Keohane saw the funny side and Scott recorded his rhyme: 'The snow is all melting and everything's afloat. If this goes on much longer we shall have to turn the tent upside down and use it as a boat.' However, Scott's diary of 6 December shows a deep despair. 'Miserable, utterly miserable. We have camped in the "Slough of Despond" . . . A hopeless feeling descends on one and is hard to fight off.' He had no option but to break into the summit rations. Men and animals had to be fed even though they were making no progress.

Scott wondered whether the bad weather was affecting Amundsen. Was it widespread or was he the victim of 'exceptional local conditions'? If the latter, it was hard to know that while his party was struggling against adversity 'others go smilingly forward in the sunshine'. In fact, Amundsen was also suffering from blizzards in early December but was still able to make progress. On his worst day he covered two and a half miles and on others was achieving over twenty-five – a tribute to the pulling power of dogs and the skiing ability of his team. His route to the Polar plateau had taken him up the Heilberg Glacier and the Devil's Glacier, reckoned by some to be an even greater challenge than the Beardmore. However, he had been able to drive eighty miles farther south than Scott before reaching the mountains. As Scott and his men shivered in their sopping tents on the third day of the blizzard and he lamented 'the horrid feeling that this is a really bad season', Amundsen had passed Shackleton's record of 88°23′S and was within a hundred miles of the Pole. The knowledge would have infuriated loyal little Bowers, who was wondering how the 'back-handed, sneaking ruffian' was faring.

It was not until 9 December that the dejected group could move on. Teddy Evans described how Oates had spent much of the blizzard crouching behind a drifted-up snow wall to be near his ponies: 'We could not help laughing at him, after the blizzard, when he wrung the icy water out of his clothing. His personal bag was in a dreadful state. His sodden tobacco had discoloured everything, and as he squeezed his spare socks and gloves a stream of nicotine-stained water flowed out.'[18] Yet despite his efforts the ponies could barely stagger, belly-deep in snow, and had to be flogged on, a task the men found sickening. That evening, at a place aptly named 'Shambles Camp' close to the entry to the glacier, Oates dispatched the last of them. Wilson's relief was palpable. 'Thank God . . . we begin the heavier work ourselves,' he wrote – a sentiment that Amundsen would have found incomprehensible, particularly as three quarters of their journey still lay ahead of them. The unsentimental and wholly pragmatic Norwegian had worked out his own plans to the last detail: 'In my calculations I figured out exactly the precise day on which I planned to kill each dog as its usefulness should end for drawing the diminishing supplies on the sleds and its usefulness should begin as food for the men.'[19]

Scott now divided his men into three manhauling teams for the ascent up the Beardmore. He took Wilson, Oates and Petty Officer Evans in his group. Teddy Evans took Atkinson, Wright and Lashly – Scott had been losing patience with Teddy Evans, believing he was not keeping his team shipshape and that their increasingly slow progress was due to lack of care. Bowers shared Scott's view, noting that he was sorry to see a deterioration in Evans. Evans, however, took the view with some justice that he and his men had been manhauling much longer than anyone else and that it was therefore quite natural that they should have less stamina. Bowers, Cherry-Garrard, Crean and Keohane were to haul together. It was a gruelling business. Pushing the heavy sledges through deep wet snow in weather so warm was such hard work that some of the men wore only singlets on their torsos. The mild temperature meant that snow goggles misted up with perspiration so quickly that they needed constant wiping. Those who dispensed with them suffered the penalty of snow blindness. However, the Lower Glacier Depot was laid beneath the glacier on 11 December. Meares and Dimitri now turned for home with the dogs. Bowers had reflected on the previous day that 'the dogs are wonderfully fit and will rush him and Dimitri back like the wind'. Cherry-Garrard agreed, writing that Amundsen seemed to have chosen the right form of transport.

Meares was carrying a letter from Scott to Kathleen:

> Things are not so rosy as they might be but we keep our spirits up and say the luck must turn. So far every turn shows the extraordinary good fortune that Shackleton had. This is only to tell you that I can keep up with the rest as well as of old, and that I think of you whenever I stretch tired limbs in a very comfortable sleeping-bag. – P.S. The thought of you is *very* pleasant.[20]

Kathleen meanwhile had been pursuing her vigorous round of social activity in London, 'the antithesis of the pathetic grass widow' as Scott called her.[21] In diaries which Scott would never have the chance to read she described such events as lunch with H.G. Wells, a 'disgusting little bounder' though witty and clever, and Nansen, who had become devoted, writing to her that 'It is nice to know there is a woman so like what one has dreamt of but never met'.

The granite cliffs of the Beardmore looked awesome, rearing above the flat expanse of the Barrier. However, half the party were not in a position to appreciate the sight as they were suffering from snowblindness. An irritable Scott blamed them for their own carelessness. He also blamed his 'tiresome fellow-countrymen' for not having become more proficient skiers. Skis would have made a big difference on the soft snowy surface with its hidden dangers. Bowers agreed, writing: 'The ski are a wonderful protection against crevasses, as the weight is distributed over such a large surface.' Scott's short temper was partly the result of such a bad acid stomach that, as he later told Cherry-Garrard, he feared that he might not be able to go on. He was also worried. The sledges weighed some 700 pounds. Could they really haul them up the 110-mile Beardmore? Moreover, the going was very soft while Shackleton had had the advantage of blue ice – another fact that Scott noted glumly. Scott was carrying the diary of Frank Wild recounting the latter's journey south with Shackleton. Raymond Priestley, geologist on both expeditions, later wrote: 'Throughout the outward journey, Shackleton's team naturally played the part of a ghostly pacemaker in the race', while Cherry-Garrard described how: 'We were working against Shackleton's averages and dates . . .' Scott was determined to outperform his rival. He was also keen to prove that Shackleton had exaggerated the difficulties, referring in his diary to 'Shackleton's overdrawn account'. The word 'overdrawn' was later edited out in the published version.

Bowers wrote a memorable account of the epic struggle which ensued: 'I have never pulled so hard, or so nearly crushed my inside into my backbone by the everlasting jerking with all my strength on the canvas round my unfortunate tummy.' He also observed that on 15 December the 'Owner was in quite a paddy with the weather and said we had not had a good piece of luck since we started. After pitching our tent we discovered a crevasse two feet from the door. I threw an empty oil can down and it echoed down for a horribly long time.' However, if they had only known it, the race was already lost. Amundsen had reached the Pole on 14 December. 'Five weather-beaten, frost-bitten fists' had 'raised the waving flag in the air, and planted it as the first at the geographical South Pole'.[22]

By 17 December, as Amundsen was preparing for his return dash to Framheim, Scott's men, all unknowing, had reached 3,500 feet below the Cloudmaker Mountain, dragging the sledges up the pressure ridges and sliding down the other side, avoiding crevasses that could have accommodated St Paul's Cathedral. To Bowers it was 'the greatest fun in our lives' zooming over the frozen switchback. Wilson was also enjoying himself. After the Winter Journey the Beardmore could hold no horrors for him. He sketched whenever he could, turning out marvellous panoramic drawings. However, they were all beginning to suffer from food fantasies, dreaming of sumptuous banquets. Cherry-Garrard dreamt of big buns and chocolate in a railway station buffet but always awoke just as he was about to sink his teeth into them. Also, as the altitude increased they were becoming increasingly dehydrated with Scott writing, 'We get fearfully thirsty and chip up ice on the march, as well as drinking a great deal of water on halting. Our fuel only just does it . . .'

The Mid-Glacier Depot was laid at 84°33′S in near perfect weather and Scott felt his spirits begin to rise at last. However, he now realized that dogs could have made the climb and it must have given him serious cause for reflection. As Amundsen later wrote: 'Not only can one get the dogs up over the huge glaciers that lead to the plateau, but one can make full use of them the whole way. Ponies, on the other hand, have to be left at the foot of the glacier, while the men themselves have the doubtful pleasure of acting as ponies.'[23]

As Scott's party climbed still higher the glacier broadened out into large fields of ice, 'a hard rippled blue surface like a sea frozen intact while the wind was playing on it', beautiful and awesome in its scale. Oates was beginning to note the poor state of his feet: 'They have been continually wet since leaving Hut Point and now walking along this hard ice in frozen crampons has made rather hay of them . . .' He was also limping from his war wound. Atkinson, who knew him best, told Cherry-Garrard that Oates did not want to go on. However, Oates did not tell Scott at this critical juncture when he was about to name the first returning party.

Scott had been watching his companions closely – he thought Wright, the young Canadian physicist, looked near the end of his tether, bearing out Scott's view, though not Markham's, that the older, more seasoned men could cope better than the youngsters. Scott's own opinion had been confirmed by the Winter Journey to Cape Crozier – Cherry-Garrard, the youngest of the three to make the journey, had been in infinitely worse shape than Wilson or Bowers and had taken longer to recover. This conclusion was personally reassuring to Scott who liked to reflect on the fact that Peary was fifty-two when he reached the North Pole. Scott now selected the youthful Wright and Cherry-Garrard, together with Atkinson and Keohane, to return but it was a painful decision – 'heart-rending' was the word he used in his diary. Cherry-Garrard was cut to the quick and said to Scott that he hoped he had not disappointed him – 'he caught hold of me and said "No-no-no".' Wilson comforted him and said it had been 'a toss up' whether Cherry-Garrard or Oates should go on.

Wright was bitterly disappointed. He had blamed Teddy Evans for some time for the slow progress of their sledge team, writing on one day that 'Teddy is a quitter' and on another 'Teddy, the damn hypocrite, as soon as he sees the Owner's sledge stopped and they watch us come up puts his head down and digs in for all he is worth.' It had come to the point where Teddy Evans was unable to do anything properly, according to Wright, who even criticized his behaviour in the tent. Now Wright gave vent to his emotions in his diary: 'Scott a fool. Teddy goes on. I have to make course back. Too wild to write more tonight. Teddy slack trace seven eighths of today.'

They parted after one last great march together when Scott pushed on like a man possessed. He was 'fairly wound up' in Lashly's words,[24] and Teddy Evans and Atkinson fell the length of their harness down a crevasse before camp was made at 85°S and the Upper Glacier Depot was laid at 7,000 feet. Before they parted Scott instructed Atkinson orally to bring the dog teams south to meet the returning Polar party if Meares had gone back with the ship. Scott also gave the returning party a letter for Kathleen. He told her that they were almost at the top of the glacier and had sufficient provisions. 'We ought to get through,' he wrote.[25]

14

'What Castles One Builds'

The outlook seemed brighter now in every sense. Sunlight danced over sparkling fields of ice and the Beardmore Glacier had been conquered. They were also closing the gap with Shackleton's performance. A more cheerful Scott opened a fresh volume in his journal and inscribed on the flyleaf the names and ages of himself, forty-three, Wilson, thirty-nine, Petty Officer Evans, thirty-seven, Oates, thirty-two, and Bowers, twenty-eight – the very men who would go to the Pole. This gave, he noted carefully, an average age of thirty-six. The entry suggests that Scott had at least decided who was in contention to go to the Pole. Perhaps he had even taken the controversial decision that the final party would consist of five men, not four as originally planned. Whatever the case, he does not seem to have shared these thoughts with anyone, not even with Wilson, whom he cared for and trusted the most. Wilson had sent a letter back for Ory which simply said: 'I am as fit and strong as a horse and have great hopes of being one of the final party.'[1]

For the moment the eight men hauled away across the plateau that would rise to over 10,000 feet. They were divided into two teams, each pulling a sledge carrying twelve weeks' supply of food and fuel. Scott's party consisted, as before, of Wilson, Oates and Petty Officer Evans. Bowers marched with Teddy Evans, Lashly and Crean. They had to concentrate on avoiding treacherous crevasses as wide as Regent Street. Wilson described how: 'Twice we had greenhouse ice with a false bottom – very disagreeable to go over. We have also crossed many wide crevasses bridged well, but sunk and with very rotten lower edges . . .' Nevertheless, they were making good progress and Scott was satisfied that he had 'weeded the weak spots'. On 23 December the surface hardened and the horizon levelled out. A more confident Scott wrote: 'To me for the first time our goal seems really in sight.'

Christmas Eve saw them cover 14 miles. On Christmas Day, Lashly's forty-fourth birthday, Scott coaxed an extra mile out of his men. They covered 15 miles and even Bowers felt the pace. Lashly fell into a crevasse but, as Scott observed, he was tough as nails and relatively unperturbed to find himself dangling in a void 50 feet deep. Lashly wrote: 'It was not of course a very nice sensation, especially on Christmas Day and being my birthday as well. While spinning around in space like I was it took me a few seconds to gather together my thoughts . . . It certainly was not a fairy's palace.'[2] Teddy Evans, Bowers and Crean hauled him out and the latter wished him many happy returns of the day. Lashly's reply was said to be unprintable.

They celebrated Christmas with what Wilson called 'a magnificent lunch' of biscuits, raisins, butter and chocolate. Dinner was 'a regular tightener' with a spectacular hoosh made of pemmican, pony meat, onion powder and curry powder and biscuit crumbs, a pannikin of cocoa, a large piece of plum pudding, five caramels and five pieces of ginger. They had reached the stage where food was becoming an obsession. Teddy Evans described their anxiety as they watched Birdie cook it: 'Had he put too much pepper in? Would he upset it? How many pieces of pony meat would we get each? But the careful little Bowers neither burnt nor upset the hoosh: it was up to our wildest expectations.' However, Bowers himself had noticed some days earlier that 'in spite of all this [food] we are getting noticeably thinner'.

Afterwards they lay contentedly in their sleeping bags and read. Scott was almost too replete to move and recorded with obvious regret that he and Wilson had been unable to finish their plum pudding. That night a sentimental Bowers said to Teddy Evans: 'If all goes well next Christmas, Teddy, we'll get hold of all the poor children we can and just stuff them full of nice things. Won't we?'[3] Their camp (on what they called 'King Edward VII Plateau', though unknown to them it had already been named after King Haakon VII of Norway, courtesy of Amundsen) was a tiny oasis of humanity in that vast frozen emptiness. Evans described their two tiny green tents, 'the only objects that broke the monotony of the great white glittering waste that stretches from the Beardmore Glacier Head to the South Pole'.

They were now at some 8,000 feet and the weather continued fine though the surface was undulating and the manhauling strenuous. As Scott wrote, 'everyone sweated, especially the second team, which had great difficulty keeping up'. Poor Bowers, who set such store by his physical prowess, fretted: '. . . it is fairly heart-breaking to know you are putting your life out hour after hour while they go along with little apparent effort.' His diary also reflected the awful effects of the weather: 'I could not tell if I had a frostbite on my face now, as it is all scales, so are my lips and nose. A considerable amount of red hair is endeavouring to cover up matters.'

They experimented with changing the loading, swapping the

sledges between the two teams. This led Scott to conclude that 'the sledge is the cause of the trouble and taking it out I found that all is due to want of care. The runners are excellent but the structure has been distorted by bad strapping. Bad loading etc.' He continued irritably: 'The party are not done, and I have told them plainly that they must wrestle with the trouble and get it right for themselves. There is no possible reason why they should not get along as easily as we do.' Scott does not appear to have seen what Teddy Evans had noticed – that everyone was losing their springy step. Evans wrote that: 'A man trained to watch over men's health . . . would have seen something amiss,' but Wilson apparently did not. He had not practised medicine since the *Discovery* expedition. The low temperatures – Scott and his men experienced a mean temperature of -19°F on the plateau – were sapping their stamina. They were also suffering from dehydration. They did not have sufficient fuel to melt enough ice to drink and yet, at altitude and in low temperatures, the body quickly loses moisture through perspiration.

Scott was feeling the pressure and the isolation of leadership. 'Steering the party is no light task. One cannot allow one's thoughts to wander as others do, and when, as this afternoon, one gets amongst disturbances, I find it is very worrying and tiring.' Other more recent leaders of Antarctic expeditions such as Roger Mear have described similar exhaustion caused by having continually to motivate and lead.[4] Bowers had earlier let his watch lose time by failing to attend promptly to the nightly instruction of 'wind watches'. An accurate watch was essential to identify noon and thereby to work out longitude by using the sun's position at this time. Scott's watch had, however, remained accurate, avoiding major problems. Scott now found that Bowers had broken their only hypsometer, an instrument used to determine altitude, and vented his frustration on him. The little man described 'an unusual outburst of wrath', mourning that it was 'rather sad to get into the dirt tub with one's leader at this juncture but accidents will happen and this was not carelessness . . .'

As December drew to a close they had reached over 9,000 feet, but the surface had worsened, making the pulling very heavy. On 29 December Scott recorded his satisfaction that the second party were now managing to keep up, but the very next day was expressing fears that they were tiring. He hoped the situation would improve after depoting some of the equipment so that they could move on with lighter loads. 'We have caught up Shackleton's dates. Everything would be cheerful if I could persuade myself that the second party were quite fit to go forward,' he wrote nervously. On New Year's Eve the next depot was laid. The two teams also halted for half a day for the sledges to be stripped down and for the 12-foot runners to be replaced with 10-foot runners to produce a lighter sledge. Lashly, Crean and Edgar Evans laboured in sub-zero temperatures without a proper carpenter's bench and made a good job of it. However, in the process Evans cut his hand – an accident that would have great significance in the days that followed.

The New Year was celebrated with sticks of chocolate and a new camaraderie. Writing two years later in the *Strand Magazine* Teddy Evans described how Captain Oates opened out for the first time that night.

> He told us all about his home, and his horses . . . He talked on and on, and his big, kind brown eyes sparkled as he recalled little boyish escapades at Eton . . . At length Captain Scott reached out and affectionately seized him in the way that was itself so characteristic of our leader, and said, 'You funny old thing, you have

quite come out of your shell, "Soldier". Do you know
we have all sat here talking for nearly four hours? It's
News Year's Day and 1 a.m.!'

This sudden outpouring was perhaps a sign that Oates was yearning for his former existence – the life in India, the pig-sticking
and hunting and polo, the comforts of Gestingthorpe. Recreating
it for others comforted him in this bleak spot.

On New Year's Eve Scott had ordered Teddy Evans's team to
leave their skis at the depot, a strange decision on the face of it. As
he himself acknowledged, it was far easier to pull on skis than to
plod along. On New Year's Day Scott was cheerful, observing that
prospects seemed to be getting brighter and that there were only
170 miles to the Pole with plenty of food left. Perhaps he was also
cheerful because he was about to take his final major decision on
the way to the Pole. On 3 January he went to Teddy Evans's tent.
As he entered Crean was coughing. Scott said, 'You've got a bad
cold, Crean,' to which the astute Irishman replied, 'I understand
a half-sung song, sir.'[5] Scott told them that he had decided that
Teddy Evans's team should return to Cape Evans. The news probably came as little surprise. Lashly and Teddy Evans had been
manhauling the longest and Evans, at least, was worn out. But
Scott then ordered everyone except Teddy out of the tent and
dropped the real bombshell. He said that he wanted Bowers to join
the Polar party and asked for Teddy Evans's consent. Although it
would leave him dangerously short-handed on his return journey,
Evans had no option but to agree. Scott was clearly pleased with
the outcome, writing in his diary: 'Bowers is to come into our
tent and we proceed as a five-man unit to-morrow. We have 5
1/2 units of food – practically over a month's allowance for five
people – it ought to see us through.'

Scott's decision to take five men, not four, to the Pole has never been satisfactorily explained. Debenham believed that Scott wanted as many of his colleagues as possible to share his success, but that is unlikely to be the whole story. Neither are the reasons behind Scott's choice of those particular companions clear, though Ponting made the interesting observation that Scott picked the four men with the most striking personalities. There seems little doubt that he always intended Wilson and Petty Officer Evans to be with him at the Pole. He had a deep personal regard for the doctor and derived great spiritual strength from him. He also had a special affection for the burly Welshman going back to the days of the *Discovery*, as well as a high opinion of his strength, endurance and resourcefulness. In *The Great White South* Ponting wrote: 'Nobody ever doubted, all through the winter, that Petty Officer Evans would be one of the ones chosen for the Pole.' There was also the presentational factor that the lower deck must be represented. However, Wilson appears to have had doubts about Evans's reliability under stress. Before Atkinson had turned back, the two doctors had agreed that of all the seamen Lashly would be the best choice for the Pole. With hindsight Cherry-Garrard also believed that Lashly should have gone, later writing that 'Lashly was wonderful'.

As far as Oates was concerned, there was also a presentational point. His presence at the Pole would allow the army a share in the glory – Wilson had told Atkinson that 'Scott was keen on his going on, he wanted the Army represented'.[6] It never occurred to Scott that Oates might be less than keen. However, Oates had told Teddy Evans that his personal ambition was simply to get to the top of the Beardmore. He did not expect to be selected for the southern journey and, though he did not say so, by this stage probably had little desire to go on. Struggling such a distance on foot and on skis with his left leg shorter than his right – the legacy of his Boer War wound – must have been sapping his strength and stamina. His diary had already mentioned problems with the tendons of his right knee as well as with his feet.

The letter Oates wrote to his mother shows his mixed feelings. He had earlier acknowledged that 'the regiment and perhaps the whole army would be pleased if I was at the Pole'.[7] He now assured her that he was delighted, feeling fit and well and that 'We shall get to the Pole alright. We are now within 50 miles of Shackleton's farthest South'.[8] However, the letter goes on to dwell with nostalgic longing on his home at Gestingthorpe and improvements there, of clothes he would like sent out for his return and of plans for a filly. He sent his love to his sisters and brother and finished with 'God bless you and keep you well until I come home' – the only mention of God in his letters. Among the other things he asked for was tobacco, cigarettes and a large box of caramel creams. He was trying to convince himself that he would come through and the letter is pathetic when seen against Atkinson's comment when they had parted earlier that Oates 'knew he was done – his face showed him to be and the way he went along'.[9]

But what was Scott's purpose in taking Bowers? There were no long-standing ties and Bowers had not originally even been a member of the shore party, but he had steadily won Scott's admiration. For one thing he was very strong. After the Winter Journey to Cape Crozier Scott described him as 'the hardest traveller that ever undertook a Polar journey, as well as one of the most undaunted' and referred to his untiring energy and astonishing physique. He also valued Bowers for his organizational abilities, phenomenal hard work but above all, perhaps, for his unswerving loyalty. The latter was a source of practical strength and comfort to Scott in the same way that Wilson gave him inner courage. Certainly, Wilson and Bowers were an impressive combination. As Cherry-Garrard later reminisced, 'It was easy to be brave when Bill and Birdie were near.'[10]

Scott may also have needed Bowers's skills as a navigator. He had originally considered taking two navigators to the Pole, so important did he consider this to be, and it was certainly an area where he was vulnerable. His own skills were rusty and he was out of practice with using a theodolite, which he had brought in preference to a sextant. Wilson and Oates and Edgar Evans's talents in that direction were even more limited. Teddy Evans was an experienced navigator, but Scott had not considered taking a man whom he basically considered played out and incompetent to the Pole. Bowers's abilities were accordingly a welcome addition.

However, the decision to take Bowers was probably, above all, a decision taken on impulse. Scott's companions on the *Discovery* expedition had often observed that he was impulsive, prone to take decisions quickly and without consulting. That would explain why he had allowed Bowers to depot his skis just three days earlier so that henceforward he would have to march on foot while the others skied, an exhausting and unnecessary strain. In just the same way Scott may have decided on impulse that five men would be more desirable than four. Certainly, time would show Scott had not stopped to consider fully the practical implications. He may simply have concluded that the benefits of another man to help pull the sledge would outweigh any logistical disadvantages. Hindsight suggests that if he wanted to take five he would have done better to have taken Crean in place of Oates or Edgar Evans. It was logical that Lashly and Teddy Evans should be sent back – they had after all been manhauling all the way from Corner Camp – but Crean had not and was still immensely strong and capable – he called himself 'The Wild Man of Borneo'.

However, Scott had made his choice. On 4 January the Polar party set out and he was in optimistic mood.

> We were naturally late getting away this morning, the sledge having to be packed and arrangements completed for separation of parties. It is wonderful to see how neatly everything stows on a little sledge, thanks to P.O. Evans. I was anxious to see how we could pull it, and glad to find we went easy enough. Bowers on foot pulls between, but behind, Wilson and myself; he has to keep his own pace and luckily does not throw us out at all.

Teddy Evans, Crean and Lashly followed in case of accident but, as soon as Scott was confident enough, the two parties stopped, said their farewells and gazed on each other for the last time. They must have been a wild-looking group of men with beards caked with ice, weather-scarred faces and split lips. Scott described the parting: 'Teddy Evans is terribly disappointed but has taken it very well and behaved like a man. Poor old Crean wept and even Lashly was affected.'

As well as Wright, both Cherry-Garrard and Bowers had criticized Teddy Evans during the march and before, Bowers on the grounds of Evans's 'sedition' in criticizing Scott before both men and officers. However, being second-in-command on an expedition such as Scott's is, as history shows, a thankless task and it would be wrong to judge Evans too harshly any more than Scott. Evans later wrote privately that he did not feel Scott treated him well but his published account in the *Strand Magazine* described how:

> The excitement was intense; it was obvious that with five fit men – the Pole being only one hundred and forty-five miles away – the achievement was merely a matter of ten or eleven days' good sledging. The last farewell was most touching, Oates being far more affected than any other of the Southern Party . . . I think his last actual remark was, 'I am afraid, Teddy, you won't have much of a "slope" going back, but old Christopher is waiting to be eaten on the Barrier when you get there.'

As a tremendous meat eater himself Oates had been dwelling on Christopher with some longing. The Last Supporting Party gave three huge cheers, turned their sledge and began the long march home. Oates, who was pulling at the rear, waved several times. Teddy Evans described how: 'We frequently looked back until the little group were but a tiny black speck on the southern horizon, and finally they disappeared.'

Evans could not have known that 'we would be the last to see them alive, that our three cheers on that bleak and lonely plateau summit would be the last appreciation they would ever know'. The Polar party were already marching into legend. Hereafter only their own records would tell their tale.

And so the Last Supporting Party turned north to face dangers of their own. Teddy Evans had given Bowers a little silk flag from his wife to plant at the Pole. In return he was carrying a letter from Scott to Kathleen, telling of his satisfaction with their progress and touching on his favourite themes of strength and leadership: 'no man will or can say I wasn't fit to lead through the last lap.'[11] Evans was also carrying an oral message which would play its part in the disaster ahead. Scott had changed the instructions yet again for the dogs. Meares was to bring the teams out to meet the returning party between 82° and 83°S, towards the middle of February to enable the returning Polar party to be in time for the *Terra Nova*. It is questionable whether these were the most effective arrangements but Scott's great mistake was to assume that Evans would deliver the message in time. Scott had predicted Evans would make a quick journey back, but he could not have been more wrong. He shared a mistaken belief, common among the expedition members, that the homeward journey must be easier than the outward one.

Scott was cheerful now. He was with men he liked and trusted, there had been no serious mishaps and the Pole seemed within their grasp. 'What castles one builds now hopefully that the Pole is ours,' he exulted. Yet the seeds of the coming disaster were already present. As Cherry-Garrard later wrote: 'We hear of trouble immediately the Last Supporting Party left them: . . . From this time onwards things went wrong.'[12] Edgar Evans's hand, injured while he was adjusting the sledges, was refusing to heal, no doubt the result of vitamin deficiency, and Wilson was having to dress it daily. Bowers was exhausted through having to march on foot, noting in his diary that it was 'more tiring for me than the others', something which Scott fully acknowledged.

Oates was worrying privately about the condition of his feet and his old war wound which, as an officer and gentleman of his day, he was loath to admit. The trouble was exacerbated by poor diet. A symptom of scurvy is that scar tissue from old wounds begins to dissolve and wounds open up and it is possible that the party were already beginning to suffer from incipient scurvy. Their diet, which had been their staple for over a hundred days was based on 16 oz. of special biscuits made by Huntley and Palmer, 0.57 oz. cocoa, 12 oz. pemmican, 2 oz. butter, 3 oz. sugar and 0.7 oz. tea. At the same time it was only producing some 4,500 calories, compared to the more than 6,000 they were probably burning, so they were also beginning to starve.

On the practical side, Scott soon became aware that cooking for five was more difficult than for four. The very day after parting from Evans he was writing that, 'Cooking for five takes a seriously longer time than cooking for four, perhaps half an hour on the whole day. It is an item I had not considered when re-organizing.' It also required more fuel. Furthermore, as Cherry-Garrard pointed out in *The Worst Journey*: 'There was 5 1/2 weeks' food for four men: five men would eat this in about four weeks'. There was also considerable discomfort as the result of the fifth man. The tents, which were of teepee construction, were about seven feet at the apex so that it was difficult for more than one person to stand. They had been designed for four so that when stretched out for the night the sleeping bags of the two outside men must have been partly off the separate floor cloth (the tent did not have a sewn-in ground sheet) and probably on the snow. The claustrophobia, difficulty of moving and long periods of confinement during blizzards must have been wearing.

The going was becoming increasingly difficult with heavy surfaces, sandy snow and falling crystals. For men already exhausted by manhauling up the Beardmore it was a struggle. There was great satisfaction when on 6 January they passed the site of Shackleton's most southerly camp, but Scott was becoming preoccupied with the difficult terrain: 'The vicissitudes of this work are bewildering,' he wrote in anguish. They were among sastrugi, frozen snow waves caused by the wind, 'a sea of fish-hook waves', some of them barbed with sharp crystals. This made skiing near impossible and Scott decided to abandon the skis. However, after marching for a mile the sastrugi disappeared and they returned to fetch their skis, wasting precious time and energy. A rueful Scott concluded that 'I must stick to the ski after this' but his indecision was a symptom of the growing strain he was under. On the same day Wilson was recording the increasingly grim conditions: 'We get our hairy faces and mouths dreadfully iced up on the march and often one's hands get very cold indeed holding ski sticks. Evans, who cut his knuckle some days ago at the last depot . . . has a lot of pus in it tonight.'

The next day a blizzard struck. Scott consoled himself that the rest would be good for Evans's hand and used the enforced break to write a tribute to his companions. His diary turns to eulogy about his sledging comrades:

> It is quite impossible to speak too highly of my companions. Each fulfils his office to the party; Wilson, first as doctor, ever on the lookout to alleviate the small pains and troubles incidental to the work; now as cook, quick, careful and dexterous, ever thinking of some fresh expedient to help the camp life; tough as steel on the traces, never wavering from start to finish. Evans, a giant worker with a really remarkable headpiece. It is only now I realise how much has been due to him . . . Little Bowers remains a marvel – he is thoroughly enjoying himself. I leave all the provision arrangement in his hands but not one single mistake has been made. In addition to the stores, he keeps the most thorough and conscientious meteorological record, and to this he now adds the duty of observer and photographer

> ... Oates had his invaluable period with the ponies;
> now he is a foot slogger and goes hard the whole time,
> does his share of camp work, and stands the hardship
> as well as any of us. I would not like to be without
> him either. So our five people are perhaps as happily
> selected as it is possible to imagine.

This Platonic view of an expedition as a mini society where every-one has their particular specialism is shared by more modern explorers. Sir Ranulph Fiennes wrote in his account of his Pole to Pole Transglobe expedition that 'much of our strength, despite our lack of experience, lay in our collective ability'.[13]

The blizzard lifted and on 9 January Scott was able to note in his diary a triumphant 'RECORD' – they had passed Shackleton's farthest south and were truly in terra incognita. However, the party were becoming increasingly weary. The Polar plateau was covered with sandy snow which clogged the runners of the sledge. Relatively warm and sunny conditions made the going worse. His diary shows that Scott now realized that the journey was going to be 'a stiff pull *both ways* apparently'. On 11 January Scott was writing: 'Another hard grind in the afternoon and five miles added. About 74 miles from the Pole – can we keep this up for seven days? It takes it out of us like anything. None of us ever had such hard work before.' He was using words such as 'fearful' and 'agonising'. The heavy pulling was soul-destroying. 'With the surface as it is, one gets horribly sick of the monotony and can easily imagine oneself getting played out . . . It is an effort to keep up the double figures, but if we can do so for another four marches we ought to get through. It is going to be a close thing,' wrote a sombre Scott.

They were feeling the cold: 'At camping to-night everyone was chilled and we guessed a cold snap, but to our surprise the actual temperature was higher than last night, when we could dawdle in the sun. It is most unaccountable why we should suddenly feel the cold in this manner; partly the exhaustion of the march, but partly some damp quality in the air, I think.' From now on the cold becomes a recurring theme – the effect of the climate was exacerbated by lack of food. Scott noticed that Oates, in particular, was feeling the chill and the fatigue more than the others. But in spite of these warning signs Scott was buoyed up as they neared the Pole, intent on his goal. On Monday 15 January he wrote like an excited schoolboy: 'It is wonderful to think that two long marches would land us at the Pole. We left our depot to-day with nine days' provisions, so that it ought to be a certain thing now, and the only appalling possibility the sight of the Norwegian flag forestalling ours.'

Of course, that is exactly what happened. Scott's diary entry for the next day tells how the 'appalling possibility' had become reality:

> The worst has happened, or nearly the worst. We marched well in the morning . . . and we started off in high spirits in the afternoon, feeling that to-morrow would see us at our destination. About the second hour of the march Bowers's sharp eyes detected what he thought was a cairn; he was uneasy about it, but argued that it must be a sastrugus. Half an hour later he detected a black speck ahead . . . We marched on, found that it was a black flag tied to a sledge bearer; near by the remains of a camp; sledge tracks and ski tracks going and coming and the clear trace of dogs' paws – many dogs. This told us the whole story. The

> Norwegians have forestalled us and are first at the Pole.
> It is a terrible disappointment, and I am very sorry for
> my loyal companions.

Curiously enough on 15 December while out sledging Gran had dreamt accurately that his fellow Norwegian had reached the Pole that day. His companions pooh-poohed it but he insisted on noting it down in Griffith Taylor's copy of Browning. Taylor later ascribed it to extraordinary coincidence rather than the supernatural, as Gran believed, but was clearly struck by the strangeness of it.

The psychological impact of the discovery on Scott's Polar party was tremendous. The shock made it difficult to sleep that night. Scott lay in his sleeping bag contemplating the weary journey back, all hope gone. His thoughts must have turned to Kathleen, then visiting relations in Berlin and attending lectures given by Nansen. This is the occasion on which Roland Huntford alleges they had an affair.[14] Kathleen certainly enjoyed the company and admiration of this virile explorer who perhaps reminded her of her husband. She may well have been strongly attracted to him. However, she was both too honourable and too sensible to embark on what she must have recognized could become a lasting and destructive liaison. Just as she had determinedly preserved her virginity in her youth while relishing the ardent admiration of her many suitors, she would have kept the relationship from becoming physical. She made no secret of their meeting, writing to Scott in a letter which he would never read: 'He really is an adorable person and I will tell you all the lovely times we had together when you get back. He thinks you are marvellous and me still more.'[15]

The next day, Wednesday 17 January, they at last reached the Pole but, as Scott wrote bitterly, in very different circumstances to those which they had imagined. To make matters worse there was a chill wind blowing and the air seemed curiously damp, penetrating into their bones. Oates, Evans and Bowers all had frostbitten noses and cheeks and Evans's hands were hurting him. They took some sightings but there is nothing but despair in Scott's diary, culminating in his anguished cry: 'Great God! this is an awful place and terrible enough for us to have laboured to it without the reward of priority.' This says it all – the back-breaking struggle, the terrible deprivation, the worry and anxiety had all been for nothing. Whatever Scott may have said and thought earlier he now knew how badly he had wanted to win. 'Now for the run home and a desperate struggle. I wonder if we can do it,' are his heroic comments in the edited version of his diary, which was later published. What he actually wrote at the Pole was: 'a desperate struggle to get the news through first.' Even if he was not the first at the Pole he still hoped to give the Central News Agency the scoop they expected.

Scott was determined to salvage something and his reaction is in interesting contrast to his colleagues'. He did not have Wilson's quiet faith that everything turned out as God meant it to. Wilson's own diary is phlegmatic: 'He [Amundsen] has beaten us in so far as he made a race of it. We have done what we came for all the same and as our programme was made out.' Bowers's letter to his mother was positively chirpy:

> Well, here I really am and very glad to be here too. It is a bleak spot – what a place to strive so hard to reach ... It is sad that we have been forestalled by the Norwegians, but I am glad that we have done it by good British manhaulage. That is the traditional British sledging method and this is the greatest journey done by man ...[16]

There is a strong hint that their approach based on 'honest sweat' was more honourable than Amundsen's. Evans's response is not recorded but it must have been a deep disappointment to him. Victory at the Pole would have set him and his family up for life, allowing him to fulfil his ambition of owning a pub. Oates's reaction was one of sardonic detachment. 'We are not a very happy party tonight,' he wrote, mentally shrugging his shoulders. 'I must say that that man must have had his head screwed on right. The gear they left was in excellent order and they seem to have had a comfortable trip with their dog teams, very different from our wretched man-hauling.'[17]

However, despite appearances, the Norwegians had been exhausted too, finding the altitude a struggle. Altitude sickness comes on at lower altitudes near the Pole. On 11 December, just four days from the Pole, Amundsen had written: 'We'll get our breath back, if only we win.'[18] He too realized the psychological boost of winning.

On 18 January, as Scott and his men continued to take observations around the Pole, they came across Amundsen's tent at his most southerly camp. It was a neat, compact affair supported by a single bamboo pole. Inside was a letter to King Haakon of Norway and a note from Amundsen asking Scott to make sure it was delivered. Amundsen was covering himself in case some accident overtook him on the way back to Framheim, though on that very day he was within one week of regaining the Bay of Whales. To Scott and his men it must have seemed the ultimate humiliation. Scott pocketed the letter and left a note to say he had visited the tent. The rest of this final day at the Pole was spent in sketching and erecting a small cairn from which to fly 'our poor slighted Union Jack'.[19] Scott and his men then photographed themselves in front of it; Birdie Bowers used a string to activate the shutter. Those pictures are among ten taken on a single roll of film at the Pole. They are the saddest of the whole expedition and not only because one knows those pictured were doomed – the weariness and sense of futility leap out. Their faces are drawn and weatherbeaten and there is no joy in them. Oates looks tired and in pain, leaning heavily on his shorter left leg.

They carried the flag a short distance northwards, fixed it to a stick then helped themselves to some of the surplus equipment left behind by Amundsen – Bowers took a pair of reindeer mitts to replace his lost dogskin ones. Amundsen had considered leaving them a spare can of fuel but had concluded that Scott's party would be so well-provisioned there was little point. Yet, as events were about to prove, this would have been the greatest service he could have rendered his defeated rivals, who now prepared for the homeward trek.

So that was that – a banal and humiliating end to an epic journey. Their ambitions had been thwarted and there was only the consolation prize. 'Well,' Scott wrote, 'we have turned our back now on the goal of our ambition and must face our 800 miles of solid dragging – and good-bye to most of the day-dreams!'

15

'God Help Us'

Retracing their steps, Scott's weary party trekked past the 'ominous black flag' which just three days earlier had blasted their hopes.[1] They took the flag staff to help make a sail, hoping to use the wind to speed them on their way. It was made of hickory, gave Wilson splinters and was soon discarded. At first they made reasonable progress, picking up their old track but showers of fine crystals rendered the surface heavy as sand and they were all feeling the cold more than on the outward journey. Scott reflected that 'the return journey is going to be dreadfully tiring and monotonous'. Over the next few days his diary is dominated by such gloomy descriptions as 'terrible bad', 'really awful', 'terribly weary'. This is in marked contrast to Amundsen's jaunty account of the Norwegians' departure from the Pole: 'The going was splendid and all were in good spirits.'[2]

Scott's men were not in good spirits. Even Bowers, 'an undefeated little sportsman'[3] to the last and engagingly optimistic, was finding the long marches tiring with his short legs and was yearning for his 'dear old ski'. Oates was clearly suffering from cold and fatigue. However, Scott was determined to keep up a good marching pace to give them the chance to be back in time to catch the ship. He did not yet seriously consider the possibility that they might not return at all. In fact the returning *Terra Nova* was spotted by Tryggve Gran on 20 January, just three days after their departure from the Pole, trying to nose her way in through the pack ice.

They made dogged progress. Bowers recorded how they watched anxiously for the chain of cairns they had built on their outward odyssey: 'We are absolutely dependent upon our depots to get off the plateau alive, and so welcome the lonely little cairns gladly.' They used the wind when they could. On 23 January Bowers was cheerfully recording that 'Filling the sail we sped along merrily doing 8¾ miles before lunch. In the afternoon it was even stronger and I had to go back on the sledge and act as guide and brakeman. We had to lower the sail a bit, but even then she ran like a bird.' However, on the same day they were depressed by Wilson's discovery that Edgar Evans's nose was badly frostbitten – 'white and hard' according to Scott. On the *Discovery* expedition Scott had noticed that Evans's nose had always been 'the first thing to indicate stress of frostbiting weather', but Evans was no longer joking about his 'old blossom' as he had once called his nose. They made camp and cooked up a good hot hoosh, but Scott was worried about his comrade. For the first time, perhaps, he realized that the man he believed to be a Goliath and the strongest of them all had suffered the most from the long haul to the Pole.

Evans was the heaviest and should, in theory, have had larger rations than the others. As Cherry-Garrard observed, larger machines need more fuel to drive them. Dr Mike Stroud, who manhauled to the Pole himself a few years ago, calculated that Evans would have lost more weight than anyone else, perhaps over 15 kilos, by the time he reached the Pole, equivalent to about one fifth of his body weight.[4] As he was 'in hard condition', the loss would have been mainly to his muscles, with consequent effects on his pulling power. A concerned Scott noted that he seemed very run down, with badly blistered fingers and frostbites. He also noticed something more disturbing – Evans seemed 'very much annoyed with himself'. The usually ebullient and self-reliant Welshman was losing confidence. Unused to physical weakness and afraid of letting his companions down he was becoming depressed and withdrawn. This hesitant, fretful Evans was a far cry from the man who had tumbled down a crevasse with Scott on the *Discovery* expedition and made calm conversation as he dangled over a chilly abyss.

Scott made an anxious survey of the rest of the team. He concluded that he himself, Wilson and Bowers were as fit as possible under the circumstances, though Wilson was suffering the torments of snowblindness as a result of trying to sketch and was using cocaine ointment as a painkiller. By 24 January Scott was referring to Wilson and Bowers as 'my standby', adding, 'I don't like the easy way in which Oates and Evans get frostbitten.' In fact, one of Oates's big toes had turned black and he was secretly worrying whether it would hinder him from marching. Scott was also increasingly concerned about the blizzards and gales they were encountering: 'Is the weather breaking up? If so, God help us, with the tremendous summit journey and scant food.' Their late start for the Pole, the result of the decision to use ponies, had inevitably left them on the plateau late in the season and vulnerable to the falling temperatures. The thin air of the plateau did not help. Amundsen's men, better fed and less stressed, had found the conditions difficult enough. Amundsen described how: 'The asthmatic condition in which we found ourselves during our six weeks' stay on the plateau was anything but pleasant.'[5] For Scott and his exhausted team it was very debilitating. It would not have comforted Scott to know that on 26 January his rival reached Framheim after a journey that had taken only ninety-nine days and with men and dogs in rude good health. Amundsen and his companions crept into the hut at Framheim at four in the morning and took delight in waking the sleeping inmates with a casual request for coffee.

They marched on – Oates with his bad foot, Evans with badly frostbitten nose and fingers, Wilson with his snowblindness and all of them increasingly hungry. Lack of vitamins and malnutrition were affecting their mental as well as their physical wellbeing. Scott was observing how thin everyone looked, particularly Evans. The conversation turned more and more to food – Bowers had begun fantasizing about the pig he would make of himself at journey's end, but with some 700 miles to go he knew such dreams were premature. His more immediate problem was that 'I am in tribulation as regards meals now as we have run out of salt, one of my favourite commodities.'

30 January was a bad day. Wilson strained a tendon in his leg, Oates had revealed that his big toe was turning blue-black, while Evans was beginning to lose his fingernails. Scott observed that 'his hands are really bad, and to my surprise he shows signs of losing heart over it'. Poor Evans's transformation had continued and he had become a different person, taciturn, introverted, concentrating on keeping going. There were none of his colourful anecdotes or wild curses about the seven blind witches of Egypt to cheer his companions. Ironically, it was on this bad day for Scott that a triumphant Amundsen set sail on the *Fram* to take his momentous news to the outside world.

Wilson's leg began to recover, much to Scott's relief. As he noted, 'it is trying to have an injured limb in the party'. However,

Evans continued to decline – 'Evans's fingers now very bad, two nails coming off, blisters burst.' Yet this was the time when Evans most needed strength and endurance. They were approaching the crazy terrain of crevasses and ice-falls heralding the gateway to the Beardmore Glacier. As they attempted to negotiate their way down a steep and slippery slope Scott lost his footing and landed on the point of his shoulder. That meant that there were now 'three out of five injured' as Scott ruefully recorded. Interestingly he did not consider Oates to be one of the sick, but the reality was that only Bowers was in reasonable shape, cheered no doubt by the retrieval of his skis on 31 January. Oates had also found the pipe he had dropped on the outward journey, which must have comforted him. The party struggled on but had difficulty in picking up their track, adding to their anxiety. Bowers ceased to keep a diary around this time, making his final entry on 'Feb 3rd (I suppose)'. On 4 February Evans and Scott both fell into a crevasse and had to be hauled out. Scott now wrote: 'The party is not improving in condition, especially Evans, who is becoming rather dull and incapable.' Also at this time Wilson observed that Oates's other toes were blackening and that his 'nose and cheeks are dead yellow'.

In this ominous situation Scott relied increasingly on Bowers, who seemed immune from the mishaps: 'Bowers is splendid, full of energy and bustle all the time.' Scott needed Bowers's resilience to buoy his own flagging spirits as they looked for their way down the glacier. Their situation was becoming critical. The next days saw them weaving through a perilous maze of crevasses as they tried to find their way to the Upper Glacier Depot and the badly needed supplies of food stored there. The depot would also point the way down the Beardmore and it was important they descended quickly. Evans was in a very bad way: 'Evans is the chief anxiety now; his cuts and wounds suppurate, his nose looks very bad, and altogether he shows considerable signs of being played out.' Scott clung to the hope that his condition might improve as they descended the glacier and the temperature rose.

However, the next day there was momentary panic with the discovery that a whole day's biscuit ration was missing. Bowers, who prided himself on his efficiency in looking after their stores, was shaken. However, by early evening they at last reached the Upper Glacier Depot. Their plateau ordeal was over and they could reprovision. They reflected that they had taken twenty-seven days to reach the Pole from this point and twenty-one days to return. Scott wrote: 'we have come through our 7 weeks' ice camp journey and most of us are fit, but I think another week might have had a very bad effect on P.O. Evans, who is going steadily downhill.'

It seems strange to read in Scott's diary that the party spent a large part of the next day 'geologising'. They veered off towards Mount Darwin and Bowers was sent ahead on skis to collect specimens. The task would normally have fallen to Wilson, but he was still suffering from his strained tendon. Later on they steered for the moraine under Mount Buckley which Scott found so interesting he decided to make camp there. Scott described a pleasant few hours of pottering:

> We found ourselves under perpendicular cliffs of Beacon sandstone, weathering rapidly and carrying veritable coal seams. From the last Wilson, with his sharp eyes, has picked several plant impressions of thick stems, showing cellular structure. In one place we saw the cast of small waves on the sand. To-night Bill has got a specimen of limestone with archeo-cyathus . . . Altogether we have had a most interesting afternoon . . .

Wilson even managed to do some pencil sketches of Mount Buckley.

No doubt the break from manhauling and the relief of being in a sheltered spot out of the harsh summit winds had their effect on hungry and weary men. More important to their morale, however, was the fact that they were doing what they had come for – scientific research. They could regain some pride after the ignominy of their arrival at the Pole, reminding themselves of the differences between their carefully planned programme of scientific work and Amundsen's opportunistic Viking raid. Indeed on his return journey to Framheim, Amundsen made a conscious decision not to let anything deflect him from making a dash straight back to Framheim, not even the prospect of discovering some new geographical features. Whether Scott's geologizing was a magnificent example of dedication or a foolish diversion depends on your point of view. It added some 35 pounds to a sledge already piled with five kitbags, a cooker, an instrument box, biscuit boxes, a paraffin tank and a tent. On the other hand these rocks were to prove for the first time that Antarctica had once been covered in vegetation and had formed part of a great semi-tropical southern continent – the so-called 'Gondwanaland' – once believed to be only a myth. As scientists of the British Antarctic Survey have acknowledged:

> The plant fossils collected ... from the Beardmore Glacier and found with their bodies, were of particular significance. Although the expedition failed to reach the Pole first, its scientific achievements were more than sufficient to justify it. Amundsen won the race but his efforts provided virtually nothing in terms of scientific information.[6]

They geologized again the next day during their march, enjoying the milder temperatures now they had left the dreadful Polar plateau. Scott sounds more relaxed and confident: 'It is remarkable to be able to stand outside the tent and sun oneself. Our food satisfies now, but we must march to keep in the full ration, and we want rest, yet we shall pull through all right, D.V. We are by no means worn out.' There are no references here to the state of Evans or of Oates, suggesting that they too were benefiting from the change in conditions. Alternatively, Scott may have been trying to convince himself that everything would indeed turn out all right. We can never know.

However, on 11 February everything went wrong again. The surface was wretched and their journey rapidly became a nightmare as they got lost in a maze of pressure ridges. It was the worst day of their whole trip and stemmed from a fatal decision to steer to the east in the hope that this would lead them out of the pressure. However, after hours of hauling they seemed to be trapped in a mass of crevasses. Twisting this way and that, they at last glimpsed a smoother slope, but it lay far away across a surface riven by deep chasms. At about 10 p.m., after twelve hours of appalling grind, they were back on the right track. However, they had made little progress towards their next depot and food was beginning to run out. They reduced their rations, squeezing an extra meal out of pemmican only meant for three meals and halving their meagre lunch ration.

The next day they again became disorientated, plunging into a labyrinth of crevasses and fissures and wandering about 'absolutely lost for hours and hours' as Wilson recorded. There was clearly debate if not argument about what to do. Scott described how 'Divided councils caused our course to be erratic' and they were forced to make camp in 'the worst place of all'. Oates recorded that: 'We are in rather a nasty hole tonight.' They were grimly aware that they now had only one meal left. The wording in Scott's diary is tense. He speaks of endurance, of how the group must and will get through and how they can cope with less food.

The next morning brought thick snow cloaking everything around them. The only option was to remain in their sleeping bags, hungry and anxious. However, they were able to get under way by mid-morning and after struggling through a chaotic expanse of broken ice hit an old moraine track. It was easier to make progress on this smoother surface. Evans, confused by a shadow on the ice, shouted out, believing they had reached the next depot, but not long after Wilson spotted the real depot flag. Scott was not exaggerating when he wrote that it was 'an immense relief'. They now had a further three and a half days' food. Wilson even geologized for an hour or two as they tramped on. They were also relieved to learn from messages left for them that the two supporting parties had passed through safely, though Teddy Evans 'seems to have got mixed up with pressures like ourselves'.[7] In fact at that very moment Teddy Evans was not safe. He had collapsed from scurvy with some hundred miles to go and that day was still on the Barrier.

Scott brooded over the unnerving experiences of the last days: 'In future food must be worked so that we do not run so short if the weather fails us. We musn't get into a hole like this again.' Recent events had made him feel very insecure and it was being brought home to him that he had cut things too finely. He was revising the opinion he had expressed earlier in the year that: 'it must be sound policy to keep the men of a sledge party keyed up to a high pitch of well-fed physical condition as long as they have animals to drag their loads. The time for short rations . . . comes when the men are dependent on their own traction efforts.' He also had time to assess the condition of his companions. Bowers and Wilson were suffering badly from snowblindness. However, the news of Evans was much worse. This once hearty and vigorous giant had 'no power to assist with camping work' but Scott does not explain why. Perhaps his wounded and frostbitten hands were preventing him, or perhaps it was a further manifestation of the slowness which Scott noted after Evans fell down the crevasse.

They set off again the next day, carrying their new provisions but covered only six and a half miles. Scott knew a crisis was coming:

> There is no getting away from the fact that we are not going strong. Probably none of us: Wilson's leg still troubles him and he doesn't like to trust himself on ski; but the worst case is Evans who is giving us serious anxiety. This morning he suddenly disclosed a huge blister on his foot. It delayed us on the march . . . Sometimes I fear he is going from bad to worse, but I trust he will pick up again when we come to steady work on ski like this afternoon. He is hungry and so is Wilson.

Hunger had also affected the returning Norwegians, but as Amundsen wrote: 'Fortunately we were so well supplied that when this sensation of hunger came over us, we could increase our daily rations.'[8]

There are hints that their morale was breaking down. All of them must have been reaching the end of their tether, while Scott was becoming frustrated and disappointed with their progress. The goal of reaching the *Terra Nova* in time was slipping away – she was due to sail northwards around the end of February.

'We are inclined to get slack and slow,' he complained. 'I have talked of the matter to-night and hope for improvement.' They were now some thirty miles from the Lower Glacier Depot with nearly three days' food in hand, but on 15 February Scott was again noting that provisions were running low. In desperation he had reduced both their rations and their rest time so they could reach the depot before the rations ran out. Perhaps, as they hauled their heavy sledge, his thoughts turned to home and Kathleen as a source of strength and comfort. In fact, on 15 February, she was lunching with the Prime Minister, Asquith, no doubt in the hope of charming some funds out of him.

The next day heralded tragedy. Scott's diary for 16 February records: 'A rather trying position. Evans has nearly broken down in brain, we think. He is absolutely changed from his normal self-reliant self. This morning and this afternoon he stopped the march on some trivial excuse.' If this sounds unsympathetic it must be remembered that Scott was under great mental and physical strain. He probably also felt responsible for the poor state of his comrade and hence guilty. Oates's verdict sounds equally callous: 'It is an extraordinary thing about Evans, he has lost his guts and behaves like an old woman or worse,' and yet Oates was the most popular officer among the men of the lower deck. Wilson's verdict was that: 'Evans's collapse has much to do with the fact that he has never been sick in his life and is now helpless with his hands frost-bitten.'

The next day they pressed on, hoping to make the depot, but it was 'anxious work with the sick man'.[9] The crisis was about to break and it was, in Scott's words, 'a very terrible day'. Evans had slept well and prepared for the march, gamely declaring, as he always did, that he was fit and well. He took his place in the traces but within half an hour had to drop out because his ski shoes had loosened. The others plodded on with the groaning sledge over a thick treacly surface. Evans slowly caught them up again and once more took his place. However, after half an hour he again dropped out and asked Bowers to lend him some string. Scott told Evans to catch up when he could and the seaman apparently answered him cheerfully.

Again the others continued to haul, anxious to reach the depot and sweating heavily. At lunchtime they sat and waited, expecting the lonely shambling figure of Evans to come into view. When he failed to appear they went to look for him and caught sight of him still some way behind. It was obvious something was wrong. Scott was the first to reach Evans and was shocked at his appearance: 'He was on his knees with clothing disarranged, hands uncovered and frostbitten, and a wild look in his eyes.' Asked what had happened he replied that he did not know but thought that he must have fainted. He could no longer walk and was showing signs of complete collapse. Oates remained with him while the others hurried to fetch the sledge. By the time they managed to get him into the tent he was comatose and died quietly that night without regaining consciousness. He had been out from Cape Evans for three and a half months and had marched over 1,200 miles. In his final letter to his wife he had written: 'I am always thinking of you on this great ice platform ten thousand feet above the sea level.'[10]

His shocked companions debated the cause of his death. They concluded that he had begun to weaken before reaching the Pole and that his downward spiral had been hastened by the discovery of his frostbitten fingers, his falls on the glacier and his loss of confidence. Wilson believed he must have injured his brain during a fall. Whatever the cause of their companion's death it was a chilling moment for the four survivors, emphasizing their own vulnerability, with so many miles still to go. Yet at the same time it was the solution to a horrible dilemma. As Scott commented, 'It is a terrible thing to lose a companion in this way, but calm reflection shows that there could not have been a better ending to the terrible anxieties of the past week . . . what a desperate pass we were in with a sick man on our hands at such a distance from home.'

Later on, when Scott knew that he himself was probably going to die, he wrote that Evans's death had spared them a terrible decision since 'the safety of the remainder seemed to demand his abandonment'. He also noted gratefully that Evans had died a natural death – meaning he had not had to resort to suicide or even that his comrades had not been required to give him a merciful release with the opium they carried. They would never have left him while he lived, yet it would have been impossible to pull him on the sledge. As it was, both Scott and Wilson could record their pride that their record 'was clear'.

Scott and his companions kept vigil for two hours after Edgar Evans died – the first victim of a journey that would prove too far for them all. What they did with his body is not recorded.

16

'Had We Lived . . .'

The next day, as the surviving quartet marched grimly on their way, Kathleen wrote in her diary: 'I was very taken up with you all evening. I wonder if anything special is happening to you. Something odd happened to the clocks between 9 and 10 p.m.' She felt uncharacteristically depressed and had to shake off a sense of foreboding. There is a story that around this time Peter asked to be lifted down from his rocking horse and ran to the door holding out his hands and calling: 'Hello Daddy', but Kathleen did not believe in the supernatural.[1] She was, however, brooding over Scott's perennial bad luck and told Sir Compton Mackenzie, who was sitting for her at the time, that she feared it would prevent him from reaching the Pole. Kathleen was not to know that her husband had reached the Pole, only to be disappointed, and was now struggling against the odds to return.

After snatching five hours' sleep at the Lower Glacier Depot Scott and his three companions reached Shambles Camp, the desolate spot where the last of the ponies had been slaughtered, but a 'fine supper' of pony meat revived them a little. As Scott wrote: 'New life seems to come with greater food almost immediately.' They could take comfort that the plateau and the treacherous glacier lay behind them, but they now faced a slog of nearly 400 miles across the Barrier where the only certainty would be the mind-numbing monotony of a featureless landscape. They prepared as best they could, swapping their sledge for a new one which had been left at the depot and loading it with pony meat. However, they soon discovered that the surface was coated with soft, slushy snow. Scott described miserably how it was 'like pulling over desert sand, not the least glide in the world'. He knew they must maintain a reasonable momentum to reach the depots containing the vital supplies, strung out across the Barrier, before their food and fuel ran out. There are echoes here of Shackleton's return from his great southern journey when he wrote the morbid line: 'Our food lies ahead and death stalks us from behind.'[2]

Scott pinned his hopes on a change in the weather. A brisk southerly wind would enable them to hoist their sail and be blown across the ice. Even a moderate blizzard would have helped by sweeping away the loose ice crystals that clogged the sledge. Yet no kindly wind came to their aid. As he hauled, Scott pondered whether the loss of the tragic fifth man was a help or a hindrance. He concluded that: 'The absence of poor Evans is a help to the commissariat, but if he had been here in a fit state we might have got along faster.' On 20 February they staggered into Desolation Camp where the blizzard had imprisoned them for a disastrous four days on their outward journey. They searched hopefully for more pony meat but found none.

Scott was lost in gloom. Trudging on, the only 'rays of comfort' were finding the tracks and cairns of the outward journey. This was not easy and they sometimes found themselves veering off-course. Scott was on tenterhooks, straining for the sight of each new cairn, anxiously assessing the weather, the surface of the Barrier and wondering what the weather held in store. On 24 February Scott set down the challenge: 'It is a race between the season and hard conditions and our fitness and good food.' He might have added that it was also a race to cover the distance before their fuel ran out. That very day while collecting supplies from the Southern Barrier Depot they had found a worrying shortage of oil. The fuel allowance had been carefully calculated – two one-gallon tins had been left at each depot for the returning parties. However, the oil had been exposed to extremes of heat and cold. In particular, the tins were often left in an accessible place on the top of the cairns and in the sun's warmth the oil vaporized and escaped through the stoppers. The problem was exacerbated by the fact that the leather washers around the stoppers were prone to perish in the cold and that the tins had been disturbed by being opened by the other returning parties. Scott noted that they would have to be '*very* saving' and from now on his diaries are peppered with worried references to the fuel situation and the need to cover greater distances. Scott's anxiety expressed itself in various ways. The next day he nagged Bowers about his ability to pull on skis, writing that he 'hasn't quite the trick and is a little hurt at my criticisms, but I never doubted his heart'.

As the month drew to a close the temperature dropped steadily. By 27 February Scott was describing it as 'desperately cold'. The surface of the ice was deteriorating. It was now 'coated with a thin layer of woolly crystals . . . These are too firmly fixed to be removed by the wind and cause impossible friction on the runners'. Scott knew their position was critical. Everything now depended on reaching each depot in time. He made endless calculations – how many days would it take to reach the next depot? How many days' supply of food and fuel was left? Apart from everything else the Barrier itself depressed him – there was nothing to see, no warmth, no comfort on this great shelf of ice. 'There is no doubt the middle of the Barrier is a pretty awful locality,' he wrote in the knowledge that there were nearly 300 miles to go. Wilson's diary ceased from this time. Living up to his ideal of being 'entirely careless of your own soul or body in looking after the welfare of others' left him neither time nor energy to write.[3] Oates had abandoned his diary on 24 February, the day the poor meat-loving soldier had dug up Christopher's head, only to find that it had gone rotten. From now on Scott became the only one to record the unfolding tragedy day by day.

On 1 March they reached the Middle Barrier Depot to discover a trio of misfortunes. First, there was a further serious shortage of oil – there was barely enough to carry them on to the next depot over sixty miles away. Second, Oates, no longer able to conceal the appalling state of his feet, disclosed his frostbitten gangrenous toes on which the bitter temperatures on the Barrier had taken their toll. Third, that night the temperature fell to below -40°F, leaving them so chilled that it took them an hour and a half to struggle into their foot gear the next morning. Scott was not mincing his words when he wrote: 'We are in a *very* queer street.'

Indeed, from now on Scott's account descends into thinly veiled despair as they battled along, barely managing a mile an hour, although he acknowledged the bravery of his companions: 'Amongst ourselves we are unendingly cheerful, but what each man feels in his heart I can only guess. Pulling on foot gear in the morning is getting slower and slower, therefore every day more dangerous.' It was also taking longer and longer to push painful and sensitive frostbitten limbs into sleeping bags which were becoming ever heavier and more rigid with frozen sweat and exhaled breath. Scott derived his strength and comfort from Wilson and Bowers, knowing he would not be able to cope if they 'weren't so determinedly cheerful over things'. He was painfully aware of Oates's condition, knowing that a colder snap would spell disaster for the soldier. On 5 March he was writing: 'Our fuel dreadfully low and the poor Soldier nearly done. It is pathetic enough because we can do nothing for him . . .' None of them had expected such dreadfully low temperatures on the Barrier and the one suffering most, after Oates, was Wilson, 'mainly, I fear, from his self-sacrificing devotion in doctoring Oates's feet'.

By 6 March poor Oates could no longer pull. He never complained and, indeed, was growing daily ever more silent. There seems little doubt that he knew what lay ahead and was coming to terms with the fact that he would never again see Gestingthorpe, nor ride to hounds nor see his mother. He knew he was now a drag on the others. So did Scott, writing: 'If we were all fit I should have hopes of getting through, but the poor Soldier has become a terrible hindrance, though he does his utmost and suffers much . . .' The obvious solution stared Oates in the face. He must have remembered his discussions with Ponting at Cape Evans when he had asserted that suicide was the only honourable course for a sledger who was imperilling his companions.

The days that followed were harrowing – three men struggling to pull what had become an impossible load, the fourth wondering how much longer he should continue to be a burden. On 7 March Scott wrote that the soldier's crisis was near, but implying that it was fast approaching for them all. He himself was determined to keep going: 'I should like to keep the track to the end,' he wrote defiantly. Much would depend on what they found at the next depot. Had the dogs been out there with fresh supplies? Would there be enough fuel? Arriving at the depot at Mount Hooper on 9 March they found everything in short supply and only 'cold comfort' – 'the dogs which would have been our salvation have evidently failed,' Scott recorded grimly. The dogs had actually been awaiting the Polar party at One Ton Depot since 3 March, but a week later after depoting some supplies their drivers Cherry-Garrard and Dimitri had turned northwards again.

Meanwhile, in early March London was abuzz with rumours that Scott had been first to the Pole. Kathleen, however, confided in her diary that: 'I was certain there was something wrong.' On 7 March, with Amundsen's arrival in Tasmania, came proof positive that the Norwegian had in fact been the victor. The reaction in Britain was predictably muted and praise of Amundsen was tempered by the suggestion that he had not really played the game. *The Times* declared that his sudden decision to go south rather than north and the secrecy which surrounded it 'were felt to be not quite in accordance with the spirit of fair and open competition which had hitherto marked Antarctic exploration'. Kathleen reacted with characteristic dignity and generosity to the Norwegian's triumph but wrote: 'I worked badly and my head rocked. I'm not going to recount what I have been feeling.' Perhaps her little son was trying to cheer her up when he said: 'Amundsen and Daddy both got to the Pole. Daddy has stopped working now.'

Out on the Barrier Oates's crisis was approaching. On 10 March he 'asked Wilson if he had a chance this morning, and of course Bill had to say he didn't know. In point of fact he has none,' Scott wrote, staring reality in the face. 'Apart from him, if he went under now, I doubt whether we could get through.' The next day Scott wrote:

> Titus Oates is very near the end, one feels. What we or he will do, God only knows. We discussed the matter after breakfast; he is a brave fine fellow and

> understands the situation, but he practically asked for advice. Nothing could be said but to urge him to march as long as he could. One satisfactory result to the discussion; I practically ordered Wilson to hand over the means of ending our troubles to us ... We have 30 opium tabloids apiece and he is left with a tube of morphine. So far the tragical side of our story.

What bleak thoughts were now playing across their minds? They would have agreed with Cherry-Garrard that: 'Practically any man who undertakes big Polar journeys must face the possibility of having to commit suicide to save his companions.'[4] On the Winter Journey even the indomitable Bowers had 'had a scheme of doing himself in with a pick-axe if necessity arose, though how he could have accomplished it I don't know: or, as he said, there might be a crevasse and at any rate there was the medical case.'[5] However, Scott had not abandoned hope and was still making frantic calculations. They had seven days' food left and were about fifty-five miles from One Ton Camp. Averaging about six miles a day, the limit of their endurance, they would be just thirteen miles short of the depot when their food ran out. Could they get through?

On 12 March they managed a further few miles at terrible cost. 'The surface remains awful, the cold intense, and our physical condition running down. God help us!' They awoke the next day to a strong northerly wind and a temperature of -37° which they simply could not face. They stayed in camp till afternoon when they managed just over five miles. The next day brought even lower temperatures of -43° at midday. Wilson was so horribly cold he could not even take off his skis for some time and 'poor

Oates got it again in the foot'. Scott wrote, 'It must be near the end, but a pretty merciful end.' Under the pressure of 'tragedy all along the line' Scott was now beginning to lose track of dates and, instead of writing his diary at lunchtime and again at night, was simply making notes at midday. That he kept writing at all is remarkable.

On 16 or 17 March Oates decided he could go on no longer and asked to be left in his sleeping bag. Wilson had been reading Tennyson's 'In Memoriam' earlier on the journey. It contained lines which could have been written for the broken cavalry officer: 'This year I slept and woke with pain, I almost wished no more to wake.' His comrades persuaded him to continue and he hobbled gamely on but at night his condition was so bad it was clear he could go no further. Scott recorded his end:

> Should this be found I want these facts recorded. Oates's last thoughts were of his Mother, but immediately before he took pride in thinking that his regiment would be pleased with the bold way in which he met his death. We can testify to his bravery. He has borne intense suffering for weeks without complaint . . . He did not – would not – give up hope to the very end. He was a brave soul. This was the end. He slept through the night before last hoping not to wake; but he woke in the morning – yesterday. It was blowing a blizzard. He said, 'I am just going outside and may be some time.' He went out into the blizzard and we have not seen him since . . . We knew that poor Oates was walking to his death, but though we tried to dissuade him, we knew it was the act of a brave man and an English gentleman. We all hope to meet

the end with a similar spirit, and assuredly the end is not far.

March 17 was Oates's birthday. He was thirty-two.

The forlorn trio marched onward. They had jettisoned their theodolite, Oates's sleeping bag and a camera, but were still dragging their geological specimens 'at Wilson's special request'.[6] Bowers was now the fittest. Both he and Wilson continued to talk of winning through but, Scott wondered, could they really believe it? They were all suffering frostbitten feet and Scott's right foot was so bad that amputation was the least he could fear. However, this seemed increasingly academic – he had begun to write his farewell letters.

By 19 March they were only eleven miles from One Ton Camp but the next day a severe blizzard descended. It was decided that Wilson and Bowers would try to battle through to the depot to fetch fuel, but Wilson's letter to Oriana suggests it was a forlorn hope: 'Birdie and I are going to try and reach the Depot 11 miles north of us and return to this tent where Captain Scott is lying with a frozen foot . . . I shall simply fall and go to sleep in the snow . . . Don't be unhappy – all is for the best.'[7] Bowers's last letter to his mother is in similar vein: 'God alone knows what will be the outcome of the 22 miles march we have to make but my trust is still in Him and in the abounding Grace of my Lord . . . There will be no shame however and you will know that I have struggled to the end . . . you will know that for me the end was peaceful as it is only sleep in the cold.' It was his firm belief that 'nothing that happens to our bodies really matters'. A sad little postscript added, 'My gear that is not on the ship is at Mrs. Hatfield's, Marine Hotel, Sumner, New Zealand.'[8]

However, malign fate again took a hand. The blizzard was too thick for any such attempt and their plan changed. They decided they would all march for the depot when the blizzard lifted and die in their tracks if necessary. Yet even this was denied them. The blizzard seems to have continued to blow and their lives ebbed away with it. Perhaps, as he lay there, Scott reflected on the ill luck during the depot journey and his sensitivity to the ponies' suffering, which had resulted in One Ton Depot being laid thirty miles further north than he had originally intended. Perhaps he still hoped against hope to hear the yapping of dog teams loping through the snowstorm to their rescue. Yet in his heart he must have known it was the end.

He completed his letters. In his message to Oriana Wilson he paid tribute to Bill and also revealed his sense of guilt: 'I should like you to know how splendid he was at the end – everlastingly cheerful and ready to sacrifice himself for others, never a word of blame to me for leading him into this mess.' To Bowers's mother he wrote of her son's 'dauntless spirit' and that 'he has remained cheerful, hopeful, and indomitable to the end'. He asked Barrie to help his own wife and child but also appealed for others: 'Wilson leaves a widow, and Edgar Evans also a widow in humble circumstances. Do what you can to get their claims recognized.' He also wrote to a number of those involved with the expedition including the treasurer Sir Edgar Speyer and his agent Mr Kinsey. His 'Message to the Public' justified the decisions he had taken, aware that in death, as in life, there would be those to criticize him. He did not write directly to Markham, telling Kathleen: 'I haven't time to write to Sir Clements, tell him I thought much of him, and never regretted his putting me in command of the *Discovery*.'

Of course, Scott's deepest thoughts and feelings were reserved for his 'dear, dear' mother and for Kathleen. As he confessed to Hannah Scott: 'For myself I am not unhappy, but for Kathleen, you and the rest of the family my heart is very sore.' In a letter addressed 'To my Widow' he wrote: 'What lots and lots I could tell you of this journey. How much better has it been than lounging in too great comfort at home. What tales you would have for the boy. But what a price to pay.' Inspired perhaps by the faith of his two companions he urged Kathleen to try and make their son believe in a God because 'it is comforting'. He also told her to guard their son against indolence. In his dying hours perhaps he thought back to his own boyhood, to the little daydreamer they had called 'Old Mooney' and to the hardship caused by his father's fecklessness. He urged Kathleen to 'make the boy interested in natural history' and encouraged her to remarry: 'When the right man comes to help you in life you ought to be your happy self again – I wasn't a very good husband but I hope I shall be a good memory.' In fact as he lay dying Kathleen was giving a party in London, hoping hourly for news of him. Her brother Rosslyn was there and saw the strain she was under but he also noted that 'a new beam of courage has grown into her face'.[9]

On 29 March, believed to be the day of his death but by no means certain, Scott made one last entry in his diary, recounting the bitter frustration of their final days as each morning they had prepared to march for 'our depot *11 miles* away' only to find that 'outside the door of the tent it remains a scene of whirling drift'. He was now looking death in the eye: 'I do not think we can hope for any better things now. We shall stick it out to the end, but we are getting weaker, of course, and the end cannot be far. It seems a pity, but I do not think I can write more. R. Scott.' The diary ends with a raggedly written appeal: 'For God's sake look after our people.' This has a bitter pathos. Ever since early adulthood Scott had carried the burden of responsibility for others, with all the concomitant feelings of guilt and inadequacy. Now he was leaving mother, wife and child alone as well as the loved ones of those who had followed him unquestioningly to the Pole.

As they lay frozen and starving in their small tent out on the Barrier, Scott, Wilson and Bowers must have wondered whether the outside world would ever learn their fate – their tent was neatly pitched along the line of cairns between the depots but would soon be shrouded by drifting snow. In fact it would be eight months before their bodies would be discovered and their stricken comrades would find their letters and diaries and read Scott's spirited 'Message to the Public': 'Had we lived, I should have had a tale to tell of the hardihood, endurance, and courage of my companions which would have stirred the heart of every Englishman. These rough notes and our dead bodies must tell the tale.'

17

'We Have Got To Face It Now'

Meanwhile at McMurdo Sound the other members of the expedition watched and waited. The first supporting party consisting of Atkinson, Cherry-Garrard, Wright and Keohane reached Hut Point safely on 26 January though a ravenous Atkinson had so gorged himself on supplies at One Ton Depot that he was not at all well during the final leg of the journey. The first clue that all might not be well with the Polar party came about three weeks later. At 3.30 a.m. on 19 February the dogs began barking and an exhausted Crean staggered into Hut Point. He had walked thirty miles across crevassed ice to bring news that Teddy Evans was lying dangerously ill with scurvy near Corner Camp with Lashly to nurse him. It was pure chance that Atkinson and Dimitri happened to be there with the dog teams. Aghast at the news they hastily prepared to go to Evans's aid but a thick blizzard descended within half an hour of Crean's arrival and delayed their departure. In the afternoon they made a dash over the ice and Dimitri spotted the black cloth Lashly had fixed to the sledge to attract attention.

Evans, Lashly and Crean were, of course, the men of the

Last Supporting Party. They had bidden farewell to Scott and the Polar team on 4 January, less than 150 miles from the Pole, and had faced a return journey of nearly 700 miles. Like Scott, they had had an appalling time navigating down the Beardmore Glacier, which shook even the phlegmatic Lashly: 'We have today experienced what none of us ever wants to be our lot again. I cannot describe the maze we got into and the hairbreadth escapes we have had to pass through today . . . The more we tried to get clear the worse the pressure got; at times it seemed almost impossible for us to get along, and when we had got over the places it was more than we could face to try and retreat.' He wrote of fathomless pits and deep crevasses 'where it was possible to drop the biggest ship afloat in and lose her'.[1] Teddy Evans removed his goggles to help find the way and suffered agonies of snowblindness which left him unable to pull. He could only walk helplessly beside the sledge, hoping a poultice of used tea leaves would bring some relief. The strain took its toll. Evans felt despondent and guilty to have led his men into such a mess. He later wrote of his feelings at seeing silhouetted against the sun 'two tiny disconsolate figures, one sitting, one standing' patiently waiting for him to find a way out of the maze.

On 22 January they escaped the toils of the glacier but on this very day Evans began to display symptoms of scurvy, complaining of a stiffness behind the knees. Lashly guessed at once what it was: 'Tonight I watched his gums, and I am convinced he is on the point of something anyhow . . . It seems we are in for more trouble now, but let's hope for the best.' However, the best did not happen. As the month drew on Evans began to suffer bowel problems. On 29 January Lashly was writing: 'His legs are getting worse and we are quite certain he is suffering from scurvy, at least he is turning black and blue and several other colours as well.'

By early February Evans was in great pain. Unable to lift his legs, he had to be strapped on his skis. By the middle of the month he was passing blood and increasingly helpless. As well as his physical weakening he later admitted to some mental anguish: 'The disappointment of not being included in the Polar party had not helped me much.' Though he hid it from the men, his morale had suffered in much the same way as the Polar party's had done on finding that Amundsen had beaten them. Bowers had written on 1 January: 'Teddy was fearfully upset at not going to the Pole – he had set his heart on it so . . . I am sure it was for his wife's sake he wanted to go.'

Evans fainted on the march: 'Crean and Lashly picked me up, and Crean thought I was dead. His hot tears fell on my face, and as I came to I gave a weak kind of laugh.' Their progress was becoming worryingly slow in the low temperatures and Lashly and Crean decided the only solution was to carry Evans on the sledge. They jettisoned everything but the essentials and laid him carefully on it. He asked them to leave him behind but as Lashly wrote: 'this we could not think of'. By now Lashly was suffering from a frostbitten foot and Evans suggested he place it on his stomach to warm it up. Lashly reluctantly agreed and it worked. He paid tribute to their mutual care for each other in his diary: 'I think we could go to any length of trouble to assist one another.' He did not know of Evans's later wry comment that: 'there is something objectionable about a man's frostbitten clammy foot thrust against one's belly in the middle of the Great Ice Barrier with the thermometer at fifty below.'[2]

They pressed on, sometimes using a sail to help them along, Evans grinding his teeth with the pain. They were hoping to run into dog teams on their way out to meet the Polar party. On 17 February they thought they spotted a tent in the deceptive light of the Barrier but it turned out to be only a piece of biscuit box. Marching on, they reached one of the abandoned motor sledges which lifted their spirits and they made camp. However, the next morning it was clear that Evans was dying. Crean was almost in tears. They made the wise decision that he should strike out alone to fetch help. He set out with just a little chocolate and a few biscuits, a staunch figure struggling alone and on foot because the skis had been among the equipment jettisoned.

Evans's account of their wait shows what Scott and his companions must have gone through in their last days: 'The end had nearly come, and I was past caring; we had no food, except a few paraffin-saturated biscuits, and Lashly in his weakened state without food could never have marched in. He took it very quietly – a noble, steel true man.' However, on 20 February they heard a sound which made their hearts leap. Lashly described the wonderful moment: 'Hark! from us both. Yes, it is the dogs near. Relief at last.' One of the dogs rushed into the tent and slobbered over the prostrate Evans: 'Perhaps to hide my feelings I kissed his old hairy, Siberian face with the kiss that was meant for Lashly. We were both dreadfully affected at our rescue.'

In fact, the delight which greeted the rescue of the Last Supporting Party, coupled with their news that on parting from Scott he had been marching strongly for the Pole, obscured the significance of what had happened to Teddy Evans. Tryggve Gran, however, hit the nail on the head:

> My conversation with Evans had not lasted long, but from what I heard . . . the prospects of our five-man Polar party were not so bright as most of the members of the expedition imagined. Evans's frightful return journey was a pointer to what Scott and his men

would be bound to undergo. There was also another matter which caused me anxiety. Since the Beardmore Glacier's suitability for dogs had been established, I took it for granted that Amundsen had reached the Pole before Scott. The consequence would probably be a fall in morale for our Polar party. Of course I kept these dark broodings to myself for . . . my pessimism could only cause damage.[3]

It was some time before the rest of the party at Cape Evans began to worry seriously about Scott. The main preoccupation was what to do about sending dog teams to meet the Polar party. The various messages sent back by Scott had caused some confusion. There had been plans for Meares and his dog teams to take extra rations for the returning parties and dog biscuit out to One Ton Depot, provided they returned from the Polar trip in the first half of December. However, they did not return to Cape Evans in time. As a result, some of the extra rations but no dog biscuit were manhauled to One Ton Depot by Day, Nelson, Clissold and Hooper. It was not until 13 February that the dog teams set out again, under Atkinson since Meares was returning on the *Terra Nova*. Their mission was to run further supplies south to One Ton Depot for the returning party. The fateful encounter with Crean at Hut Point meant that Atkinson, as the doctor, was now required to nurse Teddy Evans.

Cherry-Garrard took his place, arriving with Dimitri at One Ton Depot on 3 March. He wondered whether he would find Scott already there. Of course he was not. He was still over a hundred miles away with Oates fast approaching his end. Faced with a lack of dog food and heavy winds Cherry-Garrard decided the best course was to wait at the depot. If he headed south there was every chance he might miss Scott. It never crossed his mind that the Polar party would be running out of food and fuel – as far as he knew adequate provisions had been left at the depots. Also, Atkinson had stressed that the Polar party was not dependent on the dogs to get them home and had reminded him of Scott's orders that under no circumstances were the dogs to be risked. The only way Cherry-Garrard could take the dogs south was to kill them for dog food as he went. He therefore waited six days until, on 10 March, dwindling supplies and the fact that Dimitri was suffering from the cold, decided him to turn northwards again. As he later learned Scott was just sixty miles away. It was a decision for which he would never forgive himself.

Scott had been expected back at any time from early March and by the end of the month at the latest. The men at Cape Evans waited for a signal from Hut Point to say that they were in. The telephone cable had been washed out to sea so they had agreed that rockets would be fired. However, as the month drew on there was an ominous silence from Hut Point while the storms and blizzards which raged around Cape Evans boded ill for anyone out on the Barrier. As Gran wrote: 'It can't be easy to travel on the Barrier in such God-forsaken weather.'[4] Sometimes the dogs would 'sing', something they often did when a party was approaching. The men in the hut would rush outside only to find that there was nothing. The position became more critical with every day that passed: 'Atkinson and I look at one another, and he looks, and I feel, quite haggard with anxiety. He says he does not think they have scurvy,' wrote Cherry-Garrard. Atkinson and Keohane made a sortie out onto the Barrier but could find no trace of any living thing and dared not venture much beyond Corner Camp. Their return to Cape Evans with Dimitri sparked false hopes. As Gran described: 'I heard someone shout, "The Polar party's coming."

I rushed into the hut to the gramophone to get out the national anthem to greet Scott. I stood and waited long, but no one came. I went out again, and there stood three men, bearded, and coated with ice, dirty as sweeps.' A mournful Cherry-Garrard confided to his diary in early April: 'We have got to face it now. The Pole Party will not in all probability ever get back. And there is no more that we can do.'

Atkinson had taken command as the only naval officer left. Teddy Evans had returned on the *Terra Nova*, while Campbell and his men were marooned in an igloo at Evans Coves, along the coast from Cape Adare where they had landed after finding Amundsen ensconced at the Bay of Whales. Atkinson now led an abortive attempt to get through to Campbell. However, on 24 April the sun disappeared and with it any realistic hope of rescuing anybody. The members of the expedition tried to keep busy and not fall prey to morbid thoughts. However, it must have been hard faced with the empty bunks of their companions. There was no Scott sitting at his lino-covered table calculating sledging rations with the eager little Birdie, no wise 'Uncle Bill' to look up from his sketching and dispense some kind word, no Oates to tease the scientists and indulge in horseplay and no Edgar Evans to roar his way around the mess-deck. The men with the most striking personalities, as Ponting had remarked, were gone for ever.

The dilemma facing Atkinson was whether to devote his resources to rescuing Campbell or to try and discover what fate had overtaken Scott once the sledging season came round again. He had put the question to Cherry-Garrard at the beginning of the winter and his reply had been to go for Campbell: '. . . just then it seemed to me unthinkable that we should leave live men to search for those who were dead.' However, the *Terra Nova* might have managed to pick up Campbell and his men on her voyage north. Alternatively, if Campbell had not been rescued but had survived the winter, the *Terra Nova* should be able to reach him on her way back to Cape Evans, although a land party might reach them earlier.

Scott and his companions had undoubtedly perished – the general view was that they had fallen down a crevasse, probably in the hellish labyrinth of the Beardmore, though Lashly and Crean believed they had contracted scurvy. However, dead or alive, there was surely a duty to try to discover what had happened. As Cherry-Garrard observed: 'The first object of the expedition had been the Pole. If some record was not found, their success or failure would for ever remain uncertain.' Even if the chance of finding the bodies was remote Scott had been meticulous about leaving notes at the depots. On Midwinter Day in June 1912 Atkinson gathered the whole party round the table and put the arguments. The decision was unanimous. When the weather permitted they would go south and seek the fate of the Polar party. It was a decision that would be vindicated. Campbell and his party returned safely under their own steam in mid-November.

And so it was that towards the end of October the search party set out. On 12 November, eleven miles south of One Ton Depot, they made their grim discovery. Wright saw what he thought was a cairn with something black by its side to his right and veered off towards it. 'It is the tent,' he said quietly to the others who had hurried in his wake.[5] Someone brushed off an overhanging pile of snow to reveal the green flap of the ventilator. Atkinson crawled in taking Lashly with him because he was the oldest member of the group and the last to have seen Scott and the Polar party. When he came out Lashly did not say a word but tears were rolling from his eyes.

Cherry-Garrard described what they had found:

> Bowers and Wilson were sleeping in their bags. Scott
> had thrown back the flaps of his bag at the end. His
> left hand stretched over Wilson, his life-long friend.
> Beneath the head of his bag, beneath the bag and the
> floor-cloth, was the green wallet in which he carried his
> diary. The brown books of diary were inside: and on
> the floor-cloth were some letters.

Scott lay between his two companions whose appearance was
serene, as if they had died very quietly, Bowers lying flat, his arms
crossed, Wilson half-reclining, his head and upper body against
the tent pole, and 'traces of a sweet smile' on his lips.[6] Scott, with
arm outflung towards Wilson, looked as if he had 'fought hard
at the moment of death'.[7] Their skin was yellow and glassy and
scarred by frostbite. By Scott's side was a lamp made from a tin
where he had burned the remnants of the methylated spirit as he
wrote. Some tobacco and a bag of tea lay by his head. The tent
itself was well-pitched and ship-shape. No snow had penetrated
the inner lining and all their equipment was neatly stowed –
pannikins, spare clothing, chronometers, finnesko, socks and a
flag as well as more letters, and movingly the 'chatty little notes'[8]
the supporting parties had left for Scott as they returned to Cape
Evans. There were also detailed records. Despite all the obstacles
and hardships, Bowers had kept a meticulous meteorological log
until days before their death.

Scott had left instructions on the cover of his diary that the
finder was to read it and then bring it home. Atkinson read
enough to discover what had happened to the Polar party. He
then gathered his comrades around him and read Scott's 'Message

to the Public' and the account of Oates's death which Scott had expressly asked to be made known.

It seemed sacrilege to move the bodies. The months during which they had lain beneath their canopy of snow had made them as one with the white and hostile world on which they had trespassed. Instead, the bamboos of the tent were removed and the tent itself collapsed over them. The men then built a cairn on which they placed a cross made by Lashly from Gran's skis and Atkinson read the lesson from the Burial Service from Corinthians and other prayers for the dead. Cherry-Garrard was deeply affected and left a description of Arthurian grandeur:

> I do not know how long we were there, but when all was finished, and the chapter of Corinthians had been read, it was midnight ... The sun was dipping low above the Pole, the Barrier was almost in shadow. And the sky was blazing – sheets and sheets of iridescent clouds. The cairn and Cross stood dark against a glory of burnished gold.

Atkinson wrote his own tribute: 'There alone in their greatness they will lie without change or bodily decay, with the most fitting tomb in the world above them.'[9]

After a miserable and eerie night an abortive attempt was made to locate Oates's body. However, they found only his sleeping bag with the great slit down its front which he had made to help him climb in and out with his bad feet. The party erected a cairn to him at the point where he had walked out to meet his death and left a note recording how this 'very gallant gentleman' had sacrificed himself for his comrades. The search party then retraced its steps, minds still benumbed with the horror of their discovery and the knowledge that the party had died just eleven miles from One Ton Depot. Gran wore Scott's skis so that they completed the journey. The note they left at the cairn gave the cause of death as 'inclement weather and lack of fuel' but there was more to it than that.

18

The Reason Why

Why the Polar party came to grief puzzled Scott's contemporaries as well as subsequent generations. Was it bad luck, bad judgement or a combination? Why should Amundsen the adventurer and interloper have prospered while a carefully organized British naval expedition ended in disaster? Was there too much reliance on the British talent for 'muddling through'? Was Scott merely a gifted amateur who should have done things differently?

Scott's 'Message to the Public', written under enormous stress with his two friends dying at his side, was a careful vindication of his conduct of the expedition. He wanted the public to know that the disaster was not 'due to faulty organization, but to misfortune in all risks which had to be undertaken'. He cited the loss of ponies during the depot-laying journey which had obliged him to start out later than he had intended and limited the amount of supplies which could be transported; the bad weather and in particular the gales which delayed them for four days in early December; the soft snow on the lower reaches of the Beardmore Glacier. He claimed that every detail of the food supplies, clothing and depot laying

291

had been worked out 'to perfection' but that what could not have been foreseen was the 'astonishing failure' of Petty Officer Evans which, compounded by bad weather, delayed their descent down the Beardmore. Yet these events were as nothing compared to 'the surprise which awaited us on the Barrier'.

Scott maintained that 'no one in the world would have expected the temperatures and surfaces which we encountered at this time of year' but even then, despite a hellish month and 'the severe weather', he believed the party would have come through but for the weakening of Captain Oates, the unforeseen shortage of fuel and the storm which halted their advance just eleven miles from One Ton Depot. Scott acknowledged, 'We took risks, we knew we took them; things have come out against us, and therefore we have no cause for complaint, but bow to the will of Providence, determined still to do our best to the last.'

Scott was writing not only to vindicate himself and seek comfort in his last moments but to secure financial support for the families of those who had perished, including his own – with Kathleen's full support he had invested in the expedition most of his own small capital, some £3,000. The expedition had to be seen by the public in the context of British men battling bravely against unforeseen odds and finally struck down by the hand of cruel fate. That is why he kept writing as long as he could, pencil gripped in his chilled hand – his final words a scrawled 'For God's sake look after our people'. Yet what did Scott believe in his heart as the end drew near? A man so prone to doubt, anxiety and critical self-analysis must have known there was more to it than sheer bad luck and that his arrangements while for the most part carefully thought out had not been 'perfection'.

The reasons for the failure to return safely to Cape Evans were complex. Scott was in part right to blame ill fortune. The aura of bad luck which Kathleen had divined early in their acquaintance clung to him throughout the expedition. After receiving a letter from him from Antarctica she wrote to the Royal Geographical Society, 'My husband has always the most appallingly bad luck!'[1] Amundsen would not have had much sympathy with this view. He believed that 'Victory awaits him who has everything in order – luck people call it. Defeat is certain for him who has neglected to take the necessary precautions in time – this is called bad luck.'[2] However, this is too harsh a view when applied to Scott. He did experience a series of misfortunes and they impacted on each other with the relentlessness of a Greek tragedy.

Scott was right that he encountered exceptionally bad weather, both at the base of the Beardmore Glacier in December 1911 and on his final fatal March 1912 journey back across the Barrier towards McMurdo Sound. Susan Solomon, a leading US climate scientist honoured for her work in Antarctica on the ozone hole above the continent, has shown in her book *The Coldest March* that in each case the conditions were exceptional.[3]

Using data collected over a number of years from two modern automated weather stations in the area of the Beardmore Glacier, one at the base of the glacier itself, she demonstrates that the worst December storm recorded lasted only two days with winds reaching 40 miles per hour. The storm experienced by Scott lasted four days (5 to 8 December 1911) with winds of around 80 miles per hour according to the expedition's meteorological log. On a continent where most blizzards consist of strong winds blowing existing ice crystals around and where the annual precipitation is about four to six inches and just over an inch at the South Pole, snow fell almost continuously on Scott for four days as warm, wet air pushed unusually far across the Barrier. The consequences for Scott were not just in the inability to move during the four days of the storm but also in the very difficult travelling conditions thereafter. The snow came over the tops of the men's boots and sometimes up to their knees, rendering pulling the sledges, which were themselves sinking into the snow, in Scott's understated words 'extremely fatiguing'.

Bowers kept detailed meteorological records until nearly the end, using instruments carefully calibrated by George Simpson, who later became the head of the UK Meteorological Service. Simpson himself kept detailed records back at Cape Evans. Comparing these data with those produced by automated weather stations along Scott's return route across the Barrier, Susan Solomon shows that in only one year in a fifteen-year period did the March temperatures approximate to those of March 1912 and that the March 1912 temperatures Scott experienced were between 10 and 20 degrees Fahrenheit colder than an average March.

In planning his journey Scott had used a profile of the likely weather compiled by Simpson which Susan Solomon commended as 'stunning in its accuracy'. The effect of March weather so much worse than anticipated was manifold. Not only were more calories consumed in just keeping warm, food took longer and more fuel to cook. Frostbite struck more easily and harder. It took longer to force painfully sensitive, frostbitten limbs into deeper-frozen sleeping bags and boots. But above all, the lower temperatures altered the composition of the surface of the Barrier, changing ice and snow crystals into a granular form which inhibited the sledge runners, causing Scott to write, 'Not the least glide in the world . . . on this surface we know we cannot equal half our old marches, and that for that effort we expend nearly double the energy.' In average conditions for the area at that time of year, it is possible that Scott and his men might have reached One

Ton Depot, perhaps even when Cherry-Garrard was there with the dogs.

Scott was undoubtedly extremely unlucky with the weather. However, that he reached the Beardmore Glacier when he did in December 1911 and that he was out on the Barrier in the cold of March 1912 was a result in great part of his choice of transport – using ponies and manhauling while relegating dogs to only a minor role. Using dog teams he would probably have set out about two weeks earlier, as Amundsen had done, and been beyond the effect of the Beardmore storm and back to base before the worst of the March weather.

Scott in his planning was preoccupied with the achievements of his British rival Shackleton, whose methods and route provided his template. Scott did not analyse Shackleton's experience to identify why he failed to reach the Pole. Instead he focused on why he got as far as he did. Consequently, Scott's strategy was simply to add more of the same basic ingredients as Shackleton, in terms of men and equipment, rather than to vary the recipe. Unfortunately, his rivalry with Shackleton had become so great and their relations too strained to allow him to seek Shackleton's advice direct. Scott gleaned his lessons about Shackleton's expedition at second and third hand and, during the expedition itself, from the diary of Frank Wild, which he brought with him.

Shackleton had used ponies and not dogs and therefore so did Scott. Both men had drawn the wrong lessons from the *Discovery* expedition when Scott had made much better mileages on his western journey manhauling than on his southern journey with dogs, and both had developed a blind spot. They failed to appreciate that the problems with the *Discovery* dogs were not insuperable – they derived from their own ignorance of how to handle them properly. The irony is that had either of them trained seriously with dogs and selected them well, one – probably Shackleton – might well have been first to the Pole.

However, convinced by Shackleton's success with ponies, Scott followed suit, disregarding evidence from Arctic expeditions and the advice of Nansen and others who urged the use of dogs as his main transport. True, he did take about 24 dogs on his journey south, acknowledging that dogs had some contribution to make, but he never considered it practical to take them beyond the Barrier. Thus, he never paid them the attention necessary to realize their potential, for example giving little thought to the best size of team, or to how to configure the traces for efficient pulling. He left too much to Meares, with whom his relationship was anyway an uneasy one, who was not really up to the job and soon lost interest.

In many ways Scott's attitude to the dogs was ambiguous – he acknowledged their success on the depot-laying journey in his diary but did not allow this to alter his Polar plans. Perhaps Amundsen's avowed reliance on dogs inhibited him – he did not wish to appear to be altering his plans to emulate his rival. However, his error must have confronted him starkly when he arrived at the Pole to find the surface of the ice criss-crossed with paw prints, evidence not only that Amundsen had managed to get his dogs up the glaciers to the Polar plateau but that they had whisked him quickly and efficiently all the way to his goal. In fact Amundsen's journey of 1,400 miles took him only 99 days while Scott took over 140 days to cover a comparable distance. Furthermore, Amundsen had enjoyed the benefit of his dogs, as transport and as food, for the whole trip, while from the Beardmore Glacier onwards Scott and his men had had to rely on their own pulling power, assisted occasionally by a sail to catch the wind.

In truth, despite Shackleton's success, ponies were demonstrably unsuited to the Antarctic. The greatest problem was their vulnerability to the cold. Their coats gave them little protection and snow walls had to be built to protect them from blizzards, whereas dogs could simply dig a snug hole, curl up and go to sleep. Ponies also struggled over soft ground, floundering up to their hocks, while dogs could trot lightly over the surface. The ponies therefore made poor progress on the crucial depot-laying journey in early 1911. This, in turn, meant that One Ton Depot was laid 30 miles farther north than Scott had originally intended. Scott ignored Oates's advice to force the ponies as far south as possible, and then kill them and depot the meat for dog food for the Polar journey. Yet had he taken Oates's advice it might have saved human lives. Scott, Wilson and Bowers died 19 miles north of where One Ton Depot should have been laid. It is, of course, debatable whether reaching the depot would have saved them, weak as they were and with over a hundred miles still to go to Hut Point. However, it would have given them a fighting chance. George Bernard Shaw later observed to Kathleen that Scott, whom he had never met, was 'not a man of sagacity, but a man of sentiment, when his feelings were touched his judgement ceased to exist'.[4] This is too harsh but contains a grain of truth. Scott on occasion allowed guilt about causing suffering to animals to cloud his judgement in his use of both dogs and ponies.

Interestingly, the underlying ethos of Scott's and his men's approach to travel – that the truly manly way was to strive with your own unaided efforts – is the one adopted by latter-day Polar travellers. Explorers like Ranulph Fiennes and Roger Mear have, like Scott, relied on their strength and endurance rather than on animals or motors. Helmar Hansen, who reached the Pole with

Amundsen and wrote: 'What shall one say of Scott and his companions who were their own sledge dogs . . . I don't think anyone
will ever copy him',[5] was wrong. Indeed, his own compatriot
Borge Ousland, who in 1996 became the first person to cross
Antarctica on foot, alone and unaided, echoed Scott's sentiments
exactly when he said afterwards: 'It's still possible to break fron-
tiers of human endurance in a plastic world where there are few
genuine things to do.'[6]

Given that Scott intended to rely on ponies, it seems curious
that he did not take more care over their selection. He allowed
himself to be persuaded by the loquacious and pushy Teddy Evans
to keep Oates, the horse expert, in England to help with the
preparations for the *Terra Nova* instead of sending him to Siberia
as originally intended to help Cecil Meares buy the ponies. The
net result was that Meares – certainly no horse specialist – was left
to manage the business with only the ineffectual Wilfred Bruce to
help. Also, Scott ordered Meares only to buy white ponies. This
instruction was based on a deduction from Shackleton's expedition
that these must be the most robust since they had survived the
longest. The four darkest had died even before the Polar journey
began. All other things being equal, the random probability of all
four dark ponies dying first is one in seventy and therefore Scott's
instruction may have had some theoretical validity. However, in
practice it seriously restricted Meares's choice because according
to what he told Debenham white ponies only made up around
15 to 20 per cent of those available, thus almost forcing him to
buy the group of 'crocks' that so appalled Oates.

Scott did not fully exploit the new technology of skiing, a
form of locomotion only slowly becoming appreciated in Britain
around this time. (When Ponting wrote his book about the *Terra
Nova* expedition he felt he needed to explain to the reader what

skis were.) Although quite an accomplished skier himself, and although he took an expert skier, Tryggve Gran, on the expedition and ordered practice ski sessions, Scott did not ensure that the art was taken as seriously as it should have been. Both Edgar Evans and Captain Oates remained sceptical. Scott was perhaps influenced by the fact that Shackleton had not taken skis on his Polar journey.

However, other difficulties had less to do with Scott's emulation of Shackleton than with Scott himself. Scott was interested in leading edge technology – he had experimented with balloons on the *Discovery* voyage; he used a telephone in Antarctica between Hut Point and Cape Evans on the *Terra Nova* expedition; he had thought about bringing wireless equipment and was fascinated by Ponting's cinematography, by Simpson's meteorological observations and by the work of the other scientists. He was naturally intrigued, therefore, by the possibility of using motor sledges. However, he failed to ensure that the correct higher octane fuel was taken, leading to their early breakdown on the Barrier. Had he taken Skelton, a prime mover in their development, with him instead of Teddy Evans as his second-in-command a better performance might have been coaxed from them.

Scott lost one of his three motor sledges through the ice during unloading, but there are arguments that in any case two sledges would have been quite sufficient. The extra £1,000 the third had cost would have been better spent on dogs or even ponies, which only cost around £3 and £5 respectively, as Oates had observed. However, Griffith Taylor reported that during one of Scott's lectures he had said of the motors that 'he hoped they would help; but he was not using their loads in his calculations. He realized that he was here carrying out an experiment to benefit future expeditions'.[7] In other words, while interested in the motors' performance from a scientific and engineering perspective, he did not regard them as integral to his plans.

Poor diet played a considerable role in the disaster, especially given the protracted time taken by Scott and his men on their journey. There is always a balance to be struck between the amount of food required by an expedition and the effort needed to transport it. However, despite complicated and meticulous planning, there was insufficient food and fuel at the various depots to provide a safety margin for men whose progress would be progressively slowed by bad weather, exhaustion and sick comrades. The depots themselves were not particularly well-marked and were probably too far apart. Scott studied various combinations of diet and part of his rationale for permitting the Winter Journey to Cape Crozier was to assess the effect of different diets on those taking part. However he still underestimated the number of calories needed by men who were manhauling.

For the first 36 days to the Beardmore, Scott's 'Barrier' ration allowed some 4,200 calories a day. Thereafter, the 'Summit' ration provided some 4,600 calories consisting of 210g of fat, 257g of protein and 417g of carbohydrate.[8] However, though similar to what Amundsen consumed until he increased his rations on his homeward leg, this was at least 1,500 calories too little for men who were manhauling rather than dog-driving and perhaps as much as 3,000 calories too little, based on recent evidence of manhauling in Antarctica[9] – even members of the 1955-8 Trans-Antarctic Expedition who drove Sno-Cats and had the benefits of modern Polar clothing lost weight on a diet that varied between 5,000 and 7,000 calories.[10] Other recent experience shows that manhaulers in Antarctica can at peak use up to 11,000 calories a day, around 4,000 more calories than the healthy body can absorb in any 24-hour period.[11] Undernourishment made Scott's men far more susceptible to the cold. Furthermore, poor diet had a mental as well as a physical impact on them. When the body is undernourished it starts to live off its reserves of fat which in turn produce chemicals called ketones which circulate in the bloodstream and have an enervating, depressing effect.

Not only was the diet insufficient in calories, it also lacked vitamins. Vitamins were not, of course, understood at the time. Casimir Funk who later came up with the word 'vitamin' only isolated the first vitamin (B). While the *Terra Nova* was in the Antarctic, and vitamin C was not identified until the 1930s. Doctors recognized that fresh food, especially meat and vegetables, cured scurvy. However, they had less faith than some earlier generations that they actually prevented the disease in the first place because they contained something essential to the body. Instead, they thought that scurvy was caused by some form of ptomaine poisoning or acid intoxication related to tainted tinned food. Not until the early 1930s was it finally accepted that scurvy arose from ascorbic acid deficiency. Scott's sledging rations contained no vitamin C at all. The men's only intake came when a pony was killed and eaten. Lack of vitamin C probably accounted for the failure of Edgar Evans's hand to heal and for possible problems with the scar tissue from Oates's Boer War wound.[12] All other important vitamins were also absent, notably the B group, sustained lack of which can produce mental and nervous disorders.

However, if other factors had not combined to slow their progress, poor nutrition need not have prevented the Polar party from coming through their ordeal, and Scott can hardly be blamed for not appreciating the importance of vitamins in 1912. But his decision to take five men, not four, to the Pole may have had an impact. In the first place there was less food and fuel to go around because all the preparations had been based on four men returning with the Last Supporting Party. It had never been the intention to feed a fifth man for those extra miles to the Pole and back (nearly 300 miles in all). Also, the food had been packed in units for four. The rations therefore had to be broken open and reapportioned – a time-consuming as well as tiring operation which left room for error. Furthermore, it took some twenty minutes longer and used more fuel to cook for five rather than four, while the tent was not big enough and the consequent discomfort was an added pressure on men already under stress. More food and space did become available after Evans died and, even later, when Oates left the tent, but by then the damage was done.

Scott should also have investigated more fully why fuel evaporated in the Antarctic from its storage tins. This had happened on the *Discovery* expedition and Scott believed the cause to be the cork stoppers. Therefore for the *Terra Nova*, he used metal caps and leather washers, but does not appear to have tested them since the cans still leaked. Amundsen had encountered the same problems during his Arctic travels. He had had all the welds on his cans re-soldered to reinforce them, apparently solving the problem which probably originated from leakage at the seams caused by rough jolting on the sledges. Even had the fuel not evaporated, Scott probably underestimated the amount he needed. Today, ample supplies of fuel are considered so vital that the British Antarctic Survey uses a fuel ration double the size of Scott's in warm conditions and double that again in the cold.[13]

As a result of the leakage, Scott had insufficient fuel to cook with and, almost as importantly, to melt enough drinking water. Dehydration must have had a significant effect on the party's physical well-being as they trekked across the high Polar plateau. The body needs a great deal of fluid at altitude and dehydration can lead to altitude sickness. Recent studies show that Scott's party's daily water consumption was only about the level actually required per hour when sledging.[14] In the Polar regions air pressure is less than at the equator. Thus, 11,000 feet on the Polar plateau was roughly the equivalent of 13–14,000 feet in Europe, quite high enough to cause shortness of breath and ultimately cerebral oedema. On the *Discovery* expedition one of the seamen, Handsley, collapsed with altitude sickness at around only 9,000 feet above sea level. Another consequence of insufficient fuel was that Scott and his men could not dry out their clothes and equipment thoroughly after each day's march. They therefore became progressively more frozen, heavier and stiffer and consequently painful to get into.

Scott's orders, in particular his oral instructions to Atkinson and Evans, about sending out dog teams to assist the Polar party were too vague and relied on the messengers returning safely and on time to Cape Evans. Scott himself seems to have been equivocal about what he expected the dog teams to achieve and to have been torn between preserving them for the following season's sledging and using them to speed the Polar party's return. Just as many mountaineers have died or fallen on their return from the summit, Scott, like many other Polar explorers, seriously underestimated the difficulties of the return journey, being over-focused on the achievement of the Pole itself. This probably also explains why Scott did not consider planning for supporting parties out across the Barrier towards the Beardmore to assist the Polar party to return in the same way that he had used them on the outward journey.

Some of Scott's other decisions were also doubtful, at least with hindsight. For example, he allowed Wilson and Birdie Bowers – men he must have been certain he would take on the Polar journey and, in the case of Wilson at least, probably to the Pole itself – to undertake the gruelling and debilitating winter journey to Cape

Crozier within three months of setting out for the Pole. Also, with
Evans already dead and Oates weakening fast, did it make sense
to drag some 35 pounds of rock specimens on the sledge? Gran
thought they might have saved themselves the weight. It might
have been better to store them under a cairn for retrieval during
the next sledging season and conserve their dwindling energy.
But such a conclusion lacks understanding of the Polar party's
characters. Wilson, who had written before the expedition set out
to his father that 'we want the scientific work to make the bagging
of the Pole purely an item in the results', was particularly insistent
that they kept them. It was indeed a matter of pride to them all
to prove they had stuck to the scientific spirit of their expedition.
The specimens were certainly valuable to science.

Perhaps Scott was hampered in planning and managing the
expedition by the competing claims of the race for the Pole (which
attracted the public's sponsorship) and the quest for scientific
knowledge, which genuinely enthused him. He may have had difficulty in reconciling this duality of purpose even within himself.
In any case, the twin aims demanded a larger management and
logistical effort and a greater degree of fundraising, distracting
him from concentrating in detail on any one aspect. By contrast,
Amundsen was absolutely focused on the one goal of reaching the
Pole and was not sidetracked by new technology or science. The
secrecy about his true destination allowed him to make his plans
relatively free of publicity and the burden of public expectation,
particularly once his publicly declared goal of the North Pole had
been claimed by Peary. A practical and experienced professional,
he planned carefully and applied all the lessons he had learned in
the Arctic. His depot-laying journeys in early 1911 took supplies
much closer to the Pole than Scott's. Less sensitive, and at bottom,
more emotionally self-contained than Scott, he relied exclusively

on the well-tried means of dogs for transport and unsentimentally exploited their food potential. He was similarly efficient and unsentimental in his management of his men.

All these factors beg the question of whether Scott was a good leader. He has been castigated for being doctrinaire, rigid and unapproachable. Yet while with hindsight he made some mistakes, his errors were often the result of lack of knowledge he could not have been expected to have and lack of time caused by the conflicting pressures on him. It is wrong to suggest that his leadership was inherently flawed and hence doomed to failure. Scott was as Cherry-Garrard wrote, 'a subtle character full of lights and shades'. He was perhaps not best-fitted to lead by temperament. When Kathleen Scott first heard of his death she wrote in her diary that she hoped 'the horror of his responsibility left him for there never was a man with such a sense of responsibility and duty'. In the published version of the diary 'horror' was replaced by 'weight'. Cherry-Garrard wrote similarly of Scott in the draft of his book, 'leadership to such a man may be almost a nightmare'. In the published version he replaced 'nightmare' by 'martyrdom'.[15]

However, Scott on the whole mastered his weaknesses – impatience, quick temper, oversensitivity and periodic bouts of depression. Cherry-Garrard was correct when he wrote, 'What pulled Scott through was character, sheer good grain, which ran over and under and through his weaker self and clamped it together.' Scott was generally liked and respected by his men, some of whom, including Wilson, Edgar Evans, Lashly and Crean, were veterans of the *Discovery* expedition and knew exactly what kind of leader he was. Crean wrote, 'I loved every hair on his head. He was a born gentleman . . .'[16] Wilson, who was no fool and quite capable of taking a realistic view of his fellow man, made his own feelings about Scott clear, commenting to Markham: 'With him it will be an honour to drop down any crevasse in the world! I am really *very* fond of him.'[17]

Inevitably there were flash points, especially during the long Antarctic winter. Isolation, monotony and claustrophobia take their toll and the leader becomes an obvious target for criticism. However, one must be careful not to read too much into complaints about Scott in various diaries and letters as some have done. Diaries and letters often provide a relief valve for bottled-up tensions. Oates admitted as much when he wrote to his mother, telling her not to pay too much account to his criticisms of Scott in earlier letters.[18] Bowers told his sister 'In the journal you see my feelings at the time as I have not got to play to public sentiment . . . if I seem depressed I don't think I really am.' In such notes members of expeditions let off steam by recording complaints and grievances too dangerous to voice out loud.

Naturally, Scott got on better with some of his colleagues than others – for example, he and Meares never really understood each other, neither did he communicate well with the laconic Oates and he doubted the ability of Teddy Evans. Meares himself recalled arguments between Scott and Teddy Evans which went on all day with Scott swearing repeatedly at Evans. Yet, as Debenham said, the *Terra Nova* expedition was reasonably harmonious. All expeditions experience some friction. On Shackleton's *Nimrod* expedition, one of his men, Marshall, wrote that he had 'not an iota of respect for him'[19] and that he considered Shackleton a coward, a cad and incompetent to boot: 'Following Sh. to the pole is like following an old woman. Always panicking.'[20] On the same expedition Wild regularly complained in his diary that his companions Marshall and Adams were not pulling properly. He described Marshall as a 'big hulking lazy hog'.[21] He and Adams were 'grubscoffing useless beggars' and the reason for the failure to reach the Pole.[22]

On Scott's expedition there was nothing like the rupture which occurred between Amundsen and Johansen, who had the temerity to criticize Amundsen in front of the others after the abortive first sortie to the Pole. Amundsen removed him from the Polar party and never forgave him, treating him as a pariah even after the expedition's return. Johansen shot himself in January 1913.

All these expeditions avoided the mutinies which beset some 19th century Arctic expeditions, particularly the American expeditions of Charles Hall in the early 1870s and Major Adolphus Greely, who led an American Army expedition in the early 1880s. There are strong grounds for believing Hall was murdered by an expedition member. He died from a violent sudden illness just after drinking a warming cup of coffee on returning from a sledging expedition. When his body was disinterred in 1968, tests showed that Hall had ingested arsenic just before he died. His expedition had suffered disunity before his death and there were more violent arguments and outright mutiny against his second-in-command after it. Greely's expedition got into difficulties and morale plummeted so far that he felt compelled to court-martial and execute one of his men for pilfering. When survivors were eventually rescued, concealed evidence of cannibalism was found on the bodies of some expedition members who had died.

The morale of the *Terra Nova* expedition can also be compared with more modern expeditions. Roger Mear and Robert Swan's account of a journey 'in the footsteps of Scott' in the mid 1980s refers frequently to antagonism and intolerance and stress within the party. They found it all too easy to understand the pressures:

> Imagine the frustration when, returning from the Pole, short of food and time, Scott's party hauled their single sledge across the snows of the Polar Plateau. First,

Bowers has to stop and pull up a sock that is causing trouble, then, ten minutes later, Wilson needs to
pee, and Scott who is steering their course has to halt
repeatedly to check their bearing, and each time their
progress is delayed. Imagine the brewing suspicions
that the others are not pulling as hard as they might.[23]

Ranulph Fiennes's account of leading the Transglobe expedition
– the first Pole to Pole circumnavigation of the world – is equally
frank:

Human beings are not ideally designed for getting on
with each other – especially in close quarters . . . On
many expeditions there is no way out, no means of
transport, so a situation of forced togetherness exists
that breeds dissension and often hatred between individuals or groups.[24]

On the *Discovery* expedition even the mild Edward Wilson noted
in his diary that 'familiarity breeds contempt'.[25] Fiennes confessed
to feeling 'positive hatred' towards members of his team for some
petty and irrational reason and to being hurt at the critical comments made about his leadership in a colleague's diaries. Thor
Heyerdahl pinpointed some of the same problems:

The most insidious danger on any expedition where
men have to rub shoulders for weeks is a mental sickness
which might be called 'expedition fever' – a psychological condition which makes even the most peaceful
person irritable, angry, furious, absolutely desperate . . .
until he sees only his companions' faults . . .'[26]

At a more mundane level, even those of us who have spent a wet weekend hiking and camping in a small tent with our nearest and dearest can appreciate how quickly tensions and exasperations can mount, leading to things being said that were better left unspoken.

Fiennes also gives an interesting sidelight on charges that Scott failed to consult, commenting that he himself steered clear of asking advice or seeking suggestions with one of his groups because 'to do otherwise mostly encouraged them to offer further advice when it wasn't wanted'.[27] Scott had to be a leader; neither the navy nor a Polar expedition can be run as a democracy. Against this background, Scott's leadership of the *Terra Nova* expedition and the general harmony look remarkable.

Yet though the *Terra Nova* expedition was a comradely one, it was, as Scott himself claimed, not particularly fortunate, even leaving aside the question of the weather. Constant worries about funding the expedition distracted him throughout the planning phase and dogged him even in Antarctica. Instead of being free to work on the detailed arrangements Scott was unfortunate that he had to concentrate on fund-raising and seeking sponsorship – time which would have been better spent evaluating sledging clothing and equipment, training and studying cold weather technique, all things Scott has been criticized for failing to do thoroughly enough. Scott was also unlucky in being unable to obtain the *Discovery* for the expedition. She was a quicker, more fuel-efficient vessel than the *Terra Nova* and might have helped him reach Antarctica more quickly. Amundsen in the *Fram* took ten weeks less to reach Antarctica, albeit with fewer ports of call. The *Terra Nova* was twenty-two days behind her own schedule for reaching Cape Town. The problem was compounded because Scott encountered the pack ice much farther north than he had anticipated. Consequently, the journey through the pack took twenty days compared with four on the *Discovery*. His late arrival significantly delayed the depot-laying journey. Had it started earlier, One Ton Depot might have been laid farther south.

However, perhaps the crowning piece of bad luck, at least from a psychological point of view, was Amundsen's intervention and the manner in which he made it. From the moment Scott heard the news that the Norwegian was going south he was under pressure. How should he react? According to his lights his rival had acted in a sly, ungentlemanly way. Should he alter his plans? What if Amundsen's approach proved superior? What would the world say of him if he were beaten by Amundsen? His hopes of fame and honours seemed suddenly to rest on slender foundations. The discovery of Amundsen in the Bay of Whales must have destroyed Scott's peace of mind in the months before the Polar party set out, whatever brave front he may have assumed. And then there was the horrible discovery at the Pole. Scott was not exaggerating when he wrote that 'the worst had happened'. Exhausted, malnourished and facing a gruelling return journey, the disappointment must have been tremendous. After all those years of struggle and effort there was only the dubious consolation prize of being first back with the news.

It was a devastating blow to Scott personally. He would not return a conquering hero to the wife whom he regarded with such awe and who had encouraged him to go south. As he wrote in his last letter to her: '. . . you urged me to be leader . . . I have taken my place throughout, haven't I?' Oates had astutely commented much earlier: 'If [Amundsen] gets to the Pole first we shall come home with our tails between our legs and no mistake. I must say we made far too much noise about ourselves, all that photographing, cheering, steaming through the fleet etc.'[28] As Scott trudged northwards again such thoughts must have taken their physical and mental toll. He was by his own admission given to introspection and depression. He probably also suffered from stress, hence the attacks of dyspepsia on the *Discovery* expedition and at the foot of the Beardmore Glacier which made him fear he could not go to the Pole. These characteristics probably became more pronounced on the retreat from the Pole. His diaries show how he gamely tried to take solace from the cheerfulness of Bowers and Wilson but hint at a terrible heaviness of heart.

Edgar Evans was also bitterly disappointed. Devoted to Scott since *Discovery* days, the failure at the Pole may have shaken his confidence in his captain and thus weakened his mental resistance to his physical collapse. Of course this physical weakening in turn played a part in the disaster. Not only was it unnerving to see the big Welshman decline to a state of helplessness, but it also delayed the others. There is honest relief in Scott's diary about the natural death of Evans. Some suggest that Evans would have been under stress as the only member of the lower deck in a party of officers. However, against this is that Evans knew Scott well – he had shared a sleeping bag with him on the *Discovery* expedition and had been able to persuade Scott not to banish him from the *Terra Nova* expedition because of his drinking bout in New Zealand. He was also noted in several diaries for his general affability and the easy way he mixed with scientists and officers at Cape Evans. What did have a bearing, however, was that perhaps out of loyalty to Scott and ambition to go to the Pole, Evans did not disclose how badly he had injured his hand while adjusting the sledges.

The personalities of the other members of the Polar party also contributed. Captain Oates personified the laconic Edwardian officer. He would probably have been relieved to have been asked to return with the Last Supporting Party. His war wound in his left leg was perhaps troubling him. He had already recorded problems with the tendons at the back of his other knee – the right – before the choice of the final party was made. The unbalancing effect of his shortened left leg would have placed a heavy, distorting, strain on his right leg as well as his spine and pelvis after walking and skiing so many miles.

Oates did not share the others' passionate devotion to Scott. If anything he, far more than Edgar Evans, was the odd man out – a military man from a different social stratum who had little to prove or to gain from being in the Polar party. However, he was conscious of the honour of his regiment and of the army and like others of his generation had a profound sense of duty. It would never have occurred to him to ask to return with either Atkinson or Evans. Nevertheless, his sense of duty was unfortunate. Had he disclosed his weakening, he would not have gone to the Pole. Oates's collapse, like Evans's, significantly delayed his comrades. Unfortunately Wilson, who had not been a practising doctor since the *Discovery* expedition, did not spot the problems with Oates or Evans. Had he given his colleagues even a rudimentary medical at the turning-back point, despite the cold, he might have discovered the seriousness of Evans's wounded hand and Oates's foot, perhaps, in turn, influencing Scott's choice of the Polar party. Scott had made his own views on those who concealed medical problems clear in an excised diary entry when Atkinson failed to report his injured foot during the depot journey: 'He might have wrecked it. Surely, small consideration ought to suggest to anyone that they risk others' lives beside their own in concealing ailments in this way'.[29] As already discussed in an earlier chapter, Scott's chances of survival might have been appreciably better had he taken Lashly and/or Crean in place of Edgar Evans and Oates.

Wilson's and Bowers's physical and mental stamina and devotion to Scott were a counterbalance to the decline of Evans and Oates and a source of strength to Scott. However, Wilson and

Bowers were perhaps too loyal and unquestioning towards their leader. Bowers had earlier written: 'I am Captain Scott's man and I shall stick to him right through.' They seldom, if ever, challenged his spur of the moment and sometimes illogical decisions or probed his indecision. Paradoxically, this may have put an additional onus on Scott as leader, contributing to his isolation and feelings of guilt and responsibility. Their loyalty also made it difficult for them to leave him at the end and try to break through to One Ton Depot. Bowers and – to a lesser extent – Wilson were in better shape than Scott, crippled by frostbite, and might have pressed on. Bowers wrote in his last letter to his mother: 'I am still strong and hope to reach [One Ton] depot.'

It is not clear from the diaries why they did not try to. No one will ever know what really happened in that cold green tent. The weather may simply have been too bad – though, according to Susan Solomon's meteorological research, it is unlikely that the white-out persisted the whole time they lay in the tent.[30] There is no evidence that Scott tried to dissuade them. Equally, there are no hints that Scott attempted to replicate the sacrifice of Captain Oates to make the decision easier for them. Even if he had they would probably not have allowed it. Whatever options they may have discussed, they may have chosen to lie down beside their leader and wait for death. Of course, as well as being deeply loyal to Scott, both Wilson and Bowers were deeply religious and inclined to see God's hand in everything. This gave them a calm acceptance of their fate and both met death serenely. Not so Scott, who appeared to have struggled in his dying moments, perhaps trying to free himself from his sleeping bag to allow the cold to hasten his end. If, as often said, he was the last to die, it must have been truly dreadful for a sensitive agnostic such as him to lie waiting for death by the bodies of his companions.

What were the physical causes of the deaths of the Polar party? The most likely explanation for Edgar Evans's collapse was that starvation aggravated by scurvy weakened his blood vessels and that the blow to his head when he fell down a crevasse triggered a brain haemorrhage. At the end he was probably also suffering from hypothermia – staggering and fainting are recognized symptoms of exposure.[31] An alternative thesis is that his death resulted from cerebral oedema and other effects of dehydration at high altitude, which a descent to lower levels had not improved.[32] A third but less likely theory is that he contracted anthrax from contact with the ponies or their equipment or from spores on the leather and skins with which he worked to make the sleeping bags.[33]

Captain Oates was the victim of severe frostbite in his foot. The pain must have been intolerable and his ability to march severely restricted, hence the decision to walk out into the snow and seek death. The frostbite was probably exacerbated by problems with his circulation caused by his old war wound, which may itself have been reopened by incipient scurvy. Scott, Wilson and Bowers died of starvation and exposure. The food and fuel simply ran out.

As Cherry-Garrard sadly observed: 'The whole business simply bristles with "ifs".[34] Yet, criticism is all too easy with hindsight and, tempting as it is to focus on what went wrong, the fact remains that Captain Scott and his companions achieved something remarkable, exhibiting courage, loyalty and extraordinary physical endurance. The final trio struggled for 1,450 out of a 1,600 mile journey in the worst conditions on earth. Had the weather been just a little better and had they only managed just 350 yards a day more after leaving the Pole, they would have reached One Ton Depot. The point is not that they ultimately failed but that they so very nearly succeeded.

Epilogue

On 18 January 1913 a spruce and festive *Terra Nova*, flags a-flutter, arrived at Cape Evans under the command of a healthy and renewed Teddy Evans. He and his crew leaned over the edge, eager to hear the news, but the figures on the ice seemed strangely subdued. Teddy Evans shouted through a megaphone, 'Are you all well?'[1] There was an ominous silence before Campbell could bring himself to reply that while Scott and his party had reached the Pole, all were dead. Flags were immediately lowered to half mast, the banners and ribbons decorating the wardroom taken down and the champagne and cigars put out to welcome the returning heroes removed. What should have been a joyful reunion became a sombre leave-taking. Before boarding the *Terra Nova* the men gathered around the simple nine-foot-high cross of Australian jarrah they had erected on Observation Hill. On it they inscribed the names of the five who had died and at Cherry-Garrard's suggestion their epitaph was taken from Tennyson's 'Ulysses': 'To strive, to seek, to find, and not to yield'. This quotation had been inscribed in a volume of Browning's poems found in the tent by Scott's body.

The grief of the survivors was a bond between men who had shared an extraordinary experience and suffered a common loss. However, on their return to civilization, they found their emotions mirrored on a vast scale. As Cherry-Garrard described, they landed 'to find the Empire – almost the civilized world – in mourning'. The news, telegraphed by the men of the *Terra Nova*, was made public in Britain in early February 1913. After Amundsen's victory interest in Antarctica had declined and other topics like suffragette militancy, coal strikes and tension in Ulster had dominated the headlines. Now the newspapers vied with each other in emotional and patriotic outpourings. The disaster pushed other news items such as '*Crimes passionelles* in France', 'The Motor Bandits Trial', 'Rioting in Tokyo', 'Serbian and Montenegran Attacks' and 'The Race Question in South Africa' off the front page. *The Times* of 11 February declared that: 'For a time after the arrival of the news yesterday afternoon, people hoped against hope, wondering whether the information had not been understood, since Arctic and Antarctic news at first is largely impregnated with rumour.' It also recalled Tennyson's lines on the death of Sir John Franklin while seeking the North-West Passage but changed one word:

Not here! The white south hast thy bones and
thou heroic sailor-soul
Art passing on thine happier voyage now
Toward no earthly pole

Headlines like 'How Captain Scott died', 'Eight days of starvation', 'His dying appeal to England', 'Homage to Heroes' and 'No Surrender Oates' held the public in thrall. Scott had become a national icon. The King's message of sympathy reflected the mood when he referred to 'that shocking catastrophe which the English race and the whole scientific world are lamenting'. Only ten months earlier the nation had mourned the loss of the *Titanic*.

Now, as one leader put it, 'Captain Scott died in more awful circumstances than the *Titanic*.' Emotional crowds packed into St Paul's Cathedral on 14 February for a memorial service attended by the King, while thousands stood outside. On the same day, at noon, the 750,000 children of London's County Council Schools were told the story of Scott's death by their teachers. It certainly caught the imagination of the young – the Mitford sisters nicknamed their freezing loo 'the Beardmore'.

As the news reached Britain one journalist reminded his readers that there was 'one who is still ignorant of the frightful tragedy, that hapless woman, still on the high seas, flushed with hope and expectation, eager to join her husband and to share in the triumphs of his return'. Kathleen, who would not have relished being depicted in this way, had set out in January. After 'vagabonding' with cowboys on a ranch in Mexico, sleeping round a cedar wood campfire at night and riding on the engines of trains as they tore across the Mexican prairies she had boarded the RMS *Aorangi* in San Francisco. On 19 February as the ship steamed between Tahiti and Raratonga a nervous captain handed her a wireless message: 'Captain Scott and six [sic] others perished in a blizzard after reaching the South Pole.' A stunned Kathleen thanked him politely and went off to have a Spanish lesson, have lunch and then read a book on the *Titanic*. Yet her outward display of strength, so characteristic, masked a deep anguish. She wrote that had she believed 'firmly in life after death' she would have thrown herself overboard. However, as she did not, her duty was to make the best of things and exercise the 'complete self-control' she had learned from Scott.

On Kathleen's arrival in New Zealand Atkinson handed over Scott's journals and his last letter. Their powerful, beautiful language and the spirit they conveyed were what she would have expected. However, during the months that followed, she must have been struck by the irony that so many things which had eluded Scott in life were posthumously heaped on him. Kathleen was given the status of a wife of a Knight Commander of the Order of the Bath on the grounds that this honour would have been bestowed on Scott had he survived. The money for which he had always had to struggle began to pour in as the nation responded to his 'Message to the Public'. By July 1913 the Scott Memorial Fund amounted to £75,000, more than Scott had ever raised in his lifetime. This provided grants of £8,500 to both Kathleen and Oriana, with an additional £3,500 for Peter, £6,000 to Hannah Scott and her daughters, £4,500 to Bowers's mother and her daughters and £1,250 to Lois, the widow of Edgar Evans. As Oates had been a wealthy man a donation was made to a memorial planned by his regiment. There were also government annuities and pensions – Lois Evans received £48 a year for herself and her three children while Kathleen received £100 a year plus her Admiralty pension of £200 with £25 a year for Peter. Scott's mother and sisters received an annuity of £300. The residue from the fund of some £12,000, after debts had been settled, was put towards the foundation of the Scott Polar Research Institute at Cambridge University.

Kathleen resumed her independent and gregarious life, seeking occasional solace in trips abroad to escape from the 'eulogy and sympathy and notoriety of the Antarctic disaster',[2] and was passionately, even obsessively, devoted to her son. She was gaining increasing recognition as a sculptress and her work now included busts and figures of her dear 'Con' like the bronze figure clad in full sledging gear unveiled in London's Waterloo Place by Balfour in 1916. Others were placed in Portsmouth and Christchurch, New Zealand. In 1922 she married the politician Edward Hilton

Young, later created Lord Kennet of the Dene, after flirting with the idea of T.E. Lawrence, whom she was sculpting in marble, as a suitor. She lived to see her son Peter fulfil Scott's ambition for him by becoming a renowned naturalist. She died in 1947.

But what of the others whose lives were touched by the tragedy? Amundsen was profoundly moved by Scott's death. 'Horrible, horrible,' was his response when he heard the news in Madison, Wisconsin.[3] Scott's tragedy eclipsed his own achievement. The popular feeling grew that, by robbing Scott of his rightful prize, Amundsen had broken Scott's heart. Amundsen also agonized over his decision not to leave a spare can of fuel for Scott at the Pole, now knowing that this might have made a difference to the final outcome.

Amundsen never married but continued to seek new challenges. In 1923 he tried to fly from Alaska to Spitsbergen but his plane crashed on take-off. In 1925 he and some companions set off in two planes on a flight from Spitsbergen towards the North Pole but were forced down onto the pack ice. In 1926 he commanded the first expedition to cross the Arctic in an airship called the *Norge* piloted by the Italian Umberto Nobile. Two years later Nobile crashed on a flight to the North Pole aboard the airship *Italia*. Amundsen took off in a small seaplane to his rescue, flying into a chill winter sky, and was never seen again. Some months later the plane's floats and a petrol tank were found. Amundsen and his comrades had clearly used them as liferafts but had nonetheless perished – a not inappropriate Polar end for Amundsen.

Scott's other great rival Shackleton was in New York when he first heard the news of Scott's death. Reuters quoted him as saying: 'It is inconceivable that an expedition so well equipped as Captain Scott's could perish in a blizzard,' adding that he had faced the severest blizzards without disaster.[4] Shackleton also continued to explore. In 1914 he put together an expedition with the ambitious aim of crossing Antarctica from the Weddell to the Ross Sea. However, his ship the *Endurance* was crushed by the ice. The crew, under the command of Frank Wild, sought refuge on Elephant Island while Shackleton and five of his men, including Thomas Crean, made a desperate but successful bid to row nearly 1,000 miles to South Georgia to fetch help in a 22-foot whaler. The crew was eventually rescued. In 1922 an undeterred Shackleton set out once again with Frank Wild as his second in command to explore Graham Land, but the physical weakness he had fought so hard to master overcame him. He died of heart failure on board ship and was buried on South Georgia. He was forty-seven. Wild went to Africa, but developed drink problems. He died in Transvaal of pneumonia in 1930.

Sir Clements Markham was cut to the heart by the loss of Scott. In fact, his own death was only three years away. Preferring to read by candlelight, despite the availability of electricity, his bedclothes caught fire and he died of shock at the age of eighty-five.

Hannah Scott was granted a grace and favour apartment in Hampton Court – a place with pleasant associations as it was where she had seen her son married. Oriana Wilson, who had sat so quiet and sphinx-like as the *Terra Nova* carried her husband away from her, proved as practical in her own way as Kathleen. She threw herself into activity, winning the CBE for her work with the New Zealand Red Cross during the First World War. However, the death of her husband caused her to lose her faith in God, once so central to her life and that of Edward Wilson. She later kept in close touch with the work of the Scott Polar Research Institute, never remarried and died at seventy in 1945.

Captain Oates's mother, Caroline – the only woman he had ever loved, as he confided in Wilson on the eve of his death

– never recovered. Every night she slept in the room which had been his at Gestingthorpe and she carried one of his regimental epaulettes in her bag. She also erected a brass plaque to her son on the north wall of Gestingthorpe Church which she cleaned every week, and ordered his diary to be destroyed, though not before her daughter Violet had secretly copied extracts from it. Letters of condolence flooded in – the manner of Oates's death struck a chord around the world as the epitome of what was to be expected from an English officer and a gentleman. Anton, the little Russian who became Oates's stable boy, had a strange fate – he fought in World War One, joined the Red Army during the revolution and helped establish a collective farm, but was killed by lightning in 1932.

Lois Evans, described by a condescending *Western Mail* as 'quite a superior and refined little woman', erected a memorial to her husband Edgar in Rhosili Church and settled in a Swansea suburb in a house she named 'Terra Nova'. She was thankful that her husband had been spared the later suffering of the others, but had to contend with a persistent suggestion in the press that Edgar Evans's mental and physical breakdown had cost the others their lives. In 1948 she attended the premiere of the Royal Command Film *Scott of the Antarctic* and watched James Robertson Justice play her husband. John Mills played Scott. She died in 1952.

The surviving members of the expedition had varying fates. The ebullient Teddy Evans had suffered the death of his wife Hilda from peritonitis on board ship returning from New Zealand. Later he had a highly successful naval career, winning the DSO, rising to Vice-Admiral and created a Labour Peer, Lord Mountevans of the *Broke*, in 1946. The *Broke* was the destroyer he had fearlessly commanded during a fierce engagement against a pack of German destroyers in 1917.

Oates's soulmate Dr Atkinson survived the war, winning the DSO and then the Albert Medal for rescuing men from a burning ship in Dover harbour, which cost him an eye. He died at only forty-six in 1929.

Apsley Cherry-Garrard, the sensitive and short-sighted young man who made the memorable mid-winter journey to Cape Crozier with Wilson and Bowers to collect emperor penguin eggs, never recovered from the loss of his companions and was haunted for the rest of his life by the thought that in March 1912 he should have taken the dogs beyond One Ton Depot to look for the Polar party, only some sixty miles away on the Barrier. He had a recurring dream that 'the hut door opens, letting in its mist of cold air, and the Polar party walks in, shaking the snow from their clothes and the ice from their faces . . . The disappointment of finding that it is only a dream will last for days.'[5] In 1913, as the sole survivor of the Winter Journey, he took the eggs to the Natural History Museum, where they were received without a word of thanks. He even had to insist on being given a receipt. During the First World War he commanded a squadron of armoured cars. Afterwards he lived quietly, periodically troubled by illness, both mental and physical, and died in 1959.

Thomas Crean, the muscular Irishman who had saved Teddy Evans's life, was awarded the Albert Medal for his efforts. The lure of Antarctica proved irresistible. In 1912 he bought himself out of the navy to join Shackleton in his expedition aboard the *Endurance*. He died in Ireland in 1938 at only sixty-two. His companion on the return to Cape Evans, William Lashly, also received the Albert Medal. Discharged from the navy on his return from Antarctica with a pension, he joined the reserve the next day. The First World War saw him fighting aboard HMS *Irresistible*, sunk in the Dardanelles and then transferred to HMS *Amethyst*.

He ended his working life as a customs officer in Cardiff and retired to a house he named 'Minna Bluff', dying in 1940. He left instructions that there should be no headstone on his grave.

Cecil Meares, the buccaneering adventurer who had taken charge of the dogs, continued his exotic career. During the First World War he joined the Royal Flying Corps reaching the rank of Lieutenant-Colonel. In 1921 he took part in a British air mission to Japan and received the Japanese Order of the Sacred Treasure, Third Class. Retiring to British Columbia he died in 1937 at sixty.

Herbert Ponting or 'Ponko', the expedition's talented photographer, continued his career after the *Terra Nova* expedition and derived considerable kudos both from his still photography and from his film *90° South*. However, in subsequent years various business ventures failed. He died in 1935.

Tryggve Gran, the youngest member of the party, also joined the Royal Flying Corps during the First World War, justifying his promise to Oates that he would fight for Britain when the chips were down. He later joined the Norwegian Flying Corps and took part in the search for Amundsen. He died in 1980 aged ninety-one, the last survivor of the *Terra Nova* expedition.

Frank Debenham, who founded the Scott Polar Research Institute in 1926, had a distinguished academic career and died in 1959. His fellow Australian Griffith Taylor also did well academically, becoming Professor of Geography first at Chicago and then at Toronto University and lived until 1964. Charles Wright, the expedition's sole Canadian, served as a wireless officer in the First World War and won the MC and the Legion of Honour. He went on to become a highly respected scientist with the Admiralty, was knighted in 1946 and died in 1975.

The *Discovery*, which took Scott on his first expedition, had a busy subsequent career first with the Hudson Bay Company as a merchant vessel, then as a scientific research ship and for over forty years as a Sea Scouts' training ship on the Thames. In 1979 she was put into the care of the Maritime Trust, restoration began and in 1986 she was returned to her native Dundee to the sound of bagpipes. Today she is open to visitors as part of an exhibition about Scott's Antarctic expeditions. The *Terra Nova*, that 'small queer-shaped ship' as Debenham called her, was lost off Greenland during the Second World War.

The hut at Cape Evans still stands. While researching this book, the account of a Polar explorer who had recently visited it caught my eye:

> It was impossible to feel at ease in the shadowy hall, and though the atmosphere was not malevolent, the feeling of reproach never left me while I pried into its dark corners . . . None of us . . . ever mustered enough courage to sleep a night there.[6]

Others, I knew, had been brave enough, even sleeping in Scott's own bunk, but the almost universal reaction of visitors to the hut is that it is disturbingly atmospheric – a place where people talk instinctively in whispers.

Curious to judge ourselves, in February 1997 my husband and I sailed from New Zealand for Ross Island aboard a small 2,000-ton Russian research vessel. Our route south was the same as Scott's but, like him, we ran into a terrific storm – in our case a full-scale hurricane off Cape Adare. 140-knot winds whipped off the Polar plateau, causing 70-foot high seas which hurled boulder-sized chunks of ice at the ship's bows, denting them. For forty-eight hours our chain-smoking and unshaven Russian captain held the vessel into the wind. A life-raft was blown overboard, activating a transponder which signalled to far away Moscow that the ship was in trouble – possibly lost. At last, with no sign of the storm abating and with ice accumulating so rapidly on the ship's superstructure that we were in danger of capsizing, our captain decided we must turn northwards again. As we came beam-on to the wind, heavy seas almost swamped us but we made it.

Our first emotion was relief, but this soon gave way to disappointment that we had come a long way for nothing. Later though we realized that we had at least increased our understanding of what Scott and his men endured. Like them we had found ourselves victims of this beautiful but capricious and fundamentally unwelcoming end of the earth. Also like them, we had encountered 'unseasonal weather', unfulfilled expectations and a ship with two speeds – 'slow and slower'. At least we were alive and could hope another chance would come.

It did. After a further abortive but less dramatic attempt to reach the Ross Sea, when clotting sheets of ice forced our ship to pull back or risk becoming trapped, we finally made it. In 2004 we sailed from Hobart in Tasmania on a fully-fledged ice breaker. This time the conditions were kind and the voyage south went smoothly. By 40 degrees south, we saw our first wandering albatrosses riding the air currents as they searched the silver-grey seas for squid. By 50 degrees south there was a distinct Antarctic bite to the air and by 60 degrees a gentle snow was falling. Soon after, our first iceberg – a pale turquoise cliff – came rocking gently towards us. Then came the so-called 'ice blink' – a luminous white light reflecting off the pack ice that girdles Antarctica.

We turned past Cape Adare into the Ross Sea and sailed along the dazzling wall of the Trans-Antarctic Mountains. We approached Ross Island with the sun low in the sky, pinkening the blow from a pod of killer whales spouting around us. Next day, a drifting shelf of ancient sea-ice, too thick even for an ice-breaker to smash through, was blocking the final approach to Cape Evans but we were able to land near Scott's hut by one of the ship's helicopters. Beneath its cocoon of snow and with the mighty backdrop of Mount Erebus, the hut looked touchingly small.

Slithering over the ice to the entrance, I felt suddenly and unexpectedly reluctant to enter a place so overlain with emotion and so long in my thoughts. When finally I stepped inside, I caught my breath at the fusty atmosphere. It recalled meals cooked long ago on blubber stoves impregnating everything with smoke and fat. As my eyes adjusted to the dim light, I began to make out some very human reminders of the men who once lived and worked here. The galley where Clissold the cook baked bread at night is still piled with provisions – boxes of sledging rations, bottles of Heinz tomato ketchup, tins of Lyles golden syrup and Colman's mustard. The long table where Scott's men celebrated Midwinter's Day – the Antarctic Christmas – with a feast including penguin breast with redcurrant jelly – remains. Touching the smooth wood conjures the improvised decorations, the little delicacies carefully preserved for the occasion, the cheerful eager young faces captured on film by Herbert Ponting. His small neat darkroom remains a testimony to his skill as a 'camera artist' as he liked to call himself. The 'tenements' along the north wall – where Oates and Bowers slept and plotted their schoolboy raids on the scientists living opposite them – look exactly as in Ponting's photos. Scott's private cubicle, with its narrow bed and reindeer sleeping bag, also looks achingly familiar and there is still a photograph of Kathleen and his baby son Peter on the wall. The nearby bunk of Edward Wilson lies beneath a shelf still cluttered with his medicine bottles.

Looking at the possessions of those who never came home brings a lump to the throat. So does thinking about those who waited here, hoping in vain that Scott and his party might still return. Even so, the hut at Cape Evans is more homely than haunting. The tragic ghosts that I'd sensed so vividly as I entered did not fully materialize as the minutes passed. So many things – hockey sticks resting against the wall, the scientific equipment, even socks hanging up to dry – are a reminder that for many of Scott's party the months they spent in the seductive white wilderness of Antarctica was the greatest adventure of their lives and they experienced their warmest, most intensely human moments here.

Sailing a little further south, we came to Hut Point where on his first expedition in 1904 Scott moored the *Discovery* to an ice anchor and built the Discovery Hut as a refuge. Today, this hut speaks less of Scott than of the party of Shackleton's men later stranded here during his abortive Trans-Antarctic expedition. However, the smoke-blackened interior still smells of the hay eaten by Scott's ponies when he was trapped here on his return from the depot-laying journey in 1911 and the floor still bears the scuffmarks from their hooves. The jarrah wood cross erected on nearby Observation Hill by Scott's men to commemorate their dead comrades still survives and we climbed up to it. As we stood there, purple shadows were stealing in from the Pole and, like so many before us, we felt the full force of what is one of the most compulsively alluring regions on earth.

It was sad to reflect, as we sailed northwards again, that though some measures had been taken to protect the historic huts from the effects of time and climate change, problems continue to mount. Warmer temperatures mean that pernicious wood fungi are gaining a hold while sea salt is eating away at metal containers, causing some to rust. Debate over the future of the huts and issues such as whether decaying artefacts should simply be stabilized or whether they should be replaced by similar articles of the period or even by replicas has been fierce and emotional. Some have suggested that the huts should be covered by geodesic domes, others even that they should be moved to New Zealand where more people could visit them. However, it has now been agreed that the *Terra Nova* hut at Cape Evans should be restored where it stands and by the end of 2009 nearly £3.5 million had been raised and work was under way with a planned completion date of 2014.

Meanwhile the bodies of Scott and his two companions, 'alone in their greatness . . . without change and bodily decay' in Atkinson's words lie as if only asleep beneath their frozen canopy.[7] One day, as the Barrier moves down to meet the sea, the piece of ice in which they are buried will break off and bear them northwards again. Recent calculations suggest that this will not be for another 265 years.[8]

But there we must leave a story which, though so much a part of its own time, continues to fascinate. Indeed, as our environment becomes busier, fuller, more restricting, Scott's dissatisfaction with what he called this 'dreadfully civilised world' becomes ever more relevant. We can understand the spirit that motivated those five men on their strange quest and appreciate their achievement rather than criticize them for their failure. As Cherry-Garrard put it on behalf of his dead comrades: 'though we achieved a first rate tragedy . . . tragedy was not our business.'[9]

Sources and References

This book is intended primarily for the general reader. For this reason I have tried to keep the number of textual references to manageable proportions and have not referenced the numerous quotations taken from the following primary sources, except where I felt the source might be unclear in the context:

Bernacchi L. *The Saga of Discovery*;

Bowers H.R. *Journal of the Terra Nova Expedition* (the typed version lodged in the Scott Polar Research Institute); and his letters which are also in the Scott Polar Research Institute;

Cherry-Garrard Apsley *The Worst Journey in the World*;

Debenham F. *The Quiet Land*;

Evans E.R.G.R. *South with Scott*;

Gran T. Antarctic Diary (published as *The Norwegian with Scott*);

Kennet Lady Kathleen (Lady Scott) *Self-Portrait of an Artist*;

Oates's diaries – extracts are taken from 'Captain Oates' by Sue Limb and Patrick Cordingley and his letters which are also in the Scott Polar Institute. Oates's diary was, in fact, destroyed on the orders of his mother, but not before his sister Violet was able to copy some extracts which she later gave to Sue Limb.

Ponting H.G. *The Great White South*.

Priestley R. Diary at Scott Polar Research Institute;

Scott R.F. *The Voyage of Discovery*

Scott R.F. *Scott's Last Expedition* (1913 edition);

Scott R.F. *Journals*, edited by M. Jones (contains both Scott's published account as above but also the excised entries);

Taylor G. *With Scott: The Silver Lining*;

Wilson E.A. *Diary of the Discovery Expedition*

Wilson E.A. *Diary of the Terra Nova Expedition to the Antarctic*;

Where references to the above have been made, these refer to the editions listed in the bibliography. (Please note that quotes from Cherry-Garrard's *The Worst Journey in the World* are taken from the 1994 Picador edition, while the quotes from *Scott's Last Expedition* are from the 1913 edition published by Smith, Elder and Co unless otherwise specified. Similarly, the details of the editions used for other sources referenced in the notes are given in full in the bibliography.)

Quotations from Scott's correspondence and that of his wife come from the Kennet family papers held by Cambridge University Library, letters held by the Scott Polar Research Institute, supplemented by letters published with Kathleen Scott's agreement by Stephen Gwynn, and from Louisa Young's *A Great Task of Happiness*.

Introduction

1. Cherry-Garrard, *The Worst Journey in the World*, p. 475.
2. Scott, letter to Kathleen Bruce, 11 May 1908.
3. Wells H.G. quoted by Hynes, *The Edwardian Turn of Mind*, p. 7.
4. Balfour, Hansard Vol. 89, Cols. 19 and 20.
5. Glyn, *Romantic Adventure*, p. 97–8.
6. Baden-Powell, *Scouting for boys*, p. 208.
7. MacKellar, C.D., *Scented Isles and Coral Gardens*, quoted by Huntford, *Shackleton*, p. 159.
8. Scott, *The Voyage of Discovery*, Vol. I, p. 467.
9. Gran, *The Norwegian with Scott*, p. 33.
10. Cherry-Garrard, *The Worst Journey in the World*, p. 58.

SOURCES AND REFERENCES

Chapter One – The Early Heats of the Great Race

The key sources for this chapter are the diaries of Captain Cook, from which nearly all the quotes from Cook are taken; James Clark Ross's *A Voyage of Discovery and Research in the Southern and Antarctic Regions* from which all Ross's quotes are taken and L.P. Kirwan's excellent book *The White Road* which chronicles the history of Polar exploration.

1. Kirwan, *The White Road*, p. 12.
2. Kirwan, ibid., p. 43.
3. Scott, *The Voyage of Discovery*, Vol. I, p. 14.
4. Kirwan, op. cit., p. 230.
5. Address to the Royal Geographical Society, 1900.
6. Quoted in Huxley, *Scott of the Antarctic*, p. 4.
7. Markham, *Antarctic Obsession*, p. 4–5.
8. Markham, *The Lands of Silence*, p. 447.

Chapter Two – Scott – The Early Days

1. Scott, letter to Kathleen Bruce, 26 May 1908.
2. Thompson, Sir Courtauld letter quoted by J.M. Barrie, introduction to *Scott's Last Expedition*, (1927).
3. Scott's diary, quoted by Seaver, *Scott of the Antarctic*, p. 18.
4. Scott, letter to Kathleen Scott, 1 January 1911.
5. Scott, letter to father, 29 September 1894.
6. Scott, letter to mother, 1898.
7. Scott, letter to mother, 2 December 1898.
8. Scott, letter to mother, 15 October 1898.

Chapter Three – 'Ready, Aye, Ready'

The main secondary sources for Wilson are G. Seaver's two excellent books *Edward Wilson of the Antarctic* and *The Faith of Edward Wilson*. The main secondary source for Edgar Evans is G.C. Gregor's *Swansea's Antarctic Explorer* which provides some interesting detail about the early years of this engaging and important but sometimes neglected figure.

1. Markham, *Antarctic Obsession*, p. 125.
2. Ibid, p. 133.
3. Armitage, *Cadet to Commodore*, p. 129.
4. Ibid, p. 130.
5. Ibid, p. 141.
6. Schackleton, quoted Huntford, *Schackleton*, p. 13.
7. Scott, letter to Oriana Wilson, March 1912.
8. Seaver, *Edward Wilson of the Antarctic*, p. 17.
9. Ibid, p. 56.
10. Ibid, p. 72.
11. Markham, *Antarctic Obsession*, p. 83.
12. Ibid, p. 102.
13. Ibid, p. 17.
14. Letter, *Cambria Daily Leader*, 13 February 1913.
15. Markham, *Antarctic Obsession*, p. 96.
16. Ibid, p. 88.

Chapter Four – 'Childe Harold to the Dark Tower Came'

1. Hare to Pound, letter, 21 June 1965.
2. Lashly, *Antarctic Diaries*, p. 27, 10 February 1902.
3. Ibid, p. 35, 28 March 1902.
4. Quoted by Bernacchi, *The Saga of Discovery*, p. 47.
5. Ibid, p. 44.
6. Ibid, p. 71.
7. Wilson, letter to parents, quoted by Seaver, *Edward Wilson of the Antarctic*, p. 84.
8. Scott, *The Voyage of Discovery*, Vol. I, p. 312.
9. Ibid, p. 313.
10. Ford, quoted by Seaver, *Edward Wilson of the Antarctic*, p. 95.

SOURCES AND REFERENCES

Chapter Five – 'Poor Old Schackleton'

1. Hare, letter to Pound, 21 June 1965.
2. Wilson, letter to parents quoted by Seaver, *Edward Wilson of the Antarctic*, p. 84.
3. Wilson, quoted by Seaver as above, p. 104.
4. Wilson, *Diary of Discovery Expedition*, p. 175.
5. Wilson, quoted by Seaver as above, p. 106.
6. Armitage, op. cit., p. 132.
7. Scott, *The Voyage of Discovery*, Vol. I, p. 544.
8. Shackleton, diary, 9 November 1902.
9. Ibid, 21 November 1902.
10. Armitage, memo to H.R. Mill, 24 May 1922.
11. Shackleton, diary, 25 December 1902.
12. Scott, letter to *Daily Mail*, 7 November 1904.
13. Wilson, quoted by Seaver, *Edward Wilson of the Antarctic*, p. 114.
14. Armitage, memo to H.R. Mill, 24 May 1922.
15. Barne, diary, 1 March 1903.
16. Doorly, *The Voyage of the Morning*, p. 110.

Chapter Six – 'Little Human Insects'

1. Hodgson, *Discovery Journal*, 22 June 1903.
2. Skelton, *Sledging Journal*, 19 November 1903.
3. Wilson, *Diary of the Discovery Expedition*, p. 332.
4. Colbeck, quoted by Savours, *The Voyage of Discovery*, p. 97

Chapter Seven – The Reluctant Celebrity

1. Markham, address to Royal Geographical Society's and Royal Society's welcome luncheon, 16 September 1904.
2. Wharton, comment on Scott's initial report to the Admiralty, 13 May 1904.

3. Scott, speech to the welcome luncheon, 16 September 1904.
4. Scott, letter to mother, September 1905.
5. Scott, letter to H.R. Mill, 1904.
6. Scott, speech at the Royal Geographical Society on receiving the Gold Medal of the American Geographical Society, April 1906.
7. Barrie, introduction to *Scott's Last Expedition*, p. xii. (1927 edition).
8. Shackleton, letter to Scott, 17 May 1907.
9. Scott, letter to Shackleton, handwritten on 8. above, and quoted as being among Shackleton family papers by M. and J. Fisher in *Shackleton*.

Chapter Eight – 'Captain Scott in Love'

1. Scott, letter to Kathleen Bruce, 8 November 1907.
2. Quoted by Seaver, *Scott of the Antarctic*, p. 13.
3. Bernacchi, op. cit., p. 114.
4. 'Podge' (Kathleen Bruce's sister), undated note in pencil to Kathleen recalling their childhood.
5. Lees-Milne, quoted in Young, *A Great Task of Happiness*, p. 99–100.
6. 'Podge', undated note to Kathleen, as at 4 above.
7. Ibid.
8. Scott, letter to Kathleen Bruce, 25 July 1908.
9. Scott, letter to Kathleen Bruce, November 1907.
10. Scott, letter to Kathleen Bruce, early 1908.
11. Scott, letter to Wilson, undated.
12. Scott, letter to Kathleen Bruce, 11 May 1908.
13. Lord Kennet, introduction to *Self-Portrait of an Artist*, p. 11.
14. Bruce, Kathleen, letter to Scott, 4 January 1908.
15. Scott, letter to Kathleen Bruce, 5 January 1908.
16. Bruce, Kathleen, letter to Scott, quoted in Young, op. cit., p. 89.
17. Bruce, Rosslyn, (Kathleen's brother), to Rachel Gurney (his fiancée) quoted by Young, op. cit., p. 89.

18. Scott, letter to Kathleen Bruce, 14 May 1908.

19. Exchange of correspondence recorded in Lady Kennet's *Self-Portrait of an Artist*, p. 85.

20. Scott, letter to Kathleen Bruce, 26 May 1908.

21. Scott, letter to Kathleen Bruce, 3 June 1908.

22. Bruce, Kathleen, letter to Scott, quoted by Louisa Young, op. cit., p. 98.

23. Gran, quoted by Huntford, *Scott and Amundsen* from an interview with the author, p. 278.

24. Scott, letter to Kathleen Bruce, 27 July 1908.

25. Scott, letter to Rosslyn Bruce, quoted by Anderson, *The Last of the Eccentrics*, p. 185.

26. Scott, letter to Kathleen Bruce, 18 August 1908.

27. Scott, letter to Kathleen Bruce, 27 August 1908.

28. Bruce, Rosslyn, letter to Rachel Gurney quoted in Anderson, op. cit., p. 184.

29. Scott, letter to Kathleen Bruce, 28 July 1908.

30. Sir Lewis Beaumont, quoted by Gwynn, op. cit., p. 131.

31. Scott, letter to Kathleen Bruce, 11 May 1908.

32. Scott, letter to Kathleen Scott, quoted by Young, op. cit., p. 104.

33. Letters: Kathleen Bruce to Scott, 12 November 1908; Scott to Kathleen Scott, 17 January 1909 and 17 March 1909; Kathleen Scott to Scott, 13 March 1909 and Scott to Kathleen, 25 November 1908.

34. Related by Dr Atkinson, memorandum from papers of the British Antarctic Expedition 1910–13.

35. Scott, speech at dinner given by Savage Club in honour of Shackleton, 18 June 1909.

36. Scott, letter to Shackleton, 1 July 1909.

Chapter Nine – A Matter of Honour

The main source for Oates's early life, in addition to his letters to his mother is material published in *Captain Oates* by S. Limb and P.

Cordingley. The main source for the youthful Bowers, in addition to his family letters, is G. Seaver's biography *Birdie Bowers of the Antarctic*.

1. Wilson, quoted in Seaver's *Edward Wilson of the Antarctic*, p. 190.
2. Skelton, letter to Scott, 7 April 1910.
3. *Halstead Gazette*, 18 March 1977, quoted by S. Limb and P. Cordingley, *Captain Oates*, p. 21.
4. Oates, letter to his mother, 2 May 1899.
5. Scott, diary, 22 October 1911, omitted from published version.
6. Oates, letter to his mother, 8 January 1901.
7. Oates, letter to his mother, 25 January 1901.
8. James, quoted by Cecil, *Life in Edwardian England*, p. 6.
9. *Army and Navy Gazette*, 22 February 1913.
10. Quoted by S. Limb and P. Cordingley, op. cit., p. 91.
11. Oates, letter to his mother, 21 January 1910.
12. Oates, letter to his mother, 12 March 1910.
13. Evans (Teddy), article in the *Strand Magazine*, 'Captain Oates – My Recollection of a Gallant Comrade', 1913.
14. Amundsen, *The South Pole*, Vol. I, p. 57.
15. Quoted by S. Limb and P. Cordingley, op. cit., p. 95.
16. Debenham, *The Quiet Land*, p. 126.
17. Bowers, letter to his mother, 28 August 1910.
18. Bowers and *The Watchtower*, letter of 7 April 1909; Bowers's comments on Church of England, letter of 23 April 1909; Bowers on spiders, letter 19 April 1910; Bowers's own letter to Eskimos quoted by Seaver, *Birdie Bowers of the Antarctic*, p. 10.
19. Ibid, p. 49.
20. Ibid, p. 72.
21. Bowers, letter to his sister, 17 July 1907.
22. Bowers's letter on Indian self-government, 27 June 1907; Bowers's letters on French, 2 June 1907 and 19 April 1910 and on the lure of the Southern Continent, 6 September 1907.
23. Bowers, letter to his sister, 14 November 1907.
24. Bowers, letter to mother, 9 April 1910.

25. Evans, (Teddy), *South with Scott*, p. 8.
26. Scott, letter to Edgar Evans, quoted by Gregor, *Swansea's Antarctic Explorer*, p. 30.
27. Cherry-Garrard, the memorable opening sentence in his introduction to *The Worst Journey in the World*.
28. Wilson, letter to Cherry-Garrard, 25 April 1910.
29. Wright, C., *Silas, The Antarctic Diaries and Memoir of Charles S. Wright*, 10 October 1910.
30. Ibid.
31. Debenham, op. cit., p. 109.
32. Oates, diary quoted by S. Limb and P. Cordingley, op. cit., p. 100.
33. Quoted by Young, op. cit., pp. 109–110.
34. Meares, letter to his father.
35. Ponting, *The Great White South*, p. 2.
36. Quoted by Young, op. cit., p. 265.
37. Scott, letters to Kathleen Scott – that on his love for her is quoted by Gwynn, 'Captain Scott', p. 161 and is dated Valentine's Day, 14 February 1910 and that on his socks is dated 1 February 1910.
38. Quoted by Cecil, op. cit., p. 35.
39. Scott, letter to his agent Joseph Kinsey, 22 January 1910.
40. Scott, letter to Kathleen Scott, October 1911.
41. *Daily Mail*, 12 February 1910.
42. Wilson, *Diary of the Terra Nova Expedition to the Antarctic*, 22 June 1910.
43. Gran, op. cit., p. 85.
44. Wright, op. cit., 2 October 1910.
45. Scott, letter to the President of the Royal Geographical Society, 29 March 1910.
46. Quoted by Pound, *Scott of the Antarctic*, p. 187.

Chapter Ten – 'Am Going South, Amundsen'

1. Bowers, letter to mother, 31 July 1910.
2. Cherry-Garrard, op. cit., p. 4.
3. Wright, op. cit., 2 October 1910.

4. Simpson, Antarctic Journals, 14 August 1910.
5. Wilson, letter to Scott, 25 June 1910.
6. Oates, letter to mother, 14 August 1910.
7. Ibid.
8. Bowers, letter to his sister, 1 September 1910.
9. Wright, op. cit., 2 October 1910.
10. Amundsen, op. cit., Vo. I, p. 42.
11. Ibid, p. 43.
12. Scott, quoted by Ludlum, *Captain Scott – The Full Story*, p. 151.
13. Bowers, letter to his sister, 28 November 1910.
14. Oates, quoted by S. Limb and P. Cordingley, op. cit., p. 100.
15. Oates's letter to mother, 28 November 1910. Bower's letter, 17 November 1910.
16. Bowers's letters to mother – on Mrs Evans, 7 December 1910 and on Mrs Scott, 11 September 1910 and 28 November 1910.
17. Oates, letter to mother, 23 November 1910.

Chapter Eleven – Stewed Penguin Breast and Plum Pudding

1. Bowers, letter to sister describing the storm, December 1910.
2. Evans (Teddy), *Strand Magazine*, 1913.
3. Bowers, letter to sister describing the storm, December 1910.
4. Evans, (Edgar), letter to mother, 3 January 1911.
5. Bowers, letter to sister describing the storm, December 1910.
6. Cherry-Garrard, diary, 24 December 1910.
7. Oates, letter to mother, 22 January 1911.
8. Cherry-Garrard, *The Worst Journey in the World*, p. 92.
9. Bruce, Wilfred, quoted by Pound, op. cit., p. 221.
10. Scott, letter to mother, 25 January 1911.
11. Scott, letter to Kathleen Scott, 12 January 1911.
12. Revealing exchange between Oates and Scott, as told by Gran to Huntford who quotes it in *Scott and Amundsen*, p. 367.
13. Bruce, Wilfred, letter to Kathleen Scott, quoted by Anderson, op. cit., p. 203.

14. Cherry-Garrard, *The Worst Journey in the World*, p. 147.
15. Ibid.
16. Evans, (Teddy), *Strand Magazine*, 1913.
17. Quoted by Seaver, *Edward Wilson of the Antarctic* from a discussion between the author and Debenham, p. 230.
18. Scott, letter to Kathleen Scott, 28 December 1910.

Chapter Twelve – Winter

Unless indicated otherwise, Cherry-Garrard's description of the Winter Journey contained in *The Worst Journey in the World* is the source for the account of the extraordinary expedition to Cape Crozier.

1. Debenham, letter to mother, 14 November 1911, quoted by Debenham, op. cit., p. 125.
2. Amundsen quoted by S. Solomon, op.cit., p.134.
3. Wilson, letter to wife, quoted by Seaver in his forward to *The Worst Journey in the World*, p. lxiv.
4. Cherry-Garrard, *The Worst Journey in the World*, p. 240.
5. Wilson, letter to wife, quoted by Seaver as at 2. above.
6. Bowers, letter to sister describing the Winter Journey, October 1911.
7. Scott, *Scott's Last Expedition*, p. 362.

Chapter Thirteen – 'Miserable, Utterly Miserable'

1. Bowers, letter to Kathleen Scott, 27 October 1911.
2. Scott, letter to Kinsey, 28 October 1911.
3. Oates, letter to mother, 24 October 1911.
4. Ponting, quoted by Seaver in *Scott of the Antarctic* from a conversation with the author, p. 140.
5. Oates, diary quoted by S. Limb and P. Cordingley, op. cit., p. 136.
6. Oates, letter to mother, 24 October 1911.
7. Oates, letter to mother, 28 October 1911.
8. Debenham, letter to mother, 14 November 1911, quoted op. cit., p. 125.

9. Scott, letter to Kathleen Scott, October 1911.

10. Scott, letter to mother, October 1911.

11. Scott, letter to Mrs (Edgar) Evans, 28 October 1911.

12. Scott, letter to Bowers's mother, October 1911.

13. Gran, quoted by Huntford in *Scott and Amundsen* on basis of author's interview with Gran in November 1973, p. 422.

14. Evans, (Teddy), *South with Scott*, p. 71.

15. Lashly, quoted by Cherry-Garrard, *The Worst Journey in the World*, p. 322.

16. *New Zealand Antarctic Record*, 1985.

17. Evans, (Teddy), *Strand Magazine*, 1913.

18. Ibid.

19. Amundsen, op. cit., Vol. II, p. 63.

20. Scott, letter to Kathleen Scott, 10 December 1911.

21. Scott, letter to Kathleen Scott, October 1911.

22. Amundsen, op. cit., Vol II, p. 122.

23. Amundsen, op. cit., Vol. I, p. 59.

24. Lashly, quoted by Cherry-Garrard, *The Worst Journey in the World*, p. 387.

25. Scott, letter to Kathleen Scott, 21 December 1911.

Chapter Fourteen – 'What Castles One Builds'

1. Wilson, letter to wife, 21 December 1911, quoted by Seaver in *Edward Wilson of the Antarctic*, p. 274.

2. Lashly, quoted by Cherry-Garrard, *The Worst Journey in the World*, p. 386.

3. Bowers, quoted by Teddy Evans in *South with Scott*, p. 203.

4. Mear and Swan, *In the Footsteps of Scott*, p. 199.

5. Gran, op. cit., p. 200.

6. Cherry-Garrard, diary, 4 April 1912.

7. Oates, letter to mother, 25 October 1911.

8. Oates, letter to mother, 3 and 4 January 1912.

9. Cherry-Garrard, diary, 4 December 1912.

10. Cherry-Garrard, introduction to Seaver's *Edward Wilson of the Antarctic*, p. xv.
11. Scott, letter to Kathleen Scott, 3 January 1912.
12. Cherry-Garrard, introduction to Seaver's *Edward Wilson of the Antarctic*, p. xxvii.
13. Fiennes, R., *To the Ends of the Earth*, p. 255.
14. Huntford, *Scott and Amundsen*, p. 545. See also an exchange of articles in *Encounter* between Huntford and Wayland Young (Lord Kennet) in 1980 and Louisa Young's *A Great Task of Happiness*, p. 141.
15. Young, op. cit., p. 141.
16. Bowers, letter to mother, 17 December 1912.
17. Oates, quoted by Limb and Cordingley, op. cit., 18 January 1912.
18. Amundsen, sledging diary, quoted by Huntford, *Scott and Amundsen*, p. 484, 11 December 1911.
19. Scott, *Scott's Last Expedition*, Vol. I, p. 546.

Chapter Fifteen – 'God Help Us'

1. Scott, *Scott's Last Expedition*, Vol. I, p. 547.
2. Amundsen, op. cit., Vol. II, p. 135.
3. Scott, *Scott's Last Expedition*, Vol. I, p. 549.
4. Stroud, *British Medical Journal*, 1986, pp. 1652–1653.
5. Amundsen, op. cit., Vol. II, p. 136.
6. Mear and Swan, op. cit., p. 34 quoting Walton and Bonner *Key Environment Antarctica*.
7. Scott, *Scott's Last Expedition*, Vol. I, p. 569.
8. Amundsen, op. cit., Vol. II, p. 138.
9. Scott, *Scott's Last Expedition*, Vol. I, p. 571.
10. Evans, (Edgar), letter to wife, 14 February 1913, quoted by *South Wales Daily Post*.

Chapter Sixteen – 'Had We Lived'

1. Pound, op. cit., p. 290.

2. Shackleton, *The Heart of the Antartic*, Vol. I, p. 363.
3. Introduction to Wilson's *Diary of the Terra Nova Expedition to the Antarctic*, p. xx.
4. Cherry-Garrard, *The Worst Journey in the World*, p. 587.
5. Ibid.
6. Scott, *Scott's Last Expedition*, Vol. I, p. 593.
7. Wilson, letter to wife, late March 1912.
8. Bowers, letter to mother, late March 1912.
9. Anderson, op. cit., p. 207.

Chapter Seventeen – 'We Have Got To Face It Now'

Following their return from Antarctica, Cherry-Garrard asked Lashly for his recollections of the expedition and for any diaries he had kept. Cherry-Garrard subsequently incorporated Lashly's vivid accounts into *The Worst Journey in the World* and, unless stated otherwise, all quotations from Lashly in this chapter come from Cherry-Garrard's book.

1. Lashly, quoted by Cherry-Garrard, *The Worst Journey in the World*, p. 404.
2. Evans, (Teddy), quoted by Pound, *Evans of the Broke*, from an unpublished manuscript, p. 116.
3. Gran, op. cit., p. 177.
4. Ibid., p. 182.
5. Cherry-Garrard, *The Worst Journey in the World*, p. 497.
6. Gran, quoted in introduction to Wilson's *Diary of the Terra Nova Expedition to the Antarctic*, p. xxi.
7. Gran, op. cit., p. 216.
8. Cherry-Garrard, *The Worst Journey in the World*, p. 498.
9. Atkinson, quoted by Teddy Evans, *South with Scott*, p. 254.

Chapter Eighteen – The Reason Why

1. Scott, Kathleen, quoted in *Polarboken*, 1978; 55–86 (A.G.E. Jones – 'Scott's Transport').

2. Amundsen, quoted by Thomas, op. cit., p. 233.

3. The detailed results of Susan Solomon's research on climate are published in her book, *The Coldest March*) (cf. p. 178 and pp. 286–306 in particular), and in her National Academy of Sciences paper written with Charles Stearn. In a private communication with this author of September 2009, she confirmed that 'every year I look at the data and the picture hasn't really changed. The data continues to show how unusual their year was'.

4. Shaw, letter to Kathleen Scott, 23 March 1923.

5. Hansen, quoted by Huntford, Scott and Amundsen, p.563.

6. *Guardian*, 23 January 1997.

7. Taylor, op. cit., p. 241.

8. Rogers, in *Starving Sailors*, edited by Watt, Freeman and Bynum, p. 166.

9. Stroud, *Shadow on the Wasteland*, p. 99 and Mear and Swan, op. cit. p. 64.

10. Rogers, in *Starving Sailors*, p. 166.

11. This is Ranulph Fiennes' experience, described on p. 285 of his book, *Captain Scott*.

12. Rogers, *Practitioner*, 1974, 2–12, The Death of Chief Petty Officer Evans.

13. Rogers, in *Starving Sailors*, p. 172.

14. The data underlying these calculations is given on p. 216 of Solomon, op. cit.

15. The quote on Scott's ability to command circumstances is from his letter to Kathleen, 17 January 1909. The quotes from Cherry-Garrard are from Wheeler, Cherry, p. 105.

16. Undated letter to Peter Scott.

17. Undated annotation by Kathleen Scott in the front of her 1913 diary, held among Kennet family papers.

18. Oates, letter to mother, 28 October 1911 and Bowers, letter of 8 December 1911.

19. Marshall, quoted by Huntford, Shackleton, p. 220.

20. *Ibid.*, p. 263.

21. Wild, diary, quoted by Huntford, Shackleton, p. 263.
22. *Ibid.*, p. 267.
23. Mear and Swan, op. cit., p. 160.
24. Fiennes, *To the Ends of the Earth*, p. 185.
25. Wilson, *Diary of the Discovery Expedition*, ed. Savours, p. 173.
26. Heyerdahl, quoted by Fiennes, To *the Ends of the Earth*, pp 211–212.
27. Fiennes, *To the Ends of the Earth*, p. 204.
28. Oates, letter to mother, 28 November 1911.
29. Scott on Atkinson, excised diary entry, 2 February 1911.
30. Solomon, op. cit., pp. 313–317.
31. Rogers, *Practitioner*, 1974, 2–12, The Death of Chief Petty Officer Evans.
32. Solomon, op. cit., p. 231.
33. Falckh, *Polar Record*, 1987, (145:397–403), The Death of Chief Petty Officer Evans.
34. Cherry-Garrard, *The Worst Journey in the World*, p. 565.

Epilogue

1. Cherry-Garrard, *The Worst Journey in the World*, p. 584.
2. Scott, Kathleen, quoted by Young, op. cit., p. 163.
3. *The Times*, 11 February 1913.
4. Ibid.
5. Cherry-Garrard, introduction to Seaver, *Edward Wilson of the Antarctic*, p. xii.
6. Mear and Swan, op. cit., p. 86.
7. Conversation between the author and Baden Norris, Antarctic Curator, Canterbury Museum, Christchurch, New Zealand.
8. The work on the movement of the bodies of Scott and his companions is by Professor Charles Bentley and is referred to in several places, including *USA Today*, 24 February 1999 and p. 261 of Michael Smith's book on Captain Oates.
9. Cherry-Garrard, *The Worst Journey in the World*, p. 562.

Bibliography

UNPUBLISHED SOURCES

('SPRI' is the Scott Polar Research Institute)

ARMITAGE, A.B., Memo to H.R. Mill, 24 May 1922 (SPRI)

BARNE, M., *Discovery* Journals, (SPRI)

BOWERS, H.R., Extracts from Journal and typed copy of Journal of Polar journey (SPRI)

British National Antarctic Expedition Papers 1910–1913 (SPRI)

BOWERS, H.R., Letters to mother and sisters (SPRI)

BROWNING, F., Diary 1910–1911 (SPRI)

CHERRY-GARRARD, A., Diaries and Notebooks 1910–1913 (SPRI)

HODGSON, T.V., *Discovery* Journal 1901–1904 (SPRI)

Kennet Papers Diaries and Letters of Kathleen Bruce (Lady Scott and later Lady Kennet), 1901–1920 (Cambridge University Library)

LASHLY, W., Diaries 1910–1904 and 1911–1912 (SPRI)

MEARES, C.H., Letters and Papers (SPRI)

OATES, L.E.G. Letters to mother 1899–1912 (SPRI)

POUND, R., Correspondence relating to research for his book *Scott of the Antarctic* (SPRI)

SCOTT, R.F., Correspondence with Kathleen Bruce, R.V. Skelton, E.H. Shackleton, Sir J.J. Kinsey, Hannah Scott (mother) and others (SPRI)

SHACKLETON, E.H., Diary of Southern Journey, (SPRI)

SIMPSON, G., Antarctic Journals 1910–1912 (SPRI)

SKELTON, R.V., *Discovery* Diaries and Sledging Journals 1901–1904 (SPRI)

WILD, F., Sledging Diary of Southern Journey 1908–9 (SPRI)

WILSON, E.A., Correspondence with wife, parents and A. Cherry-Garrard (SPRI)

PUBLISHED SOURCES

Books

(All titles published in Great Britain unless otherwise stated)

AMUNDSEN, R., *The South Pole* (Two Vols) (John Murray, 1912)

ANDERSON, V., *The Last of the Eccentrics* (Hodder and Stoughton, 1972)

ARMITAGE, A.B., *Cadet to Commodore* (Cassel and Co., 1925)

BADEN POWELL, LORD, *Scouting for Boys* (Horace Cox, 1908)

BAINBRIDGE, B., *The Birthday Boys* (Duckworth, 1991)

ed. BEAGLEHOLE, J.C., *The Journals of Captain James Cook Vols 1 and 2* (Cambridge University Press, 1961)

BERNACCHI, L., *The Saga of the 'Discovery'* (Blackie and Sons, 1938)

BRENT, P., *Captain Scott and the Antarctic Tragedy* (Weidenfeld and Nicholson, 1974)

CAMPBELL, V., *The Wicked Mate* ed. H.G. King (Bluntisham Books, Erskine Press, 1988)

CECILE, R., *Life in Edwardian England* (Batsford, 1969)

CHERRY-GARRARD, A., *The Worst Journey in the World* (Constable, 1922; Picador, 1994)

COOK, CAPTAIN JAMES, *Voyage Towards the South Pole and Around the World* (1777)

CRANE, D., *Scott of the Antarctic* (Harper Collins, 2005)

DEBENHAM, F. ed. J. Debenham Back *The Quiet Land* (Bluntisham Books, Erskine Press, 1992)

DOORLY, G.S., *The Voyage of the Morning* (Bluntisham Books, Erskine Press, 1995)

EVANS, E.R.G.R., *South with Scott* (Collins, 1921)

FIENNES, SIR RANULPH, *To the Ends of the Earth* (Arbor House (New York), 1982)

FIENNES, SIR RANULPH, *Captain Scott* (Hodder and Stoughton, 2005)

FISHER, M. and J., *Shackleton* (Barrie, 1957)

FOTHERGILL, A., *Life in the Freezer* (BBC Books, 1993)

GLYN, E., *Romantic Adventure* (E.P. Dutton (New York), 1937)

GRAN, T., *The Norwegian with Scott, Tryggve Gran's Antarctic Diary, 1910–1913* ed. G. Hattersley-Smith translated by E.J. McGhie (HMSO, 1984)

GREGOR, G.C., *Swansea's Antarctic Explorer* (Swansea City Council, 1995)

GWNN, S., *Captain Scott* (John Lane, The Bodley Head, 1929)

ed. HANLEY, W.S., *The Griffith Taylor Collection – Diaries and Letters of a Geographer in Anartica* (University of New England (NSW Australia))

HOUGH, R., *Captain James Cook – A Biography* (Hodder and Stoughton, 1994)

HUNTFORD, R., *Scott and Amundsen* (Weidenfeld and Nicholson, 1993)

HUNTFORD, R., *Shackleton* (Hodder and Stoughton, 1985)

HUXLEY, E., *Peter Scott – Painter and Naturalist* (Faber and Faber, 1993)

HUXLEY, E., *Scott of the Antarctic* (Weidenfeld and Nicholson, 1977)

HYNES, S., *The Ewardian Turn of Mind* (Oxford University Press, 1968)

JONES, M., *The Last Great Quest* (Oxford University Press, 2003)

KENNET, LADY (Kathleen, Lady Scott), *Self-Portrait of an Artist* (John Murray, 1949)

KIRWAN, L.P., *The White Road* (Hollis and Carter, 1959)

LASHLY, W., *Under Scott's Command* W. Lashly's Antarctic Diaries ed. A.R. Ellis (Gollancz, 1969)

LIMB, S., and CORDINGLEY, P., *Captain Oates* (Batsford, 1982)

LUDLUM, H., *Captain Scott – The Full Story* (Foulsham, 1965)

MARKHAM, SIR CLEMENTS, *Antarctic Obsession* (Bluntisham Books, Erskine Press, 1986)

MARKHAM, SIR CLEMENTS, *The Lands of Silence* (Cambridge University Press, 1921)

MEAR, R. and SWAN, R., *In the Footsteps of Scott* (Jonathan Cape, 1987)

MILL, H.R., *The Life of Sir Ernest Shackleton* (Heinemann, 1923)

A FIRST RATE TRAGEDY

MITFORD, N., *The Water Beetle* (Penguin, 1965)

PONTING, H.G., *The Great White South* (Duckworth, 1921)

POUND, R., *Evans of the Broke* (Oxford University Press, 1963)

POUND, R., *Scott of the Antarctic* (Cassell, 1966)

ROSS, CAPTAIN SIR JAMES CLARK, R.N., *A Voyage of Discovery and Research in the Southern and Antarctic Regions* (John Murray, 1847)

SAVOURS, A., *The Voyage of Discovery* (Virgin, 1994)

SCOTT, R.F., *Journals – Captain Scott's Last Expedition*, ed. Max Jones (Oxford University Press, 2006)

SCOTT, R.F., *Scott's Last Expedition* (2 Vols) arranged by Leonard Huxley with preface by Sir Clements Markham (Smith, Elder and Co., 1913)

SCOTT, R.F., *Scott's Last Expedition* with introduction by J.M. Barrie (John Murray, 1927)

SCOTT, R.F., *The Voyage of the 'Discovery'* (Smith, Elder and Co., 1905)

SEAVER, G., *Birdie Bowers of the Antarctic* (John Murray, 1938)

SEAVER, G., *Edward Wilson, Nature Lover* (John Murray, 1937)

SEAVER, G., *Edward Wilson of the Antarctic* (John Murray, 1933)

SEAVER, G., *The Faith of Edward Wilson* (John Murray, 1948)

SEAVER, G., *Scott of the Antarctic* (John Murray, 1940)

SHACKLETON, E.H., *The Heart of the Antarctic* (Heinemann, 1909)

SMITH, M., *An Unsung Hero. Tom Crean – Antarctic Survivor* (Headline, 2001)

SMITH, M., *'I am Just Going Outside'. Captain Oates – Antarctic Tragedy* (Spellmount, 2006)

SOLOMON, S., *The Coldest March* (Yale University Press, 2001)

——*South – The Race to the Pole* (National Maritime Museum 2000) [collection of authors.]

SPUFFORD, F., *I May Be Some Time – Ice and the English Imagination* (Faber and Faber, 1996)

STROUD, M., *Shadows on the Wasteland* (Jonathan Cape, 1933)

TAYLOR, G., *With Scott: The Silver Lining* (Smith, Elder and Co., 1916)

THOMAS, D., *Scott's Men* (Allen Lane, 1977)

ed. WATT, J., FREEMAN, E.J., BYNUM, W.F., *Starving Sailors* (HMSO, 1981)

BIBLIOGRAPHY

WHEELER, S., *Cherry. A Life of Apsley Cherry-Garrard* (Random House, 2002)

WILSON, E.A., *Diary of the 'Discovery' Expedition* ed. A. Savours (Blandford Press, 1966)

WILSON, E.A., *Diary of the Terra Nova Expedition to the Antarctic* 1910–12 ed. H.G.R. King (Blandford, 1972)

WRIGHT, C., *Silas, the Antarctic Diaries and Memoir of Charles S. Wright* ed. C. Bull and Pat F. Wright (Ohio State University Press, USA, 1993)

YOUNG, L., *A Great Task of Happiness* (MacMillan, 1995)

ANON, *Like English Gentlemen* (Hodder and Stoughton, 1915)

Newspapers
Cambria Daily Leader
Daily Chronicle
Daily Express
Daily Mail
The Daily Telegraph
Evening Standard
The Guardian
Morning Post
South Polar Times (for both *Discovery* and *Terra Nova* Expeditions) (SPRI)
South Wales Daily Post
South Wales Evening Post
The Times
Western Mail
Press cuttings for both the *Terra Nova* and *Discovery* expeditions (SPRI)

Magazines, periodicals, journals and other published sources
Antarctic, 1991 12(5): 165–168, Anon.– re. plans to recover Scott's sledge

BECK, P.J., *Comtemporary Review*, 1987, 250(1452): 31–34, 'The Legend of Captain Scott after 75 years'

DEBENHAM, F., *Geographical Magazine*, 1962, 35(1): 1–7, 'An Expedition in Harmony'

349

DIAMOND, J., *Discover*, 1989, 10(4): 73–77, 'The Price of Human Folly'

DOUGHERTY, G.J., *New Zealand Antarctic Record*, 1985, 6(2): 43–44 – re. the analysis of motor sled fuel

EVANS, E.R.G.R., *Strand Magazine*, 1913: 615–626, 'Captain Oates – My Recollection of a Gallant Comrade'

FALCKH, R.C.F., *Polar Record*, 1987 (145): 397–403, 'The Death of Chief Petty Officer Evans'

GALLAGHER, M., *The Scots Magazine*, 1982: 178–186. '"Birdie" Bowers: the Scot in Scott's Shadow'

Hansard, 1900–1913

JACOBSON, D., *New Statesman*, 1971, 81(2076): 24–25, 'A Simple Message'

JONES, A.G.E., *Polarboken*, 1978: 55–86, 'Scott's Transport, 1911–1912'

ROGERS, A.F., *Practitioner*, 1974: 2–12. 'The Death of Chief Petty Officer Evans'

SCOTT, SIR PETER, *National Geographic*, 1987, 171 (4): 538–543, 'The Antarctic Challenge'

SHEARING, T., *Quarterly Bulletin of the South African Library*, 1985, 39(9): 152–157, 'The Antarctic Tragedy – A Legacy of the Boer War?'

SOLOMON, S. AND STEARN, C.R, *Proceedings of the US National Academy of Sciences* (November 1999, Vol. 96., No. 23 'On the Role of the Weather in the Deaths of R.F. Scott and his Companions).

STROUD, M., *British Medical Journal*, 1986, 293: 1652–1653, 'Scott 75 Years On'

YOUNG, W., *Encounter*, 1980, 45(5): 8–19, 'Scott and Amundsen'

YOUNG, W., and HUNTFORD, R., *Encounter*, 1980: 85–89, 'An Exchange on Scott and Amundsen'

Open Earth 1980 No. 8:6–7 – commentary on exchange between W. Young and R. Huntford

Films

90° South (Ponting's Documentary of *Terra Nova* Expedition) Great Britain, 1933, Academy Video (British Film Institute)

Scott of the Antarctic (Feature film, Ealing Studios) Great Britain, 1948

Index